LEGACY OF MUSLIM CIVILIZATION

LEGACY OF MUSLIM CIVILIZATION

Tanbir Ahmad

RANDOM

RANDOM PUBLICATIONS

NEW DELHI - 110 002 (INDIA)

Legacy of Muslim Civilization

ISBN 978-93-51117-27-8

Published in 2015 in India by

RANDOM PUBLICATIONS

4376-A/4B, Gali Murari Lal, Ansari Road
New Delhi-110 002
Phone: +9111-43580356, 23289044
E-mail: randomexports@gmail.com; sales@randompublications.com; info@randompublications.com

Reprinted 2024

Type Setting by: Friends Media, Delhi-110089
Digitally Printed at: Replika Press Pvt. Ltd.

Preface

Since the seventy century A.D., the culture of the Arab world has been dominated by the last of the three great monotheistic religions to have emerged from the region: Islam. Islam, faith of the vast majority of Arabs, is more than just a religion; it is the focal point of Arab society for Muslims and non-Muslims alike, permeating their culture at every level—political, social, economic, as well as private. To appreciate the enormous force of Islam in the Arab world, one must understand the basic tenets of the faith—how it emerged and grew. Arabic calligraphy is characterized by flowing patterns and intricate geometrical designs. This fine writing—which the Alexandrian philosopher, Euclid, called a "spiritual technique"—has poured forth from the pens of Arabs for the last thirteen centuries. For some five hundred years, Arab learning and scholarship played a major role in the development of education in the West. The Arabs brought with them well-developed techniques in translation and research and opened new vistas in areas of medicine, the physical sciences and mathematics. Application of empiricism in all fields of study was rapidly incorporated into the learning system of those who became familiar with Arab methodology.

The history of Arab mathematics began with Muhammad ibn Musa al-Khawarazmi who, in the ninth century, journeyed east to India to learn the sciences of that time. He introduced Hindu numerals, including the concept of zero, into the Arab world. This number system was later transmitted to the West. Prior to the use of "Arabic" numerals, as we know them today, the West relied upon the somewhat clumsy system of Roman numerals. Whereas in the decimal system, the number of 1948 can be written in four figures, eleven figures were needed using the Roman system: MDCCCXLVIII. It is obvious that even for the solution of the simplest arithmetic problem, Roman numerals called for an enormous expenditure of time and labor. The Arab numerals, on the other hand, rendered even complicated mathematical tasks relatively simple. The scientific advances of the West would have been impossible had scientists continued to depend upon the Roman numerals and been deprived of the simplicity and flexibility of the decimal system and its main glory, the zero. Though the Arab numerals were originally a Hindu invention, it was the Arabs who turned them into a workable system; the earliest Arab zero on record dates from the year 873, whereas the earliest Hindu zero is dated 876. For the subsequent four hundred years, Europe laughed at the method that depended upon the use of zero, "a meaningless nothing." Without question, the greatest name in physics during the Arab/Islamic Empire was Ibn al-Haytham, born in the city of Basra, Iraq, in 965 A.D. By the time he died in 1030, he had made major contributions to optics, astronomy and mathematics, some of which would not be improved upon for six centuries. Ibn al-Haytham's main field of interest and the one to which he made his greatest contributions, was the branch of physics we call optics. Striking parallels exist between his work and that of the seventeenth century English physicist, Isaac Newton, one of the greatest scientists of all time. The development and, indeed, the very creation of European medicine is unthinkable without the Arabs' contribution. For its basis was the legacy of the ancient Greeks, and that legacy was unknown to Europe until the moment when it became available in Arabic translations and with the commentaries of Arab scholars. The first contribution of the Arabs to Western medicine is, thus, the transmission of Greek knowledge. Between 800 and 900 A.D., they had discovered, translated, commented upon, and assimilated the entire Greek heritage in practically all branches of science. Of medical works they translated not only those of such giants as Hippocrates and Galen, but also of Dioscorides, Paul of Aegina, Oribasius and Rufus of Ephesus. The foundation of all great buildings in Islam was Faith. The earliest major work of Islamic architecture was undertaken during the lifetime of the Prophet Muhammad: the rebuilding of the sanctuary of the Ka'aba at Mecca. Since, Islamic architecture has created a unique design concept, style and form which have survived to this day. The principal architectural types of Islamic buildings are the mosque, with its minaret, the madrassa (school), the tomb (mausoleum), the khan (rest house), the fort, and the palace. Since Islam emerged in Arabia, it is hardly a surprise that the Muslim civilisation is a mixture of Islam according to various religious interpretations and numerous traditions from the Arab societies.

This brief chronology illustrates the richness of Islamic history, which helps shape the identity and worldview of modern Muslims.

I thank all members of my team who have helped in the preparation of the book. My special thanks go to "Random Publications" who have published the book.

— *Tanbir Ahmad*

Contents

Chapter 1

Introduction

Impartial Decision

Justice is one of those attributes of God that pervades the whole universe. In fact, the cosmos rests on it. It is the principle of life and the guarantee for its sustenance, progress and survival. Without it develops neither the character of the individual nor of the community. According to etymology of word for justice *'Adl* means dividing something into two equal halves.'

The Quran Uses the Word 'Mizan' (Balance) : In the Quran the reality of justice is brought home to us by the word *Mizan* which means Balance. If one pan of the balance is tilted, disorder results instead of order, and so the Quranic emblem is of tremendous significance :

And the Firmament has He
Raised high, and he has set up
The Balance (of Justice), *(LV - 7)*
We sent aforetime
Our apostles with clear Sings
And sent down with them
The Book and the Balance
(Of Right and Wrong), that men
May stand forth in justice; *(LVII - 25)*

Definition of Justice According to Al Ghazali, Plato and Others : Al Ghazali has defined justice as follows:

> *It controls energy, desire and anger to such an extent that they may function according to Right Reason and the* Sharia. (Ahya, *Vol. III, P. 48)*

> *Shah Waliullah offers the following conception: Justice is, as it were, a Queen, from whom issue forth the actions that make for the smooth management of cities and villages.* (Hujjatullahil Baligha, *p. 58)*

To Plato, the essence of justice is the inner or the spiritual reality, which means that the inner life should be so well-organized that every person does his work in a proper or responsible way, and does not meddle with the work of another. Dewey, James and Rogers see justice as the cream of morality and the crown of essential virtues. If this virtue is lacking all other virtues lose their significance and purpose.

Basis of Justice in Western Culture : In Western culture the basis of justice is nationalism and patriotism, which are adopted on a nation-wide scale for the sake of extolling the nation and its progress.

Basis of Justice in the Scheme of Cultural Reconstruction: In the Islamic scheme of cultural reconstruction, the basis of justice is piety and spiritual purity. It comes into being through the concept of universal welfare and general mercy, as proclaimed by Islam—'All creatures are the children of Allah'— 'All men are brothers'. Owing to such an outlook the standard of justice in our scheme is extremely high, one which would not allow for any discrimination between the close and the distant in relation, the enemy and the friend, the rich and the poor etc. Thus, the Quran says:

> *O ye who believe!*
> *Stand out firmly*
> *For justice, as witnesses*
> *To God, even as against*
> *Yourselves, or your parents,*
> *Or your kin, and whether*
> *It be (against) rich or poor:*
> *For God can best protect both.*
> *Follow not the lusts*
> *(Of your hearts), lest ye*
> *Swerve...* *(IV-135)*
> *O ye who believe!*
> *Stand out firmly*

For God, as witnesses
To fair deasling, and let not
The hatred of others
To you make you swerve
To wrong and depart from
Justice. Be just: that is
Next to Piety: and fear God. *(V-9)*

Once a gentle woman of the clan of Makhzoomia committed a theft. When appeals regarding her reached the Holy Prophets he said:

> *People before you were destroyed (by God) simply for the reason that if a person of high status among them committed a theft he was allowed to go scot free but if a weak person committed a theft he was punished to the utmost limit, By God, if my own daughter Fatima committed a theft her hand would be cut off.* (Bukhari, Muslim, Mishkat: *Babul Shafaat fil Hudud)*

Justice is of two kinds: (1) Personal, and (2) Societal.

Individual Honesty

Personal justice implies a harmony between rights and duties. The Quran speaks of it in various contexts. Thus regarding orphans it is said:

That ye stand firm
For justice to orphans *(IV - 127)*

Regarding women:

But if ye fear that ye shall not
Be able to deal justly (with them),
Then only one, *(IV - 3)*

Regarding witnesses and verdict and mutual agreement:

Whenever ye speak, speak justly,
Even if a near relative
is concerned: *(VI - 152)*
Make peace between them
With justice, and be fair: *(XLIX - 9)*

Regarding buying and selling and other affairs and transactions:

... give measures
And weight with (full) justice;— *(VI - 152)*
Let a scribe write down
Faithfully as between
The parties *(II - 282)*
Let his guardian
Dictate faithfully. *(II - 282)*

By societal justice is meant a system of justice which provides for considerations to everybody and everything. Everything should remain within its proper context and confines, and everybody should have equal opportunities according to his capabilities. This is possible only when the powers of thought and action are held in balance, and everybody, realizing that God watches him, fulfils his duty towards establishing justice. Let us turn to what the Quran says:

God doth command you
To render back your Trusts
To those to whom they are due
And when ye judge
Between man and man
That ye judge with justice: *(IV - 58)*

In this Verse, the address is made to the rulers. The term 'Trusts' includes, as pointed out above, all kinds of responsibilities, positions and ranks. Ibn-i-Taimiya rightly points out that the 'Rulers themselves are the cause of the revelation of this Verse'. *(Al Jawame' fi Siyasatil Ilahiya).* The Quran speaks more of justice:

but say: 'I believe
In the Book which
God has sent down;
And I am commanded
To judge justly between you. *(XLII - 15)*
If thou judge, judge
In equity between them,
For God loveth those
Who judge in equity. *(V - 45)*

The Opposite of Justice is Wrong-doing : The opposite of justice is wrong-doing, whether on the level of individual life or that of community life. In either case its consequence is destruction. Etymologically, the Arabic word for wrong-doing, *Zulm,* means 'putting something in the wrong place'.

(Ibn-i-Taimiya, Al Jawame' fi Siyasatil Ilahiya)

Wider Sense of the Word According to the Quran : The word, Zulm, has been used in the Quran in a variety of implied senses — blasphemy, joining partners with God, sinfulness, injustice, doing wrong to others, and oppression being some of them. But all these imply senses which are related to the etymological root-meaning of the word. Regarding blasphemy the Quran says:

Who, then, doth more wrong
Than one who utters
A lie concerning God,
And rejects the Truth
When it comes to him.
Is there not in Hell
An abode for blasphemers? *(XXXIX - 32)*
Who is more unjust
Than one who invents
A lie against God *(VII - 37)*

Concerning the joining of partners with God it is said: 'Indeed joining partners with God is great wrong-doing'. Regarding sinfulness it is said:

But there are among them
Some who wrong their own
Souls; *(XXXV - 32)*

When they have done wrong to their own souls —'Whomsoever does such a thing, verily he will do wrong to his own soul'. Then, regarding the doing of injustice and wrong to others it is said:

Say: The things that my Lord
Hath indeed forbidden are:
Shameful deeds, whether open
Or secret; sins and trespasses
Against turth or reason. *(VII - 33)*

The blame is only
Against those who oppress
Men with wrong-doing
And insolently transgress
Beyond bounds through the land,
Defying right and justice: *(XLII - 42)*

Besides the above Verses, there are others dealing with the subject of *Zulm* and its agents and victims.

Condemnation of Wrong-doing in the Traditions : We refer to certain Traditions below, which indicate the condemnation of wrong-doing in the Islamic scheme of cultural reconstruction. Once the Holy Prophet said:

> *Wrong-doing will take the shape of Darkness on the Day of Judgement.* (Bukhari, Muslim, Mishkat: *Babul Zulm)*

Once the Holy Prophet happened to pass by Hijr—the ruins of the habitations of the Thamud, the people of the Prophet Saleh. He said:

> *You should enter weeping the (ruined) houses of those who did wrong to their own souls, lest the same punishment of God seize you as it seized them'. Then the Holy Prophet bowed his head and hurriedly passed through that valley (of archaeological ruins).* (Ibid) *On another occasion the Holy Prophet said:*

> *'Help your brother, be he the agent of wrong-doing or the victim'. The Companions asked: 'O Prophet of Allah, if he is a victim, he can be helped; but if he is an agent of wrong-doing, how can he be helped?'. The Holy Prophet replied: He must be prevented from doing wrong'.*
> *(Muslim, Nasrul Akhi Zaliman au Mazluma)*

Once the Holy Prophet asked his companions: 'Who is poor?' The Companions replied: 'One among us who has no money and material goods'. At this the Holy Prophet said:

> *In my* ummat *(religious community) the poor person is one who carries (the testimony of) all the (theological) virtues like prayers (namaz), fasting and charity (zakat) on the Day of Judgment, but he is the one who has abused somebody, has falsely accused somebody, has devoured the goods of somebody, has shed the blood of somebody, and has beaten somebody. All his virtues shall be given*

over to these victims. If his virtues fall short of providing compensation for the rights of his victims, the vices of the victims will be taken off and laid on him. And then he shall be thrown into Hell.

(Muslim, Mishkat: Babul Zulm)

Kindness

Mercy is the greatest Attribute of God. The Quran says:

But My Mercy extendeth
To all things. *(VII - 156)*

Our Lord! Thy Reach
Is over all things,
In Mercy and Knowledge. *(XL - 7)*

For Thou art the Best
Of those who show mercy! *(XXIII - 109)*

Mercy has been regarded as the greatest quality of Mohammad (peace be upon him).

We sent thee not, but
As a Mercy for all creatures. *(XXI - 107)*

... to the Believers
Is he most kind and merciful *(IX - 128)*

Mercy or compassion has been emphasized even in the character of the Companions:

Compassionate amongst each other. *(XLVIII - 29)*

No Redress for Mankind Without Mercy : There can be no progress and prosperity of mankind without mercy. The Holy Prophet said:

Mercy is lacked only by the unfortunate
(Tirmidhi, Mishkat, *Al Shafqa wal Rahma alal Khalq, Fasl II).*

In the Islamic scheme of cultural reconstruction, there are certain Traditions concerning the importance of, and insistence on, mercy. Here are some of the sayings of the Holy Prophet:

Mercy is a branch which is entwined with the Merciful One.

He who does not take mercy on others is not taken mercy on.

> *Take mercy on earthly beings, and the Heavenly Beings will take mercy on you.*
>
> *He who has not taken mercy on our juniors and has not respected our seniors is not of us.*
>
> *Mercy is not confined to human beings; it encompasses the animals too. On one occasion the Holy Prophet said:*
>
> *There is reward for showing mercy to every animal.*
> *(Bukhari, Muslim)*

On another occasion he said:

> *If a person shows mercy to a slaughtered animal, God will show mercy to him on the Day of Judgment.* (Bukhari, *Al Adabul Mufrad, Bab Rahmatil Bahaim)*

The Holy Prophet has condemned hard-heartedness and lack of compassion and mercy in various ways. For example, a bedouin told him that while the Holy Prophet kissed children his own folk did not do so. At this the Holy Prophet said: 'What can I do if Allah has taken away compassion from your hearts?' (*Bukhari,* Kitabul Adab; Bab Rahmatil Maulud)

The Holy Prophet forbade the various cruel sports of making the animals fight. *(Abu Daud* Kitabul Jihad). Mercy and justice do not contradict each other, unlike what some people think. On the other hand, it is mercy that implicates justice between the good and the evil, the oppressor and the oppressed, the treacherous and the loyal, the pious and the vicious. Treating them in the same way would be a travesty of mercy.

Welfare

It means meting out such treatment to the other person as would give him happiness and relief. The Quran has repeatedly mentioned Allah as the 'Doer of Good'. The good works. He has been mentioned in various contexts, and His Servants have been ordained to do good likewise. Thus, we have the following Verse:

> *God commands justice, the doing*
>
> *Of good...* *(XVI - 90)*

Justice dispenses to every person what his due is. But with the spirit of doing good one feels concerned about the distress and comfort, misery and happiness of the people. In other words, the matter does not end with justice; doing good is also commanded for the sake of bringing redress and comfort to people. The Quran speaks of various forms of doing good. For example, giving financial help :

> *But do thou good,*
> *As God has been good*
> *To thee...* *(XXVIII - 77)*

Rescuing somebody from affliction:

> *He was indeed*
> *Good to me (says Joseph) when He*
> *Took me out of prison...* *(XII - 100)*
> *Forgiving wrongs etc. In this context it is said:*
> *For God loves those*
> *Who do goods;* *(III - 134)*

Synonymous to 'doing good' some other terms have also been used in the Quran—for example, *fazl, 'urf, ma'roof* and *bir.* If we consider all their contexts it becomes evident that 'doing good' is not confined to any one particular form; it encompasses all forms of virtue. Hence, the Holy Prophet said:

> *God has made it encumbent on you to do good with every being. Even if you have got to kill somebody, do it with good. If you want to slaughter an animal, do it with good; sharpen your knife well and let your slaughtered animal have quick relief (let it not linger in pain and agony).*
> (Muslim, *Kitabul Said Wal Zabaih)*

Doing good is not commanded merely in return for the good done to you. It is also commanded in return for the wrong, somebody does to you. The Quran says:

> *Is there any Reward*
> *For Good — other than Good?* *(LV - 60)*
> *Once a person asked the Prophet of Allah (peace be upon him): When I pass by a man he does not offer me any hospitality. If he passes by me, should I do the same?' The Holy Prophet replied: 'No, you must offer hospitality to him.'* *(Tirmidhi, Bab Ma Ja-e-fil Ahsan wal 'Afv)*

Granting Mercy

Forgiveness is also one of the most important Attributes of God. If it were not there this sinful world would have been destroyed. Divine

Names like *Ghaffar, Ghaafir, Ghafoor*—which imply forgiveness—keep recurring in the Quran. Forgiveness has been mentioned in several places. It is an important quality of the Believeres:

And, when they are angry
Even then forgive; *(XLVII-37)*
Let them forgive and overlook,
Do you not wish
That God should forgive you?
For God is Oft-Forgiving
Most Merciful. *(XXIV-22)*

The Quran makes special mention of those situations which call for forgiveness.

People are very touchy in matters of religion. They may give rise to hot disputes and enraged feelings; but in such situations forgiveness is commanded:

But forgive and overlook,
Till God accomplish
His purpose; *(II-109)*

When a man's honour is assaulted, he is enraged. In this situation too the command is forgiveness.

Let not those among you
Who are endued with grace
And amplitude of means
Resolve by oath against helping
Their kinsmen, those in want
And those who have left
Their homes in God's cause:
Let them forgive and overlook. *(XXIV-22)*

The historical occasion for the revelation of this Verse is significant. Mistah was a Kinsman of Abu Bakr who used to support him with financial assistance. But when Mistah took part in hurling slanders against Aisha, in connexion with Ifk (slander), Abu Bakr withdrew his support. At this the above Verse, which commands forgiveness, was revealed. Once a person asked the Holy Prophet: 'O Prophet of Allah, How many times should I forgive the offences of my servant?' The Holy

Prophet kept silent for sometime, and then said: 'Seventy times every day'. *(Tirmidhi,* Abwab AlBirwal Sila). Here the number is not meant to be taken literally; it means 'most frequently' according to the Arabic idiom.

Forgiveness Taught to Maintain Self-respect : In the existing New Testament forgiveness is taught in such a way as to engender feelings of meekness and lowness in the individual. But in the Islamic scheme of cultural reconstruction, it is taught in a manner which does not injure self-respect; nor does it upset the social system. Thus even revenge is sanctioned in the face of oppression and wrong-doing; but forgiveness is seen as the better policy, one which is loved by God and is worthy of reward in his eyes :

The recompense for an injury
Is an injury thereto
(In degree): but if a person
Forgives and makes reconciliation,
His reward is due
From God: for God
Loveth not those who
Do wrong. *(XLII. 40)*

To be able to forgive even when one is entitled to take revenge is a matter of great courage and moral nobility.

Providing Maximum Aid

The Self-subsisting One is He who subsists not only Himself and in His own right but also supports the subsistence of others. Etymologically, 'the self-subsisting One is he who subsists by himself, guards and takes care of everything and provides for everything the support that it needs for its subsistence.'

(Zubaidi, Tajul Urus)

At another place it has been observed:

Along with the permanent or eternal support of His own Self, He should also make for the subsistence of everything that exists, so much so that it is not possible to imagine the existence and subsistence of anything without the Self-Subsisting One. (Ibid).

When this virtue is reflected in human life it engenders endurance and independence from all that is not God. It enables man to help others and to support them with all courage and fortitude. The Quran says:

God ! there is no god
But He— the Living,
The Self-Subsisting, Eternal.
No slumber can Seize Him
Nor sleep. *(II.255)*
God! there is no God
But He,— the Living,
The Self-Subsisting, Eternal.
It is He Who sent down
To thee (step by step),
In truth, the Book, *(III.2-3)*

This virtue also leads man to discovering the reality of things. It is the reflection of the Divine Attribute of The Knower of Invisible Things. Regarding Adam, it is said in the Quran:

And He taught Adam the names
Of all things; *(II.31)*

Here the word names (Asma) is preceded by the Definite Article 'the' *(Al)*. This implies particular names which are mentioned here generically. The word *Al-Asma* has been explicated as follows:

> *God revealed to Adam, knowledge regarding the Essential nature of things, their names, the modes of knowing, the principles operating behind created things, and the knowledge of tools.* (Baizawi)

In Razi's Tafseer-i-Kabeer it is said God taught Adam the nature of things and their properties. In *Kashshaf* it is said that God taught Adam the names by which things should be called. When Adam recounted the Names and when the angels could not do so God said:

.... *"did I not tell you*
That I know the secrets of heavens
And earth, *(II-33)*

Search-after-search

Man has the ability to enquire into the reality of things, to make researches and inventions. Thus, he goes on progressing. This virtue is a reflection of the Divine Attribute of the Originator and the Inventor.

The Quran says:

To Him is due
The primal origin
Of the heavens and the earth:
When he decreeth a matter,
He sayth to it: "Be",
and it is *(II. 117)*

To Him is due
The Primal origin
Of the heavens and the earth:
How can He have a son
When He hath no consort? *(VI - 101)*

The virtue of making artifice inclines man to craftmanship and works of artifice. This whole system of creating artifice and artifacts is running because of the image of God's attribute of the Maker in man. Man, according to his capabilities, assimilates this attribute of God and creates his own work.

The Quran says:

(Such is) the artistry of God,
Who dispenses of all things
In perfect order: *(XXVII - 88)*

Specific Qualities

Under the category of distinctive attributes are manifested those qualities which are related to beauty. For example *Al-Raheem, Al-Aleem:* the Merciful, the Knower; *Al-Wahhab, Al-Ghaffar:* The Bestower of Infinite Bountees, Most Forgiving: *Al-Salam, Al-Momin:* The Source of Peace (and Perfection), The Guardian of Faith; *Al-Bari, Al-Mussawwir: The Evolver, The Bestower of Forms, Al-Razzaq, Al-Fattah:* Sustainer, The Resolver*; Al-Basit, Al-Rafe'* The Expander, The Exalter*; Al-Lateef, Al-Khabeer,* One Who understands the Finest Mysteries, The All-acquainted; *Al-Moiz, Al-Hafeez:* Giver of Power and Honour, Giver of Protection; *Al-Wajid, Al-Moqeet:* One Who Receives, One Who Provides Sustenance; *Al-Haseeb, Al-Moqsit;* One Who Calls to Account, One Who Dispenses Justice; *Al-Haleem, Al- Kareem :* The Meek One, The Generous One; *Al-Wakeel, Al-Hameed:* The Best Dispenser of Affairs, The Most Worthy of Praise; *Al-Mudda, Al-Moeed:* One Who

Brings things Into Existence, One Who Causes things to Return; *Al-Mohi, Al-Momeet:* Giver Of Life, Sender of Death; *Al-Munim, Al-Mohib-* One Who Gives Rewards, One Who Loves; *Al- Raoof, Al-Bar, Al-jameel*: Most Kind, Most Good, Most Beautiful; *Al-Mughni, Al-Moti*: Who Frees from Need, Who Bestows; *Al-Nafe', Al-Hadi:* Giver of Benefits, Giver of Guidance; *Al-Badi', Al-Rasheed:* One Who Devises, One Who Moves along the Straight Path, *AMojeeb, Al-Kafeel:* One Who accepts, One Who Provides For; *Al-Hannan, Al-Mannan:* Most Affectionate, The Greatest Doer of Good; *Al-Kamil-Al-Jawwad:* The Absolutely Perfect, The Most Generous; *Al-Kafi, Al-Shafi:* One Who is All Sufficient, One Who Heals; *Al-Wadood, Al-Shakoor:* The Greatest Lover, The Greatest Acknowledger; *Al-Wali, Al-Tawwab:* The Greatest Friend, Approver of Repentance; *Al-Naseer, Al-Mughees; Al-Mujeer:* The Greatest Helper, One who Listens to Cries of Help, One Who Gives Shelter, Zul-Taul Zul-Fazl: One Who Has Long Reach, Bounteous.

Amongst constructive Attributes those qualities are imaged which belong to *Al-Qabiz, Al-Khafis:* One Who Covers, One Who Spreads; *Al-Wase', Al-Mumeet, Al-Mueed:* One Who Spreads Infinitely, One Who Sends Death, One Who Causes Things to Return; *Al-Mozil, Al-Raqeeb:* One Who Lays Low, One Who keeps Watch; *Al-Qavi, Al-Mateen; Al-Shaheed:* The Powerful, The Firm, The All-Acquainted; *Al-Muntaqim, ZulJalal Wal Ikram;* The Avenger of Wrongs, The Possessor of Glory and Power and Greatness; *Al-Mane', Al-Dhar;* One Who Prevents, One Who Dispenses Losses and Adversity; *Al-Suboor, Al-Baseer:* The Most Patient, The Greatest Seer; *Al-Moazzib, Al-Dayyan:* Dispenser of Punishments, The Judge *ZulBatsh Shadeedul Iqab:* The Most Powerful in Catching and The Giver of the Greatest Punishment.

Supportive Aspects

Among complementary attributes the qualities related to Divine Perfection are reflected. For Example *Al-Rab, Al-Rahman;* The Lord and Sustainer, The Beneficent, *Al-Khaliq, Al-Adil, Al-Hakim;* The Creator, the Justicer the Wise; *Al-Samee', Al-Baseer, Al-Qayyum:* One Who Listens, One Who Sees, One Who Holds Up; *Al-Tahir, WalBatin,* The Manifest, and The Hidden; *Al-Majid, Al-Jame', Al-Bais:* The Glorious One, The Greatest Gatherer, One Who Causes everything; *Al-Muheet, Al-Mureed, Al-Qareeb:* The All-Encompassing, One Who Wills Absolutely, One Who is Absolutely Close; *Al-Ali, Al-Rafi, Al-Jalil, Al-Kaleem;* The Exalted, The High, The Glorious, The Noble; *Al-Modabbir, Al-Motakallim:* One Who Plans, One Who Speaks; *Malikal Mulk:* The Sovereign of All the Worlds; *Allamul Ghuyub:* The Knower of Secret Things; *Aleemum Bizzatis Sudoor:* The Knower of the Secrets of the Hearts; *Laisa Kamislehi Shaiun:* There Is None Like Him.

Among the above Divine Attributes there are some which overlap one another; but it makes no difference in respect of their reflection or imaging in man.

Virtues Emanating from Essential Attributes : The following virtues emanate from the Essential Attributes of God:

Owing to self-respect man is able to rise above objection and lowliness. Once he is lifted to the state of self-respect, he does not bow before any worldly power or greatness. He believes that the greatest agents of power and the greatest dispensers of profit and loss themselves depend on Almighty God. The Quran says.

... that to God
Belongs all power *(II-165)*
... the Command
Rests with none but God *(VI-57)*
Verily those whom ye
Call upon besides God
Are servants like unto you *(VII-194)*
No aid can they give them,
Nor can they aid themselves! *(VII-192)*
There is no help
Except from God,
The Exalted, the Wise *(III – 126)*
To Him belongs the Keys
Of the heavens and the earth *(XLII-12)*
If God do touch thee
With hurt there is none
Can remove it but He:
If He had designed some benefit
For thee, there is none
Can keep back His favour: *(X-107)*

Broad Vision

From the Essential Attributes is derived a comprehensive outlook. By virtue of this outlook man is able to transcendend personal, communal and national limitations so as to have his being spread over the whole universe.

In all his attitudes, in his friendship and animity, his love and hatred, his regard and disregard, he achieves a universal standard. Everything in the universe belongs to him simply because it belongs to his God.

The Quran says:

... While all creatures
In the heavens and on earth
Have, willing or unwilling
Bowed to His Will
(Accepted Islam),
And to Him shall they
All be brought back. *(III-83)*

O mankind, we created
You from a single (pair)
Of a male and a female,
And made you into
Nations and tribes, that
Ye may know each other
(not that ye may despise
Each other). Verily
The most honoured of you
In the sight of God
Is (he who is) the most
Righteous of you.
And God has full knowledge
And is well aquainted
(with all things) *(XLIX-13)*

It is He Who hath created for you
All things that are on earth: *(II-29)*

Mohammad (peace be upon him) said:

All human beings are brothers to one another.(Muslim, Abu Daud).

At another place he said:

> *Undoubtedly the earth belongs to God and human beings are servants of God.*
> (Abu Daud, Nasbul Raya).

On one occasion Ali said:

> *Their goods (the goods of other human beings) are like our goods and their lives are like our lives. (Nasbul Raya, Vol. III, Kitabul Sair)*

Another virtue is peace of heart. Owing to this virtue a man does not give way to despair, even if circumstances go against him. God is always with him.

This is such an invaluable virtue that all efforts of intellect and philosophy fail to achieve it. All the advancement of western civilization and all its material equipment cannot equal it in value. The Quran says:

> *When My servants*
> *Ask thee concerning Me,*
> *I am Indeed*
> *Close (to them): I listen*
> *To the prayer of every*
> *Suppliant when he calleth on Me:*
> *Let them also, with a will,*
> *Listen to My call,*
> *and believe in Me:*
> *That they may walk*
> *In the right way* *(XXXIX-53)*
> *... and never*
> *Give up hope of God's*
> *Soothing Mercy: Truly*
> *None despair of God's*
> *Soothing Mercy, Except*
> *Those who have no faith* *(XII-87)*

Tolerance and Strength

Through this virtue, a man's heart becomes strong and he sees the power of God with him. He learns to bear afflictions. The Quran says:

Nay seek (God's) help
With patient perseverance
And prayer: *(II-45)*
...For God is with those
Who patiently persevere *(II-153)*
And We appointed, from among
They, leaders,
Under Our command, so long
As they persevere with patient. *(XXXII-24)*

On one occasion, the Holy Prophet said: Patient perseverance is the commander of his (somebody's) army. Ali has brought out the psychological aspect of patience as follows:

> *Patience has the same relation to(the body of faith as the head to the human body. Just as on severing the head the body becomes useless and dead, in the same way the man who has lost patience cannot attain the faith.*
> *(Ibn-i-Abi Shaibah,* Musannaf; Baihaqi)

Owing to this virtue base emotions like lust and greed and jealousy are got rid of. For achieving benefit and avoiding harm a man abstains from adopting a method which may injure self-dignity and self-respect, for he knows that the ends of all things are in the hands of God. The Quran says:

... All bounties
Are in the hand of God.
He granteth them
To whom he pleaseth:
And God careth for all,
And He knoweth all things *(III-73)*
For the earth is God's
To give as a heritage
To such of His servants
As He pleaseth: *(VII-128)*
Thou enduest with honour
Whom Thou pleasest:
And Thou bringest Low

Whom Thou Pleasest:
In Thy hand is all Good.
Verily, over all things
Thou hast power. (III-26)

Purity

Chastity is the soul of all virture and the very essence of humanity. It enlightens one's life and makes for the distinction between man and animal. In Western civilization, the measure of character is worldly benefit and therefore chastity is not very much valued, nor does anybody bother to protect it and keep it up. But in the Islamic scheme of cultural reconstruction, the measure of character is Divine Attributes. So the virture of charity aquires a great salience and special attention is given to its protection and maintenance. Chastity is the integral part of Prophethood. It is the distinctive characteristic of the family of the Holy Prophet and of the saints and the godly. In the Quranic Verse, there is the evidence of the wife of the Governor of Egypt in favour of Joseph:

I did seek to seduce him
From his (true) self but he did
Firmly save himself
Guiltiness!... *(XII-32)*

Earlier it has been said of Joseph:

... thus
(Did We order) that We
Might turn away from him
All evil and shameful deeds:
For he was one of Our servants,
Sincere and purified. *(XII-24)*

Regarding Yahya the Quran say:

... and (s/c
Besides) noble, chaste,
And a Prophet,—
Of the (godly) company
And the righteous *(III-39)*

After mentioning the stories of many other Prophets. The Quran says:

They were, in Our sight,
Truly, of the company
Of the Elect and the Good. *(XXXVII-47)*

Regarding the members of the family of the Holy Prophet, the Quran observes:

These are not affected
By what people say *(XXIV-26)*

Regarding the Saints and the godly, the Quran says:

Those who invoke not,
With God, any other god,
Nor slay such life as God
Has made sacred, except
For just cause, nor commit
Fornication; *(XXV-68)*

There is very strict punishment for one who falsely accuses somebody of fornication, which implies the special importance of chastity:

And those who launch
A charge against the chaste women,
And produce not four witnesses
(To support their allegation),—
Flog them with eighty stripes;
And reject their evidence
Ever after: for such men
Are wicked transgressors;— *(XX IV-4)*

Lewdness is the Opposite of Chastity : Although the word 'lewdness' covers all kinds of evils, but it is mostly used for shamelessness and promiscuity (or adultery)—the Quran says:

If any of your women
Are guilty of lewdness, *(IV-15)*
... except
Where they have been guilty
Of open lewdness: *(IV-19)*

Encouragement of Lewdness in Western Civilization : Western Civilization has a paraphernalia which serves to deprive man of chastity and to encourage in him lewdness both on the level of thought and action. On the level of thought there are "isms" which condemn the suppression or concealment of sex desires. Then there is a hedonistic philosophy which says that man is as free to gratify his desires of sex as he is to gratify his desire for water; any interference in this matter is deemed as an interference in personal or private matters.

On the level of action, there are nude pictures of women, parties of dance and music, free mix up of sex, night clubs, blue films, dresses exposing or involving nakedness, exhibition of beauty and even beauty contests, dances charged with sexuality, sexy music and art, different types of female friends, for example, girl friend, call girl, company girl, party girl etc.

Encouragement of Chastity in the Scheme of Cultural Reconstruction : In our scheme of cultural reconstruction arrangements are made to prevent lewdness and to encourage chastity. Hence all things that directly or indirectly lead to lewdness have been rejected and disapproved of. For example, the human eye takes precedence in conveying messages of lewdness and therefore a check is put on the aberration of the eyes.

The Quran says:

Say to the believing men
That they should lower
Their gaze and guard
Their modesty: that will make
For greater purity for them:
And God is well aquainted
With all that they do. *(XXIV-30)*

The slight carelessness and forwardness on the part of women may create misunderstanding in a man and may encourage them to take liberties with them. For this reason, special checks are put on women.

The Quran says:

And say to the believing women
that they should lower
Their gaze and guard

Their modesty: that they
should not display their
beauty and ornaments except
What (must ordinarily) appear
Thereof; and they should
Draw their veils over
Their bosoms ... *(XXIV-31)*
O Prophet! tell
Thy wives and daughters,
And the believing women,
That they should cast
Their outer garment over
Their persons (when abroad):
That is most convenient,
That they should be known
(as such) and not molested. *(XXXIII-51)*

In the Traditions, there are various instructions regarding keeping away from lewdness and maintaining chastity. Once the daughter of Abu Bakr, Asma, came into the presence of the Holy Prophet wearing a very thin piece of clothing. The Holy Prophet said:

> *Asma, when a girl attains puberty, it is not decent to look at any part of her body except her face and palms.*
> (Abu Daud, Mishkat: Kitabul Libas)

As regards looking at women, the Holy Prophet said:

> *After the first glance, which is accidental, do not cast another glance. The first glance is alright for you but the second glance is not so.*
> (Tirmidhi, *Kitabul Istizan, Bab 'Maja-afi Nazratil Fuja-ah)*

It means that if one happens to cast a glance on a woman, he must not cast the glance the second time. Jarir b. Abdullah said: 'I asked the Holy Prophet regarding the casting of accidental glance. He instructed that one should turn away one's glance'.

Extreme Care Commanded: Besides this, there is prohibition against all those things that interfere with the maintenance of chastity—improper dresses and manners, immodesty of behaviour, use of perfumes, exhibition of body or dress or ornaments.

In Western Culture there are No Strict Laws Against Lewdness : One way of depriving man from chastity and encouraging lewdness in him is to have leniency in laws and punishment regarding lewdness. In Western culture lewdness is divided into "with consent" and "without consent" and thus rape is regarded as a form of amusement. But even in the case of the evidence of an assault on woman there is no very severe punishment, such as may set an example for the society and bring correction in it. At first the freedom of the West in these matters looked very commandable, particularly when it was seen as non-interference in personal matters. But when things went too far and the violation of chastity became common and open proposals like the following came up:

> *"The habitual sex criminals, should be castrated through surgery instead of being kept in prison for years and years."* (London, *14 April, quoted by* Sidq-e-Jadid, *30 April 1965). In 1965 Mary Stock, an eminent British Gynaecologist, proposed that such a law should be promulgated. It exists in Denmark where sex crimes have very much decreased, she said.*

Severe Punishment in the Scheme of Cultural Reconstruction : In the scheme of cultural reconstruction the crime of lewdness is punished very severely and there are very strict laws against it. Thus, on the one hand, criminals get their due and on the other the whole society learns a lesson. For example, for women with whom adultery is a first offence the following punishment has been prescribed:

> *If any of your women*
> *Are guilty of lewdness,*
> *Take the evidence of four*
> *(Reliable) witnesses from amongst you*
> *Against them; and if they testify,*
> *Confine them to houses until*
> *Death do claim them,*
> *Or God ordain for them*
> Some (other) way. *(IV-15)*

This commandment applies to the situation of first offence. The last phrase of the Verse has the same implication otherwise strictures against this crime would have been mentioned at one place. For men the punishment is prescribed as follows:

If two men among you
Are guilty of lewdness,
Punish them both.
If they repent and amend,
Leave them alone; *(IV-16)*

Corporeal Punishment for men and imprisonment for women are prescribed probably in view of the physical weakness of the latter. Another reason for the punishment of imprisonment in the case of women is that their immodesty creates greater mischief and therefore by shutting them up this mischief can be prevented. These punishments cover all forms of lewdness and promiscuity, be they heterosexual or homosexual. Regarding the next phase of the crime of lewdness, which is one of hardened criminality, the following punishment is prescribed for both the man and the woman guilty of lewdness:

The woman and the man
Guilty of adultery or fornication,—
Flog each of them
With a hundred stripes:
Let not compassion move you
In their case, in a matter
Prescribed by God, if ye believe
In God and the Last Day:
And let a party
Of the Believers
Witness their punishment. *(XX IV-2)*

Dishonesty in Married Life

The above punishment was meant for unmarried persons. For married persons guilty of lewdness, the Holy Prophet has ordained stoning to death. Thus a Tradition says:

> *A man called Maiz came to the Holy Prophet and confessed his adultery four times. The Holy Prophet gave orders for the stoning of the man to death (Abu Daud;* Mishkat). *The punishment for lewdness is very severe. This is why, there are very strict conditions laid down for the establishment of the crime. These details are found in books of Islamic Jurisprudence.*

To modern civilised man, these punishments appear not only severe but savage. It is because he is not very much aware of the value of chastity and the bad influences of lewdness on society, when in his society he sees lewdness being encouraged. The culture having this awareness would make severeness of punishment in such matters inevitable. In that case, severeness of punishment would be considered like some bitter medicine necessary for the health of the society.

Western Culture Not Aware of the Monstrosity of Lewdness : In fact, Western culture lacks the awareness of the monstrosity of the offence of lewdness. It is for this reason that it does not feel need of having strict laws against it, laws that may prescribe very severe punishments.

If the awareness had been there, western society would not have hesitated in prescribing such punishments against this offence, punishments similar to those it prescribes for offences like treason or spying—in which case the victim is subjected to death by various kinds of torture, electirc shocks and all. If the occurrence of sex crimes continues as such and if chastity is commonly violated in western culture, the day is not far off when western society would take recourse to very severe punishment for habitual criminals.

Monstrosity of Lewdness Realised in the Scheme of Cultural Reconstruction : In our scheme of cultural reconstruction, the monstrosity of lewdness is realised fully. This is testified by the following Traditions of the Holy Prophet:

> *Nobody commits the act of lewdness in the state of faith.*
> (Mishkat).

It means that purity and nobility of faith and the monstrosity and corruption of lewdness are incompatible. On one occasion, the Holy Prophet listed the activities of certain organs as lewdness, for these organs act as instruments of this crime:

> *The lewdness of both the eyes is looking at private or forbidden parts. The lewdness of the ear is listening to forbidden voices. The lewdness of the tongue is uttering forbidden discourse. The lewdness of the hand is to make use of the hands for forbidden actions. The lewdness of the feet is walking in forbidden ways.* (Mishkat, *Babul Qadr).*

This gives an idea of the awareness of the monstrosity of lewdness in Islamic culture. Thus, even 'going near this deed' has been forbidden:

> *Nor come nigh to Adultery,*
> *For it is a shameful (deed)*
> *And evil...* *(XVII-32)*

Once the Holy Prophet was asked: 'Which sin is the greatest?' He replied: Regarding somebody as equal to God, though it is God Who has created thee. Then he was asked: "Which sin is next in greatness ?' He replied: Slaying one's child for fear of sharing one's food with him or her.' Then he was asked: 'Which sin is next in greatness?' He replied: "Committing adultery with the wife of one's neighbourer" (*Mishkat,* Babul Kabair)

Lewdness is Hateful to Human Nature and is Disapproved by Society : On account of the monstrosity of lewdness human nature abhors it and human life is never ready to accept it. The Quran syas:

Women impure are for men impure,
And men impure for women impure
And women of purity
Are for men of purity,
And men of purity
Are for women of purity *(XXIV-26)*
Let no man guilty of
adultery or fornication marry
Any but a woman
Similarly guilty, or an Unbeliever:
Nor let any but such a man
Or an unbeliever
Marry such a woman:
To the Believers such a thing
Is forbidden *(XXIV-3)*

It is not the purpose of these Verses to lay down any law; their purpose is to underscore the revulsion of human nature and of society against lewdness. *Roohul Maani* comments by saying that this amounts to the expression of extreme disapproval of the act of lewdness. It goes on to say that the incompatibility of the act has been substituted for the absence of the act.

It is evident that both the male and the female lewd persons are not worthy of marrying a chaste partner because of the stain of corruption they bear. Therefore, marital relation between the chaste and the unchaste is forbidden. In the literature of the Arabs, descriptions like the following are used for indicating the ugliness of some act:

A king never tells lies. Which means that a dirty thing like a lie does not become an honourable man like a king.

Marrying a Lewd Person is Forbidden by Some Jurists : Some scholars of Islamic jurisprudence have argued for the taboo of marriage between the lewd and the chaste. Others have advised separation between the partners after the act of lewdness has been committed inside wedlock.

There are some people who do not differentiate between the beginning and the middle of a course. What we imply is that just as it is not lawful for a believer to marry a lewd woman in the same way if the woman commits the act of lewdness after marriage it is not lawful to keep her as a wife. Some scholars have given the verdict of unlawfulness in the case of the beginning or entry into marital career; but if the act is committed in the middle of the marital career they have not given the verdict of unlawfulness or taboo. (Razi, *Tafseer-i-Kabeer; Tafsir-i-Noor)*

This is supported by the following Traditions: The Holy Prophet once said:

"The adulterer who has been punished with public flogging should marry a woman like himself."

(Abu Daud, Kitabul Nikah)

Murthid b. Abi Murthid Ghanawi once requested the Holy Prophet to get him married to a woman of Mecca (She was Ghasaq, the notorious adulteress). The Holy Prophet kept silent for some time, till the above mentioned Verse (XXIV-3) was revealed, and then he said: "Do not marry her".

The following episode connected with the life of Ali is also enlightening:

A man married some woman. The woman committed adultery. She was punished for it. When the matter was brought to the judgement court of Ali, he gave the verdict of separation between them and told the woman to marry somebody like herself. All these punishments do not amount to any prescription of law; the government is authorised to give whatever punishment it likes in accordance with the exigencies of contemporary laws of the Shariah.

Capital Punishment for Lewdness and the Government Acting as Prosecutor : On account of the monstrosity and seriousness of the offence of lewdness this punishment is capital punishment. The state itself acts as a plaintiff for carrying out the sentence, which means that even if the wronged party Forgoes its claim, the state takes upon itself the duty (the rights of God) to execute the punishment. In Islamic Jurisprudence it is observed:

> *The rulers are justified to punish for this offence even in the absence of having it established by prosecution and even in the absence of any plaintiff. Similarly, it is justified to point witnesses in absence of any plaintiff.*

The standard for the establishment of offences for which the punishment is capital and for which the state itself acts as a plaintiff should be high and invulnerable.

There is wide possibility of escaping the punishment in this case, and the conditions for punishments are very strict and difficult to be fulfilled. In this case, the state is responsible for doing two things: (1) To propose alternative punishments which may be substituted for capital punishment, (2) To establish such courts as would hear to suits cancelled on account of the paucity of firm evidence or the lack of standard witnesses.

For such courts, there are terms like *Waliul Jaraem and Sahibulrad* in the books of jurisprudence. Such courts were supposed to propose alternative punishments in cases where the suits had been rejected because of lack of evidence. These courts adopted an outlook wider than the ordinary courts of justice (which gave the sentence of capital punishment). They adopted this wider outlook in enquiring into the offence and establishing it.

Humility and Honour of the Self

Modesty and self-respect are natural characteristic of human nature which gives rise to many moral virtures and safeguards chastity. If this virtue is cultivated from childhood it develops and acquires great significance, otherwise it dwindles away. In western civilization, this virtue is not very much valued, nor any arrangement is made for its cultivation. On the other hand, the western way of life tries to eliminate it from the very beginning. But in our scheme of cultural reconstruction it has been commanded to safeguard and cultivate this virtue from the very beginning. For example, the female parts related to sexuality are to be covered; talking of immodest things and looking at them is forbidden; the lowering of glances is commanded; nakedness and nudeness is forbidden, so much that even in bathrooms and bed rooms precautions have to be taken in this regard. All these punishments are there in order to maintain modesty and self-respect.

Modesty and Self-Respect are the Qualities of God and His Prophet : Modesty and Self-respect become God and they are amongst His Attributes:

> *Indeed, Allah would be ashamed to disappoint one who begs Him for some good.*
>
> *(Baihaqi. 'Kitabul Asma wal Sifet fil Istihya')*

At another place it is said:

> *Nobody is more self-respecting than Allah. This is why He has forbidden lewdness.*
>
> *(Op. Cit., 'Kitabul Asma Wal Sifat fil, Ghairah')*

Modesty and self-respect were the qualities of Mohammad (peace be upon him).

> *The apostle of God was more modest than a parda-observing virgin.*
>
> *(Bukhari, Kitabul Adab, Babul Haya')*

For the same reason the Quran says that the Holy Prophet was ashamed to dismiss people lingering after dinner:

> *... He is ashamed*
>
> *To dismiss you,* *(XXXIII-53)*

Modesty and self-respect is so much involved with the sense of Prophethood that its violation is not to be tolerated even in the childhood of the Prophet. For example, in his childhood Mohammad (peace be upon him) was engaged in carrying bricks for the reconstruction of the Kaaba. On the advice of his uncle Abbas he loosened his lower garment and put it on his shoulder. But at this incident Mohammad (peace be upon him) fainted out of his sense of modesty.

Modesty and Self-Respect are Constituents of Faith and the Basis of Humanity : In the Traditions, modesty and self-respect have been emphasised in such a way as to indicate that they are the integral constituents of faith and the very basis of humanity. Thus, the Holy Prophet said:

> *Faith branches of have more than seventy dimensions. The highest dimension is the formulation of* La Ilaha Illah *(There is no deity except Allah), and the lowest dimension is marked by acts like removing troublesome things off the way. Modesty is also a dimension of faith. Another Tradition says faith and modesty are mutually involved. If one goes off, the other too does not remain.*

There is a Tradition according to Ibn-i-Abbas which says:

> *"When one of these is lost the other too is lost." Another Tradition says: "Every religion has a specific temperament, and the specific temperament of Islam is modesty." Then there is a Tradition which says: "Modesty leads only to good." Another Tradition declares that "modesty is itself good incarnate." There is still another tradition which defines the psychological quality of immodesty in a manner of premonition: 'If you do not observe modesty, do whatever you like'.*

Honesty and trustworthiness are the very essence of morality and the very basis of humanity. Without them the affairs of life are not set right, nor can mutual trust be established.

This is why the Quran calls the Revelation bearing Angel 'AlAmin' which means one who is 'Faithful to the Trust' or the 'Spirit of Faith and Truth'. For if trust is not reposed in this Angel, the authenticity of the Revelation cannot be ascertained:

> *With it came down*
>
> *The Spirit of Faith and Truth—* *(XXVI - 193)*
>
> *With authority there,*
>
> *(And) faithful to his trust.* *(LXXXI - 21)*

Almost every prophet has manifested to his people his quality of trustworthiness. Thus Shoaib:

> *I am to you an apostle*
>
> *Worthy of all trust.* *(XXVI -178)*

And the people of Mecca had nicknamed Mohammad (peace be upon him) as 'Amin' or 'The Trustworthy' before he was invested with Prophethood, which indicates the absolute trust they reposed in him.

Honesty and Trustworthiness Hold Good for Every Sphere of Life : In the scheme of cultural reconstruction honesty and trustworthiness are not confined to any one sphere of life; they encompass the economic, the legal, the moral — in fact every sphere of life. For example, the principle of honesty and trustworthiness demands that one must not come slack in fulfilling one's duties (to God's creatures and to God); must return undamaged what has been borrowed; must keep a secret for the sake of the other person's honour; must refrain from being a tell-tale; must give the right advice; must be conscientious; must appoint only the deserving etc. The Quran says:

God doth command you
To render back your Trusts
To those to whom they are due;
And when ye judge
Between man and man
That ye judge with justice (IV - 58)

In this Verse, the word 'trusts' encompasses all responsibilities and duties :

Amaanaat (trusts) is the plural of amanat, and so it includes all the duties incumbent on man, the duties to God as well as to fellow-creatures.
(Syed Mahmud Alusi, Ruhul Maani, 'Surah Nisa')

Wider Sense of Honesty and Trustworthiness According to the Quran : The Verses of the Quran testify to the wider sense of honesty and trustworthiness. Thus, the responsibility of vicegerency has been described as a Trust.

We did indeed offer
The trust to the heavens
And the Earth
And Mountains
But they refused
To undertake it,
Being afraid thereof:
But man undertook it;— (XXXIII - 72)

Whatever material goods man possesses are as a trust from God. Thus, the Quran:

And spend (in charity)
Out of (substance)
Whereof He has made you
Heirs (LVII-7)
Even man's life is a trust from God
God has purchased of the Believers
Their persons and their goods;
For theirs (in return)
Is the Garden (of Paradise): (IX -111)

If one lends something to somebody and allows him to keep it, that thing is a trust. It should be returned intact and undamaged:

And if one of you

Deposits a thing

On trust with another,

Let the trustee

(Faithful) discharge

His trust, and let him

Fear his Lord. *(II - 283)*

Duty (in service) is Also a trust. Any slackness in it is the betrayal of trust and dishonesty:

... truly the best

of men for thee to employ is

The (man) who is strong and trusty. *(XXVIII-26)*

Positions and posts are also a trust; to give them to the undeserving is dishonesty and betrayal of trust. Ibn-i-Taimiya while interpreting the Verse: "God doth command you to render back your Trusts..." (IV-58) includes Government and all the resources of the State in the word "Trusts". Some exegetes have made the following observations while interpreting this Verse: "The fulfilment of the trusts also means that positions should be given only to the deserving". (Mohammad Shafi Deobandi, *Maqala Dastur-i-Qurani)*

Qadi Sanaullah Panipati says:

The fulfilment of the trusts is not confined to giving things that are due because of birth and inheritance; it includes all the duties of man. Whatever is due to somebody should be paid. (Tafsiri Mazhari)

The Wider Sense of Honesty and Trustworthiness according to the Traditions:

The Holy Prophet has included in the term "Trust" many subtleties and particularities of life. For example, he includes advice in this term: 'One who is asked for an advice has been consigned with a trust."

(Bukhari, *Al Adabul Mufrad, Al Mustasharo Motaminun)*

It means that the adviser must give the right advice. Matters related to conferences should be treated as trust: "Conferences are held on trust." It means that the deliberation of one conference should not be reported in another. From such report are excluded those intrigues that are made for the purpose of torturing or dishonouring anybody. One should convey the reports of such intrigues to the person concerned, otherwise one would incur a sin.

The greatest trust is the secrets between husband and wife, which one does one's duty to hide and honour. The Holy Prophet says:

> *On Doom's Day, the greatest violation of trust in the eyes of God would be the exposing of secrets about a man's wife before others.*

Secret or private affairs are also trust. The Holy Prophet said: "When a man talks to somebody and then turns to the other side this talk is a trust."

All these remarks go to indicate how wide a sense the word "trust" has in Islam.

The Value of the Honesty and Trustworthiness: The value of honesty and trustworthiness and the harm of its violation are brought out by the following saying of the Holy Prophet:

> *He who is not trustworthy has no faith. He who does not pray has no religion. The religion prayer has the same status as the head has in the body.*
>
> (Kanzul, Ummal, *Vol. II, Al Amanat)*

Another Tradition says:

> *Trustworthiness makes one achieve his sustenance: dishonesty produces poverty.* (Ibid)
>
> *Still another Hadith says: Trustworthiness is wealth.*
>
> *(Ibid)*

Trustworthiness is not something externally imposed. It is something related to the inner most being of man.

> *Trustworthiness is related to the very roots of the hearts of the people (it is related to man's inner most nature). People have learnt it from the Quran, and then from the Sunnah.* (Mishkat, *Kitabul Fitan, Falt I)*

The loss of trustworthiness is the first thing that happens when *a* community degenerates. Prayer is retained and is the last thing that is lost. A Tradition says:

(By this community) trustworthiness will be lost first; and the thing that is retained in its religion till the very end will be prayer (namaz). But there are many worshippers (namazis) who will have no reward in the eyes of God. *(Kanzul 'Ummal, Vol II)*

Another Tradition says:

The first thing that you will lose in your religion is trustworthiness. *(Baihaqi, Vol. VI)*

Thus in the scheme of cultural reconstruction every duty and every responsibility which has been entrusted is a Trust. Man's status is that of a Trustee, and without fulfilling his Trust he cannot hope to achieve well-being. The other sub-category of Distinctive Attributes, one related to the welfare of human beings, has the following implications:

Losses due to Factories

These qualities go to engender the spirit of industry and hard work in man. He is unable to take challenges and perform difficult tasks. These qualities are the image of the Divine Attributes of being the Powerful and the Firm One and of being One Who Hath a Long Reach :

And hath a Long Reach

(In all things) *(XL-3)*

Truly strong is the Grip

(And power) of thy Lord *(LXXXV.12)*

Owing to this virtue, a man does not sit contented with one state but goes on striving continually to advance from state to state. This is an image of the Divine Attributes of the Ever Developing One :

Raised high above ranks

(or degrees),

(He is) the Lord

Of the Throne (of authority): *(XL.15)*

Every day in (new) splendour

Doth He (shine); *(LV.29)*

Subjection of the Universe to Man : This quality enables man to subject the universe to him, to exploit it in his interest, to enquire into the reality of things and to control nature. This is an image of the Divine Attribute of being— The All-Conquering One. In the Quran, we have many Verses in this connection:

It is He who has made
The sea subject, that ye
May eat thereof flesh
That is fresh and tender,
And that ye may extricate
Therefrom ornaments to wear; *(XVI. 14)*
He has made subject to you
The Night and the Day;
The Sun and the Moon;
And the Stars are in subjection
By His Command... *(XVI-12)*
Glory to Him Who
Has subjected these
To our (use), for we
Could never have accomplished
This (by ourselves) *(XLIII-13)*

Control Over Beneficial and Harmful Things : This quality enables man to have control over beneficial and harmful things in nature so as to establish his supremacy. This is an image of the Divine Attributes— One Who Directs to Good, Restrains and Dispenses Harm. Thus the Quran says :

If God do touch thee
With hurt, there is none
Can remove it but He:
If He had designed some benefit
For thee, there is none
Can keep back his favour: *(X.107)*
If God touch thee
With affliction, none
Can remove it but He;
If He touch thee with happiness,
He hath power over all things. *(VI-17)*

These qualities make for the power of resistance, for avenging of wrongs and for acting as a scourge. They bring about the eradication of evils. They reflect the Divine Attributes of the Avenger and the Punisher. The Quran says:

And God is swift
In taking account. *(XXIV-39)*
And verily thy Lord
Is (also) strict in punishment. *(XIII.6)*
Then shall anyone who
Has done an atom's weight
Of good, see it!
And anyone who,
Has done an atom's weight
Of evil, shall see it, *(XCIX—7-8)*

Thus, from the Divine Attributes of Glory, emanate constructive qualities that bring about discipline in life and manifest man's stature of vicegerency. In the scheme of cultural reconstruction, the Attributes of both Beauty and Power must have scope for manifestation. If any of these is neglected, life would become lop-sided and man would fail to achieve his proper status.

Virtues Emanating from Complementary Attributes : From the Complementary Attributes, the following virtues emante:

Durability

In Arabic language *Rabubiat* means sustaining somebody or something according to various needs. It means: sustaining and cultivating something according to various needs and in such a way as to make it reach perfection (Raghib Asfahani, *Mufridatul Quran).* From this virtue the emotion of parental care emanates. Man is able to sustain, bring up and look after things and persons with love and affection. The Quran says:

Praise be to God,
The Cherisher and Sustainer of the worlds *(I.1-2)*
(When this message was delivered),
(Pharaoh) said: 'who, then,
O Moses, is the Lord
Of you two?
He said: "Our Lord is
He Who gave to each
(created) things its form

And nature, and further,
Gave (it) guidance." *(XX.49-50)*
All sustenance, life and death come from God
Such is God, your real
Cherisher and Sustainer *(X-32)*

Simplicity

Owing to the virtue of humility self-respect is created, and the self-respect so created does not lead to any pride. On the other hand, a man always feels himself humble and low before the power of the Almighty.

The Quran says:

He is the Irrestible, (watching)
From above over his worshippers *(VI-61)*
But God is free of all warts
And it is ye that are needy. *(XLVII-38)*
And the servants of (God)
Most Gracious are those
Who walk on the earth
In humility, and when the ignorant
Addressed them, they say,
"Peace!" *(XXV-63)*

Through this virtue, a man does not continue to have real trust in material means. His trust is established only in God. The Quran says:

The parable of those who
Take protectors other than God
Is that of the Spider,
Who builds (to itself)
A house: but truly
The flimsiest of houses
Is the Spider's house:— *(XXIX-41)*
If God hellps you,
None can overcome you: *(III-160)*
...whoever
Rejects evil and believes

In God hath grasped
The most trustworthy
Underhold, that never breaks. (II-256)

Doubtful Mind

Through these virtues man becomes fearless and independent of everything except God. Only with God he establishes a relation of hope and fear.

In this way, his life acquires a centrality and his conviction acquires a force. This attitude makes for success and well-being. We can quote the following Verses from the Quran:

(God) who begets no son
And has no partner
In (His) dominion: (XVII-111)
Who is there can intercede
In His presence except
As He permitteth? (II-255)
God forgiveth not
(The sin of) joining other gods
With Him: but He forgiveth
Whom He pleaseth other sins
Than this. (IV-116)
Do no mischief on the earth,
After it hath been
Set in order, but call
On Him with fear
And longing (in your hearts). (VII-56)

It is a strange fact in history that when the intellectuals of Greece wanted to break the yoke of their tyrinnical rulers they encouraged polytheism.

They came forward with the idea that just as the universe is not ruled by one God, in the same way government on earth should not be the sole monopoly of one person. The idea worked with the Greeks; they were able to dethrone their ruler from his position of autocracy.

Similarly the philosophy of history ascribes the real greatness of the Romans to two things:

(1) Limited resources for the needs of life and

(2) The force of Conviction, because of which an individual sacrifices his life, property, family and everything for the sake of some conviction.

This virtue inculcates realistic outlook and self-confidence in a man. He stops relying on false trust and hope and does not hesitate in making the greatest sacrifice for the sake of achieving his goal or ideal.

The following Verses of the Quran throw light on the subject:

That man can have nothing
But what he strives for: *(LIII-39)*
And say: "work (righteouseness):
Soon will god observe your work,
And His Apostle, and the Believers" *(IX-105)*
That (the fruit of) his striving
Will soon come in sight;
Then will he be rewarded
With a reward; *(LIII-40-1)*
God hath purchased of the Believers
Their persons and their goods;
For theirs (in return)
Is the garden (of Paradise):
They fight in His Cause,
And slay and are slain: *(IX-111)*

Virtues Emanating from Distinctive Attributes : The virtues that emanate from Distinctive Attributes are of two kinds: (1) Those that are related to the goodness and nobility of personal character; and (2) Those that are related to the well-being of other human beings. The first kind has the following implications.

Honesty

The greatest virtue emanating from Distinctive Attributes are truth and sincerity. The Quran says:

And whose word can be
truer than God's? *(IV-87)*
God's promise is the truth. *(IV-122)*

Truth is of many kinds: the truth of the tongue, the truth of the heart and the truth of action. The truth of the tongue means that falsehood should not be spoken. The truth of the heart means that what the tongue speaks should be supported by a conviction from the heart. The truth of action means that what is expressed through the tongue and the heart should correspond to action. This last is the perfect form of truth. It is called sincerity. The Quran says:

Only those are Believers
Who have believed in God and His Apostle,
And have never things doubted, but
Have striven with their
Belongings and their persons
In the cause of God:
Such are the sincere ones. *(XLIX-15)*

Falsehood And Hypocrisy are the Opposites of Truth And Sincerity: Falsehood is the opposite of truth. Falsehood too is of many kinds. There is the falsehood of the tongue, which means speaking lies so that the heart does not go with what is spoken by the tongue. It may even go contrary to it and what is spoken may not be translated into action, rather the action may be contrary to what is spoken.

This is called hypocrisy:

And invoke the curse
Of God on those who lie! *(III-61)*
... they solemnly
Invoke the curse of God
On themselves if they
Tell a lie. *(XXIV-7)*

To say one thing and to have another thing in the heart is hypocrisy: and it is worse than a lie.

For this reason, the Quran harshly condemns hypocrites:

And God beareth witness
That the Hypocraites are
Indeed liers *(LXIII-1)*

The hypocrites say one thing and have another thing in their hearts:

Saying with their lips
What was not in their hearts *(III-167)*

The hypocrites say something and do something else:

... because
They broke their Covenant
With God, and because they
Lied (again and again). *(I-77)*

Once, the Holy Prophet was asked if a Believer can be a coward. He said: 'Yes'. Then he was asked if a believer can be a miser. He said: 'Yes' and then he was asked if a believer can be a lier. He said: 'No' (Moatta Iman Malik)

There are other forms of falsehood. For example: simultation; speaking falsehood for the sake of amusement; propagating mere hearsay.

The Quran says:

And pursue not that
Of which thou hast no knowledge;
For every act of hearing
Or of seeing
Or of (feeling in) the heart
Will be enquired into
(On the Day of Reckoning). *(XVII-36)*

The Holy Prophet once said:

This is enough of a lie for a man if he goes reporting what he has merely heard.
(Mishkat; Muslim; Preface)

Charity or generosity means doing the utmost good to others. It has many forms. For example:

(1) Foregoing one's right;
(2) Giving priority to the needs of others over one's own needs;
(3) Deploying one's goods, energy and intellect for the well being of others;
(4) Undergoing loss for the sake of the benefit of others;
(5) Sacrificing one's self interest for the sake of the survival of others.

Without charity there can be neither sympathy nor love, which are the very essence of humanity. Nor can there be any perfection of virtue, which is the embellishment of humanity. This is why the Quran incites on spending out of what one has in the way of God:

O ye who believe!
Spend out of (the bounties)
We have provided for you,
before the day comes
When no bargaining
(Will avail), nor friendship
Nor intercession
Those who reject faith— they
Are the wrong doers. (II-254)

By no means shall ye
Attain righteousness unless
Ye give (freely) all that
Which ye love. (III-92)

Owing to charity a man gets rid of inordinate love for material wealth, which is the root cause of many evils:

The Evil One Threatens
You with poverty
And bids you to conduct
Unseemly. God permitteth
You His forgiveness
And bounties.
And God careth for all
And He knoweth all things. (II-268)

By virtue of charity a man acquires wisdom. Hence the next Verse in the Quran:

He granteth wisdom
To whom He pleaseth:
And He to whom wisdom
Is granted receiveth
Indeed a benefit overflowing. (II-269)

Wisdom is such an invaluable gift of God that it has been mentioned with reference to almost all the Prophets. Defining wisdom Imam Raghib Asfahani says: 'To reach the truth through knowledge and intellect is wisdom.' In Lisanul Arab we have the following definition:

"To attain knowledge of higher values through higher sciences is wisdom." Ibne Maskoya lists the following features of the wisdom: "Sharpness of mind; power of understanding; clear headedness; intellectual acumen; aptitude for learning etc. He says: 'Through these qualities the power capacity for wisdom is constituted'. Exegetes have given various interpretations of wisdom which can be summarised as follows:

> *Wisdom is a kind of power through which the knowledge of realities is attained, as also the ability to order experience. Furthermore after attaining wisdom a man's attention is focussed on the cultivation of moral sense and he directs his attitude towards this Holy task.*

The Quran states an extremely high standard of charity. For example, it prescribes that (1) no useless thing should be given to the other person, none that the giver would not like to have for himself; (2) that after giving something no benefit should be obtained in return; (3) that the receiver of obligation should not be put to any uneasiness or trouble; (4) the receiver should not be taunted with the mentioning of obligation; (5) the receiver should not be made small by the reminders of obligation; (6) recompense should not be expected:

> *O ye who believe!*
> *Give of the good things*
> *Which ye have (honourably) earned*
> *And of the fruits of the earth*
> *Which We have produced*
> *For you, and do not even aim*
> *At getting anything*
> *Which is bad, in order that*
> *Out of it ye may give away*
> *Something when ye yourselves*
> *Would not receive it*
> *Except with closed eyes.* *(II-267)*
> *O ye who believe!*
> *Cancel not your charity*
> *By reminders of your genoriosity*
> *Or by injury.* *(II-264)*
> *Those who spend*

Their substance in the cause
Of God, and follow not up
Their gifts with reminders
Of their gernorisity
Or with injury, — for them
Their reward is with their Lord: (II-262)

Usually there are two considerations which hinder charity or generosity: (1) Why should one give away one's things to others? (2) By giving away things to others one would suffer from scarcity and therefore it would cause trouble. The Quran repudiates the first consideration by proclaiming that Allah is the owner of everything. Man is only a trustee and the trustee is bound to the wishes of the owner in making use of the trusted goods. The second consideration is repudiated by the idea that scarcity and bounty, comfort and discomfort, are all in the power of Allah. His servant depends on him in every conditions:

And what cause have ye
Why ye should not spend
In the cause of God?
For to God belongs
The Heritage of the heavens and the earth. (LVII—10)
And spend (in charity) out of the (substance)
Whereof He has made you
Heirs. (LVII—7)
To him belong the keys
Of the heavens and the earth:
He enlarges and restricts
The Substance to whom
He will: for He knows
Full well all things. (XLII-12)

The Opposite of Charity or Generosity is Miserliness : The Opposite of charity or generosity is miserliness which is the source of many evils and discourtesies. For example, greed, lust, dishonesty, ingratitude, cruelty, hard-heartedness, narrow mindedness, timidity, unfair dealings, selfishness etc. This is why, the Quran condemns it harshly and dwells on its evils:

and there are those
Who bury gold and silver
And spend it not in the Way
Of God: announce unto them
A most grievous penalty—
On the Day when heat
Will be produced out of
That (wealth) in the fire
Of Hell, and with it will be
Branded their foreheads,
Their flanks, and their backs,
— "This is the (treasures) which ye
Buried for yourselves: taste ye
Then, (treasures) ye buried!" *(IX—34-5)*
By no means! for it would be
The fire of hell!—
Plucking out (his being)
Right to the skull!—
Inviting (all) such
As turn their backs
And turn away their faces
(From the Right) *(LXX—15-18)*
Seest thou one
Who denies the Judgement
(To come)?
Then such is the (man)
Who repulses the orphan
(With harshness), and encourages not
The feeding of the indigent. *(CVII—1-3)*
Who pileth up wealth
And layeth it by
Thinking that his wealth
Would make him last

For ever!
By no means! he will
Be sure to be thrown into
That which Breaks the Pieces. (CIV—1-4)
Nay Nay! but ye
Honour not the orphan!
Nor do ye encourage
One another
To feed the poor!—
And ye devour inheritance—
All will greed,
And ye love wealth
with inordinate love! (LXXX IX—17-20)
For God loveth not
The arrogant, the vainglorious,
(Nor) those who are niggardly
Or enjoin niggardliness on others,
Or hide the bounties
Which God bestowed
On them, (IV—36-7)

The harm of miserliness or niggardliness is not restricted to an individual or a few individuals only; it encompasses the whole society. For this reason, very often it happens that the increase of miserliness destroys faith and degrades the whole society:

Behold, ye are those
Invited to spend
(Or your substance)
In the Way of God:
But among you are some
That are niggardly. But any
Who are niggardly are so
At the expense of
Their own souls.
But God is free

Of all wants,
And it is ye that are needy
If ye turn back
(From the Path) He will
Substitute in your stead
Another people; then they
Would not be like you! (XLVII-38)

According to one of the Quranic Verses, the consequence of niggardliness is hypocrisy which destroys faith:

So He hath put as a consequence
Hypocrisy into their hearts,
(To last) till the Day Whereon
They shall meet Him: (IX-77)
And spend of your substance
In the course of God,
And make not your own hands
Contribute to (your) destruction; (II-195)

For all these reasons, Mohammad (peace be upon him) has always prayed for refuge against niggardliness. He says: "I seek refuge with God against niggardliness." It would not be irrelevant to mention that niggardliness is not found only in matters of wealth or goods; it applies to knowledge and power as well as to material wealth. Whatever God has bestowed upon man is meant for giving away to others, and the question of niggardliness arises in relation to every gift of God. One who is niggardly of knowledge and power also deserves punishment from God.

Chapter 2

Islam and Family Life

Social Norms

Relations between individuals in an Islamic community can be harmonious if certain rules are adhered to. These consist, firstly, of duties toward others, secondly, cultivating essential personal characteristics, and thirdly, avoiding bad personal characteristics.

Duties toward Others

- Speech is an important element and an important means of social relations. It is therefore essential that what is said and how it is said are wisely considered.
- Honesty makes a person likeable and helps in building and strengthening social bonds. It is also an essential attribute of a good Muslim.
- Amiable facial expressions during conversation are of great importance and should be understood as part of a person's duty towards others.
- A Muslim should judge people by their deeds. He should treat well those who treat him well. No man knows another's hidden intentions and feelings - those are for God to judge. But he who shows evil, is not to be trusted, even if he expresses good intentions.
- Relations with others should be based on respect and kindness.
- A Muslim should make sure before making a promise that he can keep it. He should not break promises by making excuses, thinking this will be enough. To think that others' acceptance of his excuses is the end of the matter leaves a bad effect on him.

- Care should be taken not to make many promises at one time or to many people, lest one is unable to keep them.
- Among social duties towards others is to visit them if they become sick and to attend the funerals of their dead.
- 'He who does not thank people does not thank God' (Hadith). The best way for a Muslim to thank a person for doing good to him is to say: Jazak Allah Khayran (May God reward you well).
- A Muslim should help anyone who seeks his help, unless he asks for something forbidden or undesirable. He should not hesitate to do good to others, especially when asked to do so.
- It is a duty to accept invitations; an important one not to be turned down is to a wedding ceremony.
- It is a Muslim's duty not to displease others with unpleasant odours from his clothes, body or mouth such as that caused by onions or garlic.

Personal Traits

Generally speaking, there is no goodness better than a good character. The best people are those with the best character, and the worst people are those with an evil character. The following are some aspects of a positive character which should be aspired to. A Muslim should:

- Be humble and should not boast to others.
- Fulfil his trust when put in a position of trust.
- Speak the truth always, and carry out his actions in accordance with it.
- Show mercy and tenderness to others, Muslims and non-Muslims alike.
- Supply help to one who needs help, and aid the distressed, even though he is not asked to do so.
- Forgive when in a position of power and authority.
- Harbour good thoughts of others.
- Be disposed in friendship to others, and treat them in a friendly way.
- Advise sincerely when consulted by others.
- Leave alone and never speak about what does not concern him.
- Never ask others for anything unless it is urgent or necessary.
- Keep his appointments.

- Restrain his anger and refrain from negative reactions.
- Attach special importance to his relationship with those who practise Islam.
- Be patient always.
- Greet whom he has quarrelled with previously.
- Guarantee the well-being of his family and kin.
- Be modest.
- Be satisfied and contented with what is given to him by God.
- Put trivialities aside, concentrate on important things.
- Be wise when dealing with evil people.
- Exchange gifts with others.
- Guide those towards good deeds who want to perform good deeds.
- Mediate between disagreeing parties.
- Contemplate his actions before performing them.
- Be kind to others.
- Keep secret that which others have confided to him or he has discovered about others.
- Ask forgiveness if he has committed a deed affecting a Muslim's honour.
- Forgive someone who has treated him badly, as though he were a close friend.
- Meet others with a cheerful countenance.
- Mix with others, if they are good; if not, then solitude is better for him.
- Defend others who are absent when they are slandered in his presence.
- Direct someone who has lost his way, especially some one who has bad eyesight.
- Be uncomplicated but not naive.
- Be generous, but without extravagance.
- Show gentleness toward the weak and affection toward his parents.
- Not take revenge on someone who reviles or reproaches him for something he knows about him, by reproaching that person for something he knows about him.

Dark Side

To be successful in developing social relations, it is necessary to avoid some negative characteristics and just as necessary to practise some positive ones. The following are a list of negative characteristics. A Muslim should avoid:

- Being nervous, highly strung or liable to sudden anger.
- Bad relations with others.
- Speaking about what does not concern him.
- Arrogance, especially if it comes from a poor person, who considers himself to be great but is in fact, not so in the eyes of others.
- Slandering anybody.
- Listening to other people's talk when they do not want him to hear, or they are trying to avoid him.
- Being two-faced.
- Reviling other people's genealogies.
- Displaying pleasure at a fellow-Muslim's misfortune.
- Boasting about ancestors who have died or who are of high rank.
- Seeking out others' faults in order to expose them.
- Avoiding a Muslim for more than three days, if he has had difficulties with him.
- Being a mischief-maker, spreading slander.
- Saying something about a Muslim which he or she dislikes even if what he says of him or her is true.
- Being suspicious of others.
- Being inquisitive about others.
- Spying.
- Bidding against another in order to raise the price of a commodity.
- Envying others.
- Hating other Muslims.
- Speaking evil of others behind their back.
- Ridiculing others; laughing, scoffing or jeering at them.
- Acting dishonestly toward others, deceiving and misleading them.
- Self-deception or self-delusion.

- Being avaricious and miserly.
- Being a coward, unable to control his fear and running away from danger.
- Grumbling and complaining and never being satisfied with anything.
- Drawing attention to his own helpfulness, charity, or generosity.
- Being selfish, thinking chiefly of and being interested in his own needs and welfare without care for others.
- Withholding help, when he is able to offer it to others.
- Praising and flattering somebody in his presence.
- Showing undue respect to those of a sinful nature, or those who are wealthy or have a high position.
- Speaking loudly.
- Being harsh or rude to others.
- Praising himself or overestimating himself.
- Lying.
- Talking and Listening.

The Conversation: Talking is an important means of communication, it is also an extension and expression of a person's personality.

- Moderation in speech is an excellent quality, which a good Muslim should cultivate. A Hadith says that one should either speak good or keep silent.
- A Muslim should not talk just for the sake of talking because he thinks it is a shortcoming to be silent. The shortcoming lies in talking badly and talking too much. His duty is to say what is good or to keep silent. While being silent is a good characteristic, it should not be overdone to the extent of annoying others.
- A Muslim should adhere to the truth and speak it whether pleased or displeased. He should speak the truth, even if it is bitter.
- A Muslim should think carefully before speaking, and avoid saying something that he might regret and for which he would have to apologize.
- Simplicity and clarity should characterize speech; enunciating over-carefully and speaking gutturally should be avoided. Using strange archaic words, in an attempt to demonstrate linguistic

ability or to show that one is more knowledgeable than others, is forbidden.

- Looking pleasantly at others when speaking to them is required as a courtesy.
- There is a specific topic related to every occasion. Decorum, appropriateness, should exist between the topic discussed and the occasion concerned.
- A Muslim should be sure of the truthfulness and accuracy of what he says.
- If those listening to a person cannot follow him and need to have his words repeated, it is courteous to repeat them.
- One should not speak hurriedly. It is better to speak neither too slowly nor too quickly, neither too loudly nor too softly, for such ways of speaking may tire the listener. Nor should words be interspersed with long pauses, as this will bore the listener.

Importance of Tongue

- Colloquial and slang words and expressions should be avoided as much as possible.
- Foreign words and terms should be avoided.
- One should try to attain to a pleasant, agreeable and moral mode of expression.
- It is not fitting for a Muslim to be given to cursing. He must never invoke God's curse, God's anger, or Hell on another.
- A Muslim should not be given to using bad or objectionable language and should guard against speaking slander and abuse. Being of those whom others leave alone for fear of their ridicule or ribaldry casts a bad light on one's personality and character.
- Reviling the dead is bad conduct, and is forbidden to the same degree as reviling the living.
- Objecting to his destiny and attributing injustice to God ill-befit a Muslim and must be avoided.
- It is a bad thing to express an overpermissive attitude toward others, especially Muslims, or to life in general.
- Calling down evil upon himself, his children, his servants, etc. is forbidden to a Muslim.
- Certain expressions that contradict the basic tenets of Islamic faith - for example, expressions that seem to ascribe partners to God - must be avoided. A Muslim should never say: 'What

God Wills and so-and-so wills'; rather he should say: 'What God alone wills' or 'What God wills and afterwards so-and-so wills.' He must never say: 'I have no supporter but God and you', but rather say: 'I have no supporter but God and afterwards you.' He should never say: 'I swear by so-and-so.'

- To revile the wind, rain or other natural phenomena is forbidden, for these are under God's command. Instead of reviling the wind or rain, one should say: 'O God, make it a blessing and not a punishment.' Also, the rooster should not be reviled, for he wakes people for the dawn prayer.
- A woman must not become the intimate of another woman and then describe the latter to her husband.
- A Muslim should not try to display superior knowledge of a topic discussed; he should avoid overuse of the pronoun 'I'.
- It is better to be gentle when blaming others for something they might have done and to avoid doing so before other people.
- However good a Muslim may be, he should not disgrace or revile another's beliefs or character directly or indirectly.
- A Muslim should be careful not to say anything that might give offence or be passed on, and perhaps misquoted. Subjects that might lead to embarrassment should be avoided.
- Just as a Muslim should not disgrace or revile others in his speech, he also should not disgrace or revile himself.
- A Muslim should never praise another in his presence. If he cannot avoid it, he should be moderate in his expression; it is for God to declare anyone pure.
- It is a Muslim's duty to stop anyone who continually criticizes others.
- Discussing personal and family secrets with others should be avoided; it is better to keep such things to oneself.
- A Muslim should never allow others to tell him bad things about some third person, for it is better to meet and mix with others with no ill-feelings. If he hears people talking unjustly about others, it is his duty to defend the person spoken about.
- After having done something a Muslim should not express the wish that he had not done it or had done it another way.
- Speaking for too long is a bad characteristic. Being moderate when speaking is better.

- A Muslim should avoid talking about things which do not concern him.
- Eavesdropping on the private conversation of others should be avoided.
- The term 'brother' should be confined to fellow Muslims.
- Calling a Muslim an infidel or accusing him of unbelief is completely forbidden.
- Inquiring about something from someone should be preceded by greeting the person first, taking into consideration what he is engaged in at that moment, and then confining oneself to the necessary matter.
- It is a part of courtesy that when a Muslim mentions the Prophet or when he is mentioned in his presence he should invoke a blessing on him by saying: Sallal-Lah alayhi wa sallam (Allah's blessing and peace be upon him).
- A Muslim may not use absolute and assertive terms about future events without referring to God's will by saying: insha Allah (If God wills).
- A Muslim should not abuse or revile another person or speak of his faults, even if that person abuses and reviles him and even though he speaks of his faults.

Listening : A Muslim should:

- Try to listen to others as politely as possible.
- Avoid interrupting others when they are speaking.
- Face the person he is speaking to and show interest in what he is saying, even if he is not interested in the topic being discussed, try to control himself, unless the topic is directed against Islam, its principles or the Prophet, in which case he should either try to put an end to it or leave.
- Avoid getting involved in a pointless argument with someone who expresses views with which he does not agree.

Swearing

- As far as possible, swearing and taking an oath should be avoided.
- A Muslim should swear by Allah, one of His attributes or names, only. He is not allowed to swear by something else, such as the Prophet, Prayer, the Kaaba, the Quran, etc.
- Swearing in Allah's name, unfaithfully, is considered a great sin.

- Using the colloquial expression 'by God' should be avoided.
- If a Muslim swears to do something or to refrain from doing something, and afterwards he finds doing something else is better, he is recommended not to carry out his oath and to make proper atonement.
- It is a Muslim's duty to fulfil his oath. Therefore, he must be sure before swearing that he has the means to carry out his promise.
- Using the threat: 'If you don't do this or that, I will divorce my wife', is distasteful and unbecoming to a Muslim. Marriage must not be referred to in such a trivial and childish manner.
- Swearing oaths should be avoided in certain cases, for example, in business or financial transactions.
- Breaking an oath must be avoided. If a Muslim breaks his oath then he must make atonement by providing food for a meal for ten poor people or providing each of the ten with one article of clothing. If he is not financially able to do this, then he must fast three, successive days.
- If a Muslim vows to do something forbidden in Islam, such as to take something which does not belong to him, then it is his duty to break his oath.
- If a Muslim vows to do something not recommended by Islam, then he is advised not to fulfil his oath and to make atonement.

Nadhr (to connect a vow with the fulfilment of a wish)

- To vow, in return for a favour from God to oneself, to do some specific thing for the sake of God, is permitted but is not recommended.
- Vowing to oneself to do a certain thing should be done only for the sake of God.
- A Muslim must fulfil his vow pledged for the sake of God, and may avoid fulfilling it if pledged for the sake of someone else.
- It is not permissible for someone who has made a vow to slaughter an animal for the sake of Allah, to eat anything of it unless his initial intention included the stipulation that he would eat some.

Laughter

- There are many reasons for laughing, such as seeing a pleasant thing, hearing good news or a joke.

- To laugh because other people laugh is not recommended; there should be a reason for laughter.
- Laughter should not be characterized by loud or unpleasant sounds.
- A broad smile, such as makes the back teeth visible, is better than laughing.
- It is better always to control the sounds of laughter; excessive noise should be avoided.
- It is not fitting for a Muslim to make people laugh for the sake of laughter, especially if that leads to lying.
- One should not sit with people amongst whom is a person trying to make them laugh at any expense.
- Laughing in ridicule of another person must be avoided.

Weeping

- Weeping should be spontaneous and for a good reason.
- It is not unmanly to cry because emotions should not be suppressed. Yet it should be done with restraint and not with excessive or loud sounds.

Jokes

- It is good to share jokes with others, because always being serious is burdensome.
- When making jokes, it is better to avoid using impolite or hurtful terms, directly or indirectly.
- Over-seriousness and excessive joking should both be avoided because they will lessen self-esteem and risk hurting others' feelings.
- Attention should be given to the context in which the joke is told so as to avoid hurting others' feelings.
- A joke should not be accompanied with excessive gestures or bodily movements.
- One should not take what belongs to others while joking.
- To terrify others, in jest, is forbidden.
- Lying is not allowed even for joking purposes.

Behaviour when Meeting Others : A Muslim should observe the following:

- He should smile, for a smile is the key to a successful meeting. However, he should not smile at people because of their material wealth.

- He should be first to salute other Muslims.
- He should not bow to any person when saluting, no matter who he is and whatever the occasion.
- When meeting others and after saluting, he should extend his right hand and shake hands; this enhances mutual respect.
- He should not shake hands with anyone for whom it might be a nuisance.
- If his hand is dirty and someone wants to shake hands with him, he should politely excuse himself, explaining the reason.
- He should not feel upset about shaking hands at every meeting.
- Men shake hands with men, women with women. If a woman wants to shake hands with a man or vice versa, he/she should excuse himself/herself.
- Too many questions about the family, etc. when meeting is a time-wasting activity and is likely to lead to boredom, so he should avoid it.
- If anyone meets him and begins a conversation before saluting him, he has the right not to speak to him.
- If he is seated, it is not necessary for him to stand up to shake hands. Although there are certain occasions when he may stand up, such as meeting someone who has returned from a journey.
- There is no objection to him kissing the hand of a Muslim scholar or of his parents. However, this gesture is forbidden in the case of a wealthy or powerful person. In the first case it is allowed on condition that kissing the hand does not replace shaking hands.
- When a meeting is finished he should extend his hand to shake hands once again, saying: Assalamu alaikum (Peace be upon you).
- He should not shake hands with someone who has a contagious disease.
- It is not sunnah for him to shake hands after praying, saying: Taqabbal Allah (May God accept our prayer).

Manners of Greeting

- The habit of greeting is of great importance for it increases friendship and acquaintance. It is also an act of kindness and courtesy.
- A person who is riding should greet one who is walking, a person who is walking should greet one who is sitting, and a small group should greet a larger one. The young should greet the

old. If two people of more or less the same age and both walking meet each other, either may greet the other first.

- Flexibility should characterize observance of the above-mentioned rules, for the best of people are those who do not hesitate to greet others.
- Others should be greeted by saying: Assalamu aliykum (Peace be upon you).
- Using other expressions of greeting, such as 'good morning', 'good evening', 'hello', are allowed only after saying: Assalamu aliykum.
- Politeness requires that a salutation be returned in the same or better way. Required, at least, is that one says: Wa aliykum assalam (Upon you be peace) and the ideal and perfect form is: Wa aliykum assalam wa rahmatullah wa barakatuh (Upon you be peace, God's mercy and His blessings).
- It is a Muslim's duty to respond to a salutation by returning it without delay, unless there is a good reason for delay.
- When a Muslim greets others or is greeted by others, his greeting or response to the other's greeting should be done audibly.
- If a Muslim thinks that the other did not hear his greeting for some reason, then it is his duty to greet him another time, even for a third time, but not more.
- If meeting others is repeated within a certain period of time, it should not be thought boring or monotonous to greet them again.
- Greeting others by making a gesture with the fingers, with the palm of the hand, or with the head must be avoided.
- A Muslim should greet both those whom he knows and those whom he does not know. This increases the number of his acquaintances and friends. He cannot, however, in certain cases, such as at markets or on crowded streets, give salutations to everyone he passes or meets.
- If passing a company of people, a Muslim should not greet some of them by mentioning their names or titles. Politeness requires him to greet them all in general terms, so that everyone is greeted.
- When greeted by a company of people the salutation should be returned with a general greeting and without specifying anyone in particular.
- If someone passes a Muslim, and he is in doubt of his greeting, he is not required to respond to him.

- If someone greets a company of people, and his greeting is returned by a member of this company then this is enough, though it is recommended that all members respond.
- It is a Muslim's duty to respond to another's greeting whether he is a Muslim or non-Muslim.
- If a Muslim meets someone and he is in doubt whether he will return his greeting, it is nonetheless his duty to greet him.
- Though greeting others is recommended there are certain cases where salutations should be avoided, such as greeting someone who is in the act of relieving himself, or sleeping, or drowsing.
- If a Muslim passes a mixed company of Muslims and non-Muslims, he should greet them by saying: Assalamu alaikum (Peace be upon you).
- If a Muslim is greeted while relieving himself, he should not respond until he leaves the lavatory.
- A Muslim should not neglect to greet members of his family upon returning home.
- If passing children, it is better to greet them, even though they are supposed to greet one first.
- If someone has sent another person to a Muslim with a message which includes a greeting, he must greet both of them by saying: Assalamu alayka wa alaiyhi (Peace be upon you and upon him).
- If sending a message to a non-Muslim, he may be greeted by writing: Assalamu ala man ittabaa al-huda (Peace be upon who follows the right path).
- When approaching a group of people or meeting a person, a salutation should be given. When parting, a salutation should again be given at the end of the meeting. It is of particular importance to greet when parting; especially in the case of two parties who may have argued or disagreed during their conversation, for the greeting implies that there are no hard feelings and that both attach value to a continuing good relationship.
- When greeting other Muslims, whether orally (on the telephone) or by writing (letters, etc.), one should start and finish with: Assalamu alaikum.
- It is not un-Islamic to greet non-Muslims, but a Muslim should not use: *Assalamu alaikum*.

Asking Permission to Enter Another's House

- A Muslim may not enter another's house before asking permission to do so. Politeness requires such permission, even from those who are very close to him, such as his parents, for people in their homes may be in a state of dress or of mood in which they do not wish to be seen. This is especially important in regard to women who must have time to arrange themselves, to cover their hair, and so on.
- It is forbidden to glance into someone else's house when the door is opened to greet one.
- The visitor must greet whoever answers the door before asking permission to enter. The manner of asking permission to enter should be thus: *Assalamu alaikum*, may I enter?', or '*Assalamu alaikum*, may (mention your name) enter?' Refusal of permission to enter is justified in the absence of a greeting first.
- If the visitor is asked to give his identity before the door is opened to him, he must give it. To say merely: 'It is me', is insufficient and not approved.
- The request to enter, if permission is not granted, may be repeated three times. If permission is still not granted, the visitor should leave. If the caller does not have an appointment, then the person he wants to visit is not required to receive him. Therefore, he should not take offence if he informs him that he is busy and would rather not receive guests at this time.
- Knocking at the door or ringing the bell is not a substitute for giving a greeting and asking permission to enter.
- Knocking at the door should be done gently, for there might be someone asleep or ill inside the house. If after knocking at the door three times there is no response, the caller should leave.

At a Friend's House: Exchange of visits strengthens relationships between individuals and is valued as one of the main elements in a healthy social life. It eradicates that social isolation which is not acceptable within Islam.

- It is a recommended Islamic procedure that a Muslim should inform his host of his intention to visit him. If he visits somebody without a previous appointment, and he is unwilling to receive him for one reason or another, he should not be upset.
- Appointments must be kept promptly. If there is just cause for changing or cancelling the appointment then either party should properly inform the other.

- Suitable times to pay a visit do not include night time, evening (after 'Isha' prayer) or the siesta hour.
- It is the duty of the host to receive the guest if there is an appointment.. Otherwise the host has the right to apologize for not being able to receive him. In this case the guest should not feel offended.
- Visits should be free of any personal interest or other selfishness. The aim of visiting should be to strengthen brotherly relations with other Muslims, for the sake of God.
- Men should not visit women whose husbands are away from home, unless they are mahrams to the women visited.
- A Muslim may not enter the host's house until he has his permission, and has greeted him, even if he has an appointment with him.
- A visitor should remember that he is in someone else's home. Therefore, he should try his best to fit in with the plans made by his host, even if he finds things a little boring.
- A Muslim should not limit his visits only to those who visit him.
- A guest must not lead a host in prayer or sit in the host's accustomed place without his permission.
- Social intercourse and mixing between men and women when visiting other families is forbidden. A guest is allowed to speak to the wife or daughters of the host if there is a need. The host's wife can serve the guests provided she dresses and behaves correctly.
- A woman may not visit others if her husband objects.
- Open violation of Islamic teachings by the host or members of his family should cause the guest to leave. Such behaviour is unacceptable and intolerable to good Muslims. The host in this case is requested to show understanding toward the guest's behaviour.
- If a Muslim wants to stay as a guest with someone then he should not expect his hospitality to continue for more than three days. Anything beyond that, he receives as charity. A guest should not stay so long as to make himself an encumbrance.
- It is impolite for a guest to refuse what a host offers him unless there is a medical reason, or he is fasting. In this case he must apologize and explain the reason to him.

- If a visitor wants to relieve himself he should first inform the host. He should not leave his place until permission is given.
- When visiting others, it is not proper to stay long unless requested to do so. Becoming a nuisance by remaining too long and overstaying as a guest is not proper Islamic conduct.
- When the time comes to leave, a visitor should thank the host for his entertainment. He should ask permission to leave, and not move until permission is given. He should bid the host farewell.
- If a Muslim intends to fast while staying with others as a guest, then it is polite to inform the host of his intention.
- If a friend or relative does not visit him, a Muslim should not accord him the same treatment. He should call on him and not wait for him to return his visit.
- A Muslim should not limit his visits to only special occasions. As mentioned above, exchange of visits between individuals is always beneficial.

Receiving Guests

- A Muslim host should receive his guests heartily and with a welcoming smile. To honour and entertain a guest is an Islamic duty.
- It is the host's duty to keep all sources of annoyance away from his guests.
- It is impolite to ask the guest to perform any service.
- The guest needs no invitation to come and stay for a number of days, though it is better if the visitor can inform the host in advance of his arrival. The guest can stay three days and then should leave.
- If a guest comes to visit a Muslim, it is his duty, if he is able, to be hospitable and generous by offering him food and drink, whether or not he receives the same treatment when he visits him.
- When the visit is ended and the guest is about to leave, the host should accompany him to the outside door and give him a good farewell.

Inviting Others to Dine

- Inviting others to dine is recommended, provided a Muslim's intention is not to boast about his own achievements.

- Invitations to a banquet should not be confined to the rich and influential, the poor and needy should be included too.
- Invitations to dine should be restricted to good Muslims, though inviting others is not forbidden. Priority should be given to Muslims, however, since a result of dining together is a strengthening of friendship and brotherhood and this aim should be reserved for fellow Muslims.
- It is recommended that neighbours are among those invited to dine.
- Showing generosity to invited guests is an important matter, provided exaggeration and extravagance are avoided.
- The manners of receiving a guest, should be adhered to.
- Although the guests may begin eating as soon as the meal is served, it is nevertheless good conduct to indicate to the guests that they should begin by-saying: Bismillah (In the name of God).
- It is polite and considered a form of generosity to urge guests to eat and drink, but not to excess, and not to insist that they eat a certain kind of food.
- A Muslim should be careful when speaking not to praise his own generosity or his own table.
- Restricting invitations to dine only to special occasions is not recommended; an invitation may be offered at any time.
- A host should avoid giving his guests the impression that he is observing how much he eats or that he thinks he is eating too much.
- If a guest arrives unexpectedly, it is a Muslim's duty to see that he is adequately cared for.

When Invited to a Meal

- If a Muslim is invited to a meal, it is recommended that he accepts. It is obligatory to accept a wedding feast invitation (though not if it entails forbidden things).
- An invitation to a meal from anybody who is extending the invitation only out of personal interest should be declined.
- If a Muslim is invited by someone to a meal while fasting voluntarily, then he is free either to break his fast or to visit him and keep his fast.
- When going to a meal in somebody's house, a Muslim should not take anyone with him who has not been invited.

- If someone follows a Muslim and accompanies him without his consent when he is going to his hosts, it is his duty to inform the host of the situation. The host may accept or reject the uninvited guest, as he wishes.
- When the meal is served, it is not good manners to rush to the table. It is correct to follow the person who is to one's right.
- The invitations of people competing with each other to provide a feast for the sake of ostentation, should not be accepted.
- An invitation from a morally corrupt person should not be accepted merely because one does not wish to say no to him. The invitation may be accepted only if the intention is to bring him back to Islam, otherwise not.
- When sitting down to eat, proper table manners should be observed.
- If something among the dishes or drink offered to a Muslim is forbidden according to Islam, such as wine or pork, then he should inform the host of the necessity of removing it, otherwise of his leaving, and if it is not removed he should leave immediately.
- A guest should thank the host for his invitation and ask God to bless him. The following dua may be recited: *Akala taamukum al-abrar, wa salla alaykum al- Malaika wa aftara indakum as-Saimun* (May the righteous eat your food, may the angels invoke blessings on you, and may those who have been fasting break their fast with you).

Visiting the Sick

- Visiting the sick is one way of expressing concern for them, and it helps them feel better. It also strengthens and develops social relations. So, the sick should be visited, not only among friends and relatives, but also those who are not immediate relations or acquaintances.
- Making an appointment to visit the sick is a good thing but not necessary. One should keep in mind the proper visiting times if the sick are in hospital, and comply with all regulations, including those prohibiting taking food and drinks.
- The kind of sickness determines the nature and length of the visit. Visitors may be prevented by doctors from seeing the sick person or they may be allowed a brief visit. If doctors permit, it is recommended to stay long enough for the sick person to feel that he/she is not neglected.

- A visitor should sit close to the sick person and ask how he/she feels.
- When visiting a patient one is recommended to pray for his/her recovery and that the sickness may be the cause of purification of sins. The Prophet used to say to the patients he visited: La bas Tahur insha *Allah* (No harm will come; it is a purification, if God wills).
- A visitor should select his consoling words with care; avoiding any mention of objection to destiny, describing the sickness as evil, or any words that might have a bad effect on the sick person. Instead, he/she should be encouraged to accept the illness as something that God has planned and that one must think well of God.
- If the sick person has reached a hopeless state a Muslim may say: *Inna li-llah wa-inna ilayhi rajiun* (We belong to God and to Him we return).
- A Muslim should not deprive the sick person of his visits; he should make them as frequently as necessary, especially if the sick person feels close to him.
- Concern for the patient should not be limited to visiting him; one is also required to ask his family, from time to time, about his health.
- It is permissible to visit a non-Muslim who is sick if he happens to be a friend, neighbour or relative, or if one seeks to persuade him to become a Muslim.
- To stare at a leprous person or at others with similar diseases or deformities, should be avoided lest they feel looked down upon.

Group Meetings

- Socializing, just to kill time, should be avoided. Time is a precious asset not to be wasted. Rather, it should be spent on useful affairs. Also, friends should be selected carefully.
- Places for a gathering should be respectable, such as private houses and mosques, not pavements, markets, etc.
- Socializing, if one's body, clothes or mouth smell bad, should be avoided.
- After seeking permission to enter and greeting the house owner, a Muslim should next greet the people seated. He should shake hands with everyone, starting from the right and sit where he finds himself when he has finished.

- When joining a gathering, a person should sit where a place is made for him; otherwise he should sit in any vacant place.
- If someone offers his place to someone joining the gathering, he should apologize politely for not accepting it and sit where he finds himself or where someone makes room without getting up, or where there is enough room.
- One should be careful not to oblige anyone to leave his seat, even a child, in order to take his place.
- It is not fitting to sit between two people unless permission is given, because they may be talking privately or expressing some intimacy.
- Care must be taken when sitting not to turn one's back on anyone, since this might be interpreted as a form of dislike or disrespect.
- If more people join the gathering, those already seated should make room for the newcomers.
- Someone joining a gathering should remember that those present do not have to stand up for him.
- If someone has left his seat intending to return, he has more right to his seat and others should be careful not to take his place.
- If the company consists of three people, any two of them must not talk privately in front of the third.
- If two people are talking privately when a newcomer arrives, he should not obtrude uninvited upon their conversation.
- If more than three people are present, then two of them may talk privately or intimately.
- It is polite to listen to others and not interrupt or let one's attention wander.
- A person's sitting posture should be humble and respectful of others.
- It is necessary that in any gathering people should remember God and invoke blessings on His Messenger Muhammad, peace be upon him.
- If a Muslim hears people talking about someone behind his back, he should politely try to stop them; if they persist he should excuse himself and leave.
- What is said or done in a sitting place should continuously be noted and judged in terms of the permissible and the forbidden.

- Any secrets that people exchange and divulge in private conversation are in confidence and should always be respected.
- Gatherings are not recommended after 'Isha' prayer unless necessitated for study purposes or for the sake of a guest.
- Those who sit in an assembly, gathering, meeting, etc., where there is much clamour or meaningless talk, are recommended, at the end of the gathering and before getting up to leave, to say the following dua: *Subhanaka Allahumma wa bihamdika ashhadu an la ilaha illa anta astaghfiruka wa atubu ilayka* (O Allah, I witness Your absolute transcendence, and praise You. I testify that there is no god except You; I ask Your pardon and turn to You in repentance).

Forms of Sitting

- Sitting should be respectful of others. Stretching legs out in front of others or sitting higher up than others should be avoided.
- Private parts should always be concealed in any sitting posture.
- Sitting with the left hand behind the back, while leaning on the other hand, should be avoided.
- A person should not sit with one part of his body in the sun and the other part in the shade.
- Sitting on the floor is the best posture for eating.

Women's Conduct Outside the Home

- A woman who has used incense, make-up, or has perfumed herself, should not leave her home until the make-up is removed and no scent of the perfume remains.
- A man may not spend the night in the house of a woman unless he is her husband or a mahram.
- A man and a woman are not permitted to be alone together unless the man is a mahram to the woman or, of course, her husband.
- If a man should, happen to look at a woman, he must turn his eyes away. An accidental glance is allowed, a second look is forbidden.
- Social intercourse or mixing of men and women is of two kinds:

(a) That which is related to general public life and not confined to certain groups of people, but common to all people, such as in streets, markets and mosques. Mixing in this case is allowed, provided all the above-mentioned conditions are fulfilled.

(b) Free mixing of men and women in places confined to particular groups of people, such as in school, university or work place, is forbidden, and separation of the sexes is required.

- Outside the home when a woman speaks to a man her speech should not be inviting, but should remain objective and crisp.
- Women are allowed to indulge in all business transactions allowed to men; a woman may also hold a job if it does not affect her main responsibility of the house and family, if her husband agrees, and if she is not required to mix with men. For instance, a woman may teach in a girls' school or be a women's doctor.
- When leaving work for home, a woman should remember to wear Islamic dress.
- Islam does not consider the house to be a woman's jail; she is allowed to leave the house, as long as there is a good reason for doing so.

Celebrations

- The most important rules governing celebrations are:

(a) Mixing of men and women should be avoided.

(b) Extravagant parties and wastefulness must be avoided even if a Muslim is financially able.

- Celebrating occasions foreign to Islam, such as Christmas, New Year, Mother's Day, Father's Day, Labour Day, wedding anniversaries, birthdays and the like, is an imitation of other cultures.
- Certain other celebrations have also been introduced into Islam from outside such as the Prophet's birthday, the Prophet's Isra' and Miraj (the Prophet's night journey from Mecca to Jerusalem and then to the seven heavens), the Prophet's emigration, etc.
- Instead of forbidden occasions, Muslims are encouraged to have meetings of individual villages, towns, or city districts, to discuss different economic, political and social issues relating to the present and future; or to discuss specifically devotional matters or to read the Quran and praise God.

Behaviour Toward Relatives

- Visiting relatives and being concerned about them is extremely important.

- There is no prescribed number of visits to relatives, but they should be frequent enough so that they do not feel neglected.
- Whenever he meets his relatives, a Muslim should ask and concern himself about their welfare.
- A Muslim should remember that he has a responsibility toward his poor and needy relatives. He should extend help to them and from time to time give them as a present some of the things they need.
- If a Muslim is breast-fed by a woman other than his mother, he should remember that he has another family and relatives in breast feeding.
- It is best not to wait for a visit from relatives before visiting them.
- It is not good to answer an offence from a relative with the same. It shows moral stature to refrain from answering in that way.
- A Muslim should treat his mother's sister as he treats his mother.
- A Muslim should treat his uncle as he treats his father.
- It is permitted for a woman to sit with male relatives (other than those she is forbidden to marry), provided:

(a) That they act within the limits of proper decorum;

(b) That she is not alone with one relative.

Behaviour Toward Neighbours

- The first rule governing behaviour toward neighbours is to avoid causing them any form of material or moral harm such as by raising one's voice or having loud, noisy celebrations, especially at night.
- Visiting neighbours is important for it helps establish amiable relations, especially on major occasions such as births, weddings, sickness and death, etc.
- Being generous to neighbours is in accordance with the Prophet's teachings. One should invite a neighbour to dine from time to time, and send him food at other times.
- Doing any ill to a neighbour's children should be avoided. Care should be taken not to let children's conflicts engender misunderstandings between their parents.
- A neighbour and his family have certain special privileges on a Muslim. Extending help to them when it is needed is Islamic behaviour.

- If a Muslim knows his neighbour to be in some financial difficulty, he should not wait for him to ask for help, rather he should offer help if he can.
- A Muslim should keep secrets confided in him by neighbours, or which he may have overheard.
- A Muslim should talk well of his neighbours, defend them if people talk ill of them, because his relations with them deserve his special attention and care.
- It is the housewife's responsibility to look after relations with women neighbours.
- If a neighbour is a relative, good mutual relations become all the more important.
- Good relations should not be confined to next-door neighbours but should also extend to those further away.

Gifts : Exchanging gifts between individuals is recommended by Islam, for it strengthens relations. Therefore, if a Muslim is financially able, he should try to present gifts to relatives and friends while observing the following rules:

- Giving presents to relatives has priority over giving presents to others.
- Spending a lot of money on extravagant gifts and a lot of time choosing them are bad habits that limit the exchange of gifts and might even lead to non-exchange of gifts.
- A gift should only be bought with money earned in a legal way.
- The purpose of giving others gifts must be to honour them and to strengthen relations. Giving gifts in the hope of material gain or personal influence, is bribery, which is strictly forbidden.
- On presenting a gift, discussing anything that might make the recipient sceptical about its purpose should be avoided.
- On receiving a gift, a Muslim should open it and look at it, show satisfaction, and express thanks for it. If the one who sent him the gift is present, then he should pray for him.
- Giving someone a present and then asking for it back is not polite nor, with the exception of gifts presented to children by their parents or their grandparents, is it permitted.
- It is an act of politeness to return the courtesy of a gift received by seeking an occasion to do so.
- A Muslim should not accept a gift from someone who intends to exploit him or profit from his authority or influence in any way. In fact, such a gift is in reality a bribe.

- A Muslim must not accept gifts of things forbidden to be owned by him, such as a bottle of wine or pork meat.
- If refusing a gift for one of the above reasons, one should try to explain the reason. In this case, the one who is offering the gift should not feel offended.
- When a parent gives presents to his children he should not favour one above another.
- It is most important to remember that giving presents is recommended, not obligatory. It is an error to believe that giving presents is required: such an error may hinder exchange of visits between people who, especially if they are not financially able, will seek to avoid such visits in order to avoid giving presents.

Middle Path

The outstanding feature of Islamic life is that it is free from extremes and justly balanced, for virtue is to avoid the extremes on either side. The message of God is : 'We have moulded you into a society justly-balanced that ye might be a pattern unto others, even as the Prophet has been a pattern unto you' (a : 143); 'You are the best of peoples evolved for mankind,, enjoining what is right, forbidding what is wrong (3:110).

Islam, thus, steers clear of the extremes in life and chooses for itself the middle path or the principle of moderation. Here it may be said that this is the same as the 'Golden Mean' of Aristotle. But there is a difference between 'the moderation or mean' as a principle and 'the mean' of Aristotle which he put forward as a rule. A rule is not a special order or command, it fluctuates with the collateral circumstances of each situation and is subject to flexible reason, while a principle is the command, not variable but to be obeyed by all. In Islam it takes the form of law and is law itself. Islamic law, not given to extremes, is no other than the law which adheres to the middle course and moderation in life.

We read in the Quran : 'And be moderate in thy pace' (31 : 19). In all things we have to be moderate, we are not to be so niggardly as to keep back our wealth from the just needs of those who have a right to our help, nor is it becoming to be so lavish as to make ourselves destitutes : 'Make not thy hand tied (like a niggard's) to thy neck, nor stretch it forth to its utmost reach so that thou become blameworthy and destitute,' (17 : 29). In our spending it is wise neither to be extravagant nor niggardly but strike a perfectly just balance between these extremes : 'Those who when they spend, are not niggardly, but hold a just (balance) between those extremes' (25: 67) .Nothing in excess is allowed : 'Eat and drink but nothing in excess. Indeed He does not like; those who indulge in excesses' (7: 31). To indulge in excess is to transgress the limits ordained by God. Meticulous observance of Jaw is, therefore, essentially required and this has been well specified by the Prophet who says : 'What is lawful and unlawful is evident, yet there are some doubtful cases not known to many of the people. He who guarded himself against doubtful things saved his faith and himself from what is unlawful (Bukhari). Thus, to keep the mean is to observe the law strictly and discard what is doubtful. While the mean of Aristotle is fluctuating and subject to flexible reason and thus doubtful, the mean of Islam is free from doubt, justly balanced and without any excesses.

Islam never preaches self-abnegation, for that is the creed of Cynics, nor does it advocate repression of emotions practised by Stoics but only sets a limit to Hedonistic desires as a deterrent against the evils resulting from excesses, harmonious development of body and soul being the most desirable thing. Squandering and hoarding are both denounced, Usury or unjustifiable enrichment is forbidden, moderation or just mean enjoined.

Law with a System

'Islamic law is systematic, that is to say, it represents a coherent body of doctrines. Its several institutions are well put into relations with one another ; the greater part of the law of contracts and obligations, for instance, is construed by analogy with the contract of sale. Furthermore, the whole of the law is permeated by religious and ethical considerations; each institution, transaction or obligation is measured by religious and moral rules, such as the prohibition of interest, the prohibition of uncertainty, the concern for the just mean or average (*mithl*)'. See, Schacht, *An Introduction to Islamic Law*, p. 201.

The Causes

Adab is an Arabic term meaning custom; it denotes a habit, an etiquette, a manner of conduct derived from people considered as models.

During the first two centuries following the emergence of Islam, the term '*adab*' carried ethical and social implications. The root *db* means marvellous thing, or preparation, feast. 'Adab in this sense was the equivalent of the Latin urbanites, civility, courtesy, refinement of the cities in contrast to bedouin uncouthness.' So adab of something means good manner of that thing. The plural is *adab. Adab al-Islam,* therefore, means the good manners adopted by Islam, derived from its teachings and instructions. It is in this sense that it will be used in this book. Manners in many cultures other than the Islamic are determined by local conditions and are therefore subject to changes in those conditions. According to W. G. Sumner, 'From recurrent needs arise habits for the individual and customs for the group, but these results are consequences which were never conscious, and never foreseen or intended.'

Deliberate Behaviour

Islamic manners and customs are not in this sense 'unconscious'. They are derived from the two main sources of Islam, namely the Quran and the Sunnah, the Prophet's deeds, words and indirect commandments, and are therefore, in the strictest sense, divinely inspired. The Quran and the Sunnah contain the broad principles needed to negotiate the problems that arise in human societies in different ages. As a complete way of life, Islam orders economic, political and devotional activity as well as manners relating to everyday human exchanges and routines. Islam is not confined merely to devotional and legal manners; it embraces criteria and values, attitudes, customs and manners in all reaches of human concern and relationship. As a portion of this whole, Islamic manners are derived from the broad objectives of Islam and reflect its broad ideas and values.

Adab al-Islam should neither be conceived nor practised in isolation from the whole. Rather, their interrelation with other elements of Islam should always be kept in mind. Nor, likewise, should the different elements within adab al-Islam be treated as isolatable, for these too are closely interrelated. To give a single, conspicuous example: a Muslim is required to sleep early so that he may rise early for the Fajr (dawn) Prayer.

The divine inspiration of manners in Islam confers on them a religious character which motivates proper adherence. It does not follow from their religious character that every detail of these manners is obligatory. The prescribed manners of Islam vary, in fact, from the 'forbidden' to the 'recommended'. The former are upheld and enforced by law, the latter do not expose offenders to any formal trial or punishment except in the disapproval of other members of the Muslim community. A third group of manners are those which do not even lead to disapproval if one violates them.

Nor does it follow from the divine origin of Islamic manners that the system should be rigid and inflexible. Islam is not the sort of ideal that is impenetrable to human experience or inapplicable to existing world conditions. Rather, the nature of the system is such that it is flexible in many respects while stable in others, the element of flexibility being grounded in human reasoning to which Islam appeals and which may even be reckoned among its general sources.

The two basic sources of Islam, the Quran and the Sunnah, include, besides many detailed rules, general principles which ultimately govern all matters related to the various aspects of life, religious, social, economic, political, etc. None of these general principles are subject to historical change. But conditions do change. The means for deriving rules for new problems in new situations are provided for within Islam in Ijtihad. Ijtihad is, the disciplined use of independent individual reasoning to draw the necessary conclusions in accordance with the essencc and spirit of Islam and in adherence to its immutable general principles.

Thus, through the faith and diligence of qualified scholars, the detail of Islamic teachings can respond effectively to the problem of historical change. The teachings of Islam are, in fact, fully cognizant of human nature and human needs. Islam acknowledges the realities of life and deals with them in the most practical way. There is then no impulse to abrogate or adjust the general principles of the faith in order to adapt them to particular conditions.

The realism and practicability of Islamic manners is easily illustrated. For example, fasting the full lunar month of Ramadan is a primary obligation upon all Muslims, yet Islam understanding the vicissitudes of travelling exempts the traveller from fasting, requiring that he make up lost days when the hardship is over. Likewise, women who have recently given birth, or are in the monthly cycle, and those seriously ill, are similarly exempted.

The five daily prayers are, again, a primary obligation, yet the traveller is permitted, according to some a Hadith, to combine certain of the five occasions of Salat and perform them together, also to shorten the four- rakat prayers to two-rakat prayers, known as qasr. Islam allows that the precise, final detail of the application of manners may differ, according to the fashions and circumstances of local groups, provided, of course, that the main principles of dress, of dietary laws, etc. are adhered to Islamic manners are meant to order daily life, to give it rhythm, dignity and serenity; they are not a set of snobbish or legalistic rituals to complicate daily life.

Necessary Things

Islam determines every aspect of the life of a Muslim. This essential fact is very difficult for non-Muslims to grasp. For the believer, Islam gives the criteria for judging all of his behaviour and conduct; it determines his relationship with other individuals, with society as a whole, with the physical world, and it determines also his relationship to his own self. Many examples can be given of what in secular communities are the preserve of arbitrary individual will or the equally arbitrary demands of the social milieu. Food, for example, may be prepared only from what is allowed by Islam; a Muslim can make no use of, for example, pork. A Muslim woman may not uncover her feet in public because in Islam it is not permitted. Goods forbidden to a Muslim, such as wine, may not be exchanged as gifts. If a Muslim is invited to a wedding feast, he should (if physically possible) accept the invitation because it is obligatory to do so. Death-bed wishes may not be fulfilled if they contradict the teachings of Islam, such as a request to allocate an extra share of inheritance to one of the dead person's heirs, or to have his body cremated.

Adab al-Islam are a comprehensive code covering almost every aspect of social behaviour, a part of the complete way of life which is Islam. As the different parts of Islam make up an integral unity, the application of adab al-Islam in detachment from the rest will not bring about total realization of Islam, indeed it may, in certain respects, become meaningless. The customs and manners discussed in this book are considered suitable for Muslims: those who have a proper religious attitude will instinctively seek to observe the good manners commended or required by Islam. The various aspects of Islam, ideological, spiritual, legal, social, economic, political, etc., are mutually consistent and supplement each other. For example, faith is essential as it instals in Muslims the spirit of observing the ethical, moral, legal and other prescriptions without external compulsion. Equally, voluntary observance of those prescriptions supports and enhances faith, opening up the path from devotion to social action, linking the two in a strong, stable bond. More specifically the unitary strength of Islam may be seen in, for instance, the manners concerning women, which follow from and sustain the Islamic concept of Muslim womanhood in an Islamic community.

The breadth of adab al-Islam contrasts sharply with the limitations of 'etiquette'. The manners of Islam are not merely rules of courtesy for various occasions, but cover the whole range of human relations from the simplest actions to the most elaborate of social occasions. The true purpose of Western 'etiquette' (even after it had been extended beyond royal circles to ordinary people) 'seems to have been the protection of the upper class'. By contrast, the true purpose of adab al-Islam lies in their religious character and nature. They derive from and sustain man's need to remember God in his daily routine; they are designed to keep up his remembrance of God and to help him act rightly and correctly. This is conspicuous in the invocations of God that accompany most everyday incidents of behaviour in Islam.

A Muslim should start and end his day, when waking up and when going to sleep, by mentioning God. He should thank and praise God when taking food and drink, when buying new clothes or other articles of use. Mentioning God is recommended even when relieving oneself. It is recommended to say, when entering the lavatory: 'In the name of Allah. Allah, in You I take refuge from demons', and on leaving the lavatory, ask for His forgiveness. Remembering God and asking Him for perfection and guidance are of special importance when travelling. It may be noted here that the major festivals in Islam are in fact collective celebrations of the successful completion of two principal religious obligations, namely, fasting in the month of Ramadan and Hajj (pilgrimage to Mecca).

One of the chief foundations of adab al-Islam is morality, the cornerstone of a nation's self-confidence and strength, as surely as corruption and immorality are one of the main causes of a nation's decline and disintegration. The insistence on morality often gives to the Islamic way of life an appearance of rigidity or puritanism; as one writer has noted:'... in regard to certain aspects of morality, Islam is more rigid and more puritan than certain other systems of life in our times.' But given the importance of morality to the health of a nation, normative Islam is surely right to block all ways leading to corruption, such as illicit sex and luxurious living. Material comforts should not be at the expense of human virtues, individual and collective; politics also (considered, in non-Islamic thought, as immoral or even amoral) must conform to the goals of Islam, the development of human character, the humanity of man.

The ideal of the humanity of man is grounded in the concept of Al-amal al-Salih or virtuous deeds. The term extends beyond what is normally understood as the 'religious' domain and covers a wide range of human activities (in relation to others, to the animate and inanimate environment) sanctioned within Islamic faith and law. The Prophet's life provides many concrete instances: to act justly between two people, to help a man onto his mount, to help load his belongings, to speak good words, to remove nuisances from paths or roads, to give food and water to stray dogs and cats, to be forward in greeting others, to visit relatives, etc.; even the act of making love within marriage is valued as a good deed. The most inclusive characteristics of the ideal Muslim personality are humility, modesty and simplicity or naturalness (lack of affectation). Pride and arrogance in any aspect of conduct are not accepted, as no individual is superior to another except in his degree of faith and contribution of good deeds.

Thus, clothes that show haughtiness, that flaunt social status, are forbidden. Manners in eating should demonstrate humility before the occasion as well as respect for the meal: leaning on a cushion while eating is forbidden. Sitting on the floor when eating is a sign of humility, and therefore recommended. Furnishings should show modesty and restraint; for example, the bed should not be set too high above the ground. Gait in walking, manner of address in greeting and in speech generally, should avoid any taint of arrogance.

Position of Women

When Europe was plunged into its Dark Ages and debated on the nature of woman's soul, on whether or not it was human, Islam had already declared men and women to be of the same origin and nature, equal before God and society, and promised like rewards or punishments for their good or evil deeds.

Islamic law is just and fair for both women and men. A woman in Islam has the right to hold property, and to manage her estates. She has the right to lease, or bequeath, or exploit property for her own benefit.

Although a woman's main domain is the house, she is not excluded from making financial transactions such as selling and buying, lending and borrowing, investments, etc. In the different schools of law, women are judged legally competent and fully entitled to carry out any of these transactions. There is no-difference between men and women concerning the penalties accorded under Islamic law whether for drinking alcohol, committing adultery, apostasy or murder.

Women in Islam enjoy the right to express their views freely, and to reject marriage proposals. The contemporary position of Muslim women in some parts of the Islamic world should not be adduced as evidence or argument against the concept and position of women in Islam. The following adab should remove any misunderstanding on this point:

1. The news of the birth of a girl should be welcomed exactly as the news of the birth of a boy is usually welcomed. It is against the teaching of Islam to convey congratulations on the birth of a boy, but to refrain from doing so on the birth of a girl. Islam stresses the importance of taking special care of daughters.

2. The Prophet exhorts men to treat women respectfully and gently, not to look down upon them as inferior, but to regard them as equals.
3. Women should be consulted in matters concerning them. The fact that in Islamic marriage there must be a guardian does not mean that he has the right to make the marriage decision. The woman alone has that right, to accept or refuse marriage, free from any pressure. If a girl is betrothed to someone without her consent, she then has the right to approve or disapprove the betrothal.
4. The woman in the role of mother is deeply honoured: we have noted above the Prophet's saying, 'Paradise lies at the feet of mothers.' The one most deserving of loving care by a Muslim is his mother, who commands greater respect than even his father.
5. A married woman may retain her own family name and not necessarily relinquish it in favour of her husband's. This is a mark of respect.
6. Certain manners have been prescribed by Islam in order to protect sexual identity: viz. imitation by men of women in dress, gait, etc. or vice versa, is forbidden.
7. Safeguarding a woman's personality is required in Islam as long as her deeds are not contrary to Islamic teachings. A husband is not allowed to destroy his wife's personality and make it conform to his own.
8. A woman, during her monthly period, may be treated more gently and kindly. A menstruating woman is not considered dirty or sinful as is the case in some other religions and cultures.
9. It is the right of a woman to have sexual intercourse with her husband from time to time. If the husband had never been able to make love to her, then it is her right to have a divorce.
10. A good wife is considered by Islam to be the best asset in the world. She has an extremely important role in married life - she has responsibility for running the household and the regulation of its economy.
11. Islam requires that Muslim women maintain their cultural identity and do not imitate the manners of non- Muslim women in dress, shoes, etc. Such imitation is a clear indication of weakness.
12. In Islam, a woman's dress has to serve certain purposes among which is the protection of her honour and integrity. The

difference between men's and women's dress is due to the difference between the male and female forms and the sexual effect of that difference. For the same reason, a woman may not undertake a journey unless accompanied by her husband or a mahram (a consanguine relative whom the law forbids her to marry).

Personal Education

Islamic manners train and educate the individual to control his passions and to respond to the voice of reason. They also educate him to exhibit qualities of patience, of being content and of self-dependence, that is, not seeking the help of others unless unavoidable.

One of the most praised virtues in Islam is the ability to control one's anger and not react violently. In the words of the Prophet, a powerful human being is one who controls himself when he is angry.

Punctuality and self-discipline are also valued as most important characteristics of a good Muslim. The five daily prayers teach punctuality, and the month of fasting teaches sustained self-control.

The fruits of discipline are (a) moderation and (b) wise use of time. Moderation is one of the main aims of adab al-Islam, for it creates a life of balance and equilibrium, which is necessary if a man is to be of service to others (for how can anyone given to exaggeration or affectation ever be sufficiently free of himself to help others disinterestedly) and if he is to serve God in all that He commands? Time is a human measure of the value of the life God has given: one of the most crucial questions that every man will be asked on the Day of Resurrection is what use he made of his time.

Therefore, it is the responsibility of every Muslim to make the best use of every minute, to weigh every grain, for his own interest and for the interest of the nation as a whole.

Adab al-Islam are prescribed so as to be in full conformity with the above-mentioned principle. The following clarify this point:

1. Muslim daily life begins at dawn before sunrise, and ends early just after Salat al-isha (the night prayer) that is, about one and a half hours after sunset.
2. Socializing for the sake of passing the time is disapproved. Although it is recommended that Muslims meet one another frequently, they should make use of these meetings to discuss useful matters.

3. Spending an unnecessarily long time eating should be avoided.
4. Moderation in speaking is required. Speaking at length or just for the sake of it is a bad habit and considered a waste of time: silence is preferable.

Concern About Human Safety

It is notable that Islam concerns itself with the safety of individuals. Below are some familiar adab, but any conduct that assists in achieving this purpose and does not contradict the principles of Islam is considered as part of adab al-Islam. The following are recommended:

1. Before going to bed, one should make sure that doors are properly closed, food pots and drinking vessels covered, and all sources of fire extinguished or turned off.
2. Sleeping on the roof of a house where there is no protecting wall or in a lonely place with nobody else around in case of emergency, should be avoided. Also, mattress and pillow should be examined to ensure that no harmful insects have hidden under or inside them.
3. Before drinking from any vessel, one should check that nothing harmful has fallen into it.
4. Travelling should, as far as possible, be undertaken in company and not alone. No vehicle should be so parked as to obstruct, hinder or endanger others.
5. Before putting on shoes, they should be checked to ensure that no harmful insect has hidden in them during the night or while they have been in disuse.
6. Certain animals, considered pests, are harmful to man, and for that reason should be killed: examples are scorpions, mice and snakes.

One of the great achievements of adab al-Islam has been their contribution to the unity of Muslim peoples who belong to different races, speak different languages, and inhabit different parts of the globe. The religious character of Islamic manners, derived from the Quran and the Sunnah, plays an important role in this respect. Thus a Moroccan who travels to Pakistan will not find it difficult to understand the manners of the people there, nor feel out of place. Muslim women from Egypt will not be astonished by the sight of Turkish women wearing Islamic dress. Members of the Islamic society reassert their solidarity on each occasion of each day that they adhere to the ways of doing things which constitute their very tradition.

Adab al-Islam create common understanding among Muslims - they form a universal culture which gives shape and meaning to local cultures throughout the world. The local culture may well differ from one Islamic community to another. By contrast, the system of prayers, greetings, major festivals, dietary restrictions (e.g. on alcohol), the practice of Haram and halal, are elements of the universal Islamic pattern. Conspicuous too is the fact that everywhere Muslim women dress modestly and in most Muslim countries wear the proper Islamic dress. The local variations (e.g. in national dishes, such as biryani, popular in the Indian subcontinent, or in dress, such as the sari as worn by Muslims in India) are important in that they distinguish one group of Muslims from another - we are created in different nations, the Quran tells us, that we may know one from another- but they are completely insignificant in the sense that they do not diminish the Muslim character and Muslim identity of the particular group.

An important rule of adab al-Islam is the prohibition against imitating the manners of non-Muslim peoples. This should not be confused with seeking knowledge, in crafts, technology, science, etc. which has always been encouraged by Islam. Manners play a vital part in the maintenance of cultural identity. It is obvious that manners embodying a Muslim life should be distinguished from others by their own Islamic character.

Any intrusions of non-Muslim cultures into Muslim life do not mean that Islamic identity is being erased. This is because the Islamic way of life is so deeply ingrained that a Muslim cannot easily rid himself of it and it is so deeply ingrained because it is not a temporary improvisation of forms in response to a particular period of history but a stable structure of interrelated manners and ideals that conform to the unchanging realities of human relations between man and man, and between man and God. Let whoever doubts this consider the different states of Christianity and Islam in the Soviet Union, hated and suppressed alike by the ideology of Russian communism. No; despite the economic and political disunity that prevails on the surface, the cultural strength and unity of Islam is still a reality throughout the Muslim world.

Manners and Customs of Non-muslims : The tolerance shown by Muslims toward non-Muslims living in Muslim lands is without parallel. Islam affords protection to the religion and culture of every community within the Islamic state. Any conversion to Islam must be through free choice and conviction.

The life, property and honour of every non-Muslim individual is fully protected by Islam. Moreover, Islam has guaranteed full religious autonomy and limited judicial authority to its non-Muslim citizens. Non-Muslims have the following rights:

1. Full freedom of belief and worship, and independent religious and educational institutions.
2. Full autonomy concerning personal and family law including the rules of marriage and divorce though opposed to Islamic rules.
3. In financial, transactional and civil affairs, treatment equal to that of Muslim citizens, except in certain cases, e.g. drinking alcohol, for which they may not be punished, provided it is not done in public.
4. In social customs, non-Muslims are free to preserve their distinct character as expressed, for example, in modes of dress (as long as they do not contradict Islamic law), eating and diet.

The refusal of Islam to impose its own adab on non-Muslims has helped to avoid communal frictions and religious strife; European rule, by contrast, has exploited and exacerbated community differences for the sake of political or military advantage.

There are some restrictions upon Muslims concerning their social relations with non-Muslims. These restrictions are self-explanatory the religious occasions of non-Muslims are not part of a Muslim's faith, though it is a part of his Islam to tolerate them; it follows that he should not participate in them. Far from indicating fanaticism or intolerance these restrictions express a balance between tolerance, even respect, and the need to preserve the distinctness and stability of Muslim belief, practice and adab. The tolerance of Islam is particularly striking when compared to the intolerances inflicted upon Muslims in non-Muslim lands or under non-Muslim authority. For example, in the sixteenth century, following the collapse of Muslim rule, the Christian courts of the Inquisition burnt to death all Muslims who refused to abandon their faith and convert to Christianity. Muslims were forced to change their names, dress and customs and to behave according to Christian manners.

A further example from history is the case of the Jews who, in various parts of Christian Europe, were forced to change their clothes, names and customs to conform to Christian tradition, but who, in the Muslim world, were treated with a unique tolerance. They were allowed to practise and maintain their religious rituals and customs according to their own traditions. The golden age of Jewish literature took place during Muslim rule in Spain. When the Muslims left Spain, the Jews left with them.

The evidence of this difference in treatment is still to be found today. The Jews who have lived in the Muslim world, whether they are still living there or have migrated to Israel, have Jewish names, while those who lived or are still living in the Western world have Russian, English, German or French names.

Basic Norms of Conduct

The Islamic day has a character perhaps surprisingly different from the day as it looks and is experienced in non-Islamic countries. It begins very early (i.e. after the Fajr prayer) and also ends very early (i.e. after the 'Isha' prayer). As the Islamic calendar is lunar, dates are determined according to the moon, not the sun, with the months moving round from year to year.

Time is precious for the Muslim, and he must apportion each day wisely. Quotidian problems and difficulties are put aside to observe the prayers at the five prescribed times and observing them mitigates the intensity of these problems, setting them into proper perspective. But since that perspective is Islam it applies throughout the day. For, unlike other religions, Islam influences a Muslim's conduct from the moment he rises until the moment he retires for the night. These influences of course vary in degree, the variations broadly classifiable into five categories:

1. What is permitted most actions fall into this category.
2. What is recommended.
3. What is disapproved or abhorred.
4. What is obligatory.
5. What is forbidden.

It is interesting to note that only a very small percentage of man's actions fall into the categories of obligatory and forbidden. The dividing lines between these five categories are flexible. What is forbidden under one set of conditions may become, under another, an exceptional set of conditions, permissible or even obligatory. For instance, Muslims are forbidden to eat pork. But if a Muslim finds himself faced with starvation and all that is available for him to eat is pork, then, to save his life, he is allowed to eat it. The general rules that govern Muslim conduct have not simply been arbitrarily dictated; they are derived from the Quran and the Sunnah of the Prophet; both are divinely inspired and intended as a mercy to mankind. No Muslim may be taken to task if he commits a breach of Islamic tenets or laws, if there was an unavoidable and compelling reason resulting either from his own condition or from external compulsion.

Although practising Islam is not absolutely obligatory until the individual has passed the age of puberty, it is nevertheless recommended that children grow up in an Islamic atmosphere, thus facilitating their practise later.

The principal characteristics and rules of Islamic manners for various aspects of life can be summarized as follows:

1. In almost everything, deliberation (and not haste) is required. A Muslim should consider how a matter may turn out; then, if the outcome appears worthwhile and good, he should carry on, otherwise he should refrain.
2. Kindness and gentleness in a Muslim's dealings with others are essential.
3. Cleanliness and purity of body, place, clothes, etc., should be one of the most conspicuous characteristics of Muslim life.
4. Beauty, elegance, orderliness are values for the Muslim to observe, and whenever possible to attain.
5. According to Islam, a good deed done with courtesy beautifies that deed; impudence, on the other hand, destroys the good in it.
6. All a Muslim's deeds should express an attitude of humility and not arrogance.
7. A Muslim is commanded to avoid any act that might harm himself or some other person, physically, mentally or morally.
8. In the daily life of a Muslim, silence is preferred to unnecessary speaking.
9. A Muslim should treat others as he would wish them to treat him. Like for others what he would like for himself. Good manners without consideration for others are an impossibility.
10. A Muslim should never order or ask anyone to do something that he would not do himself.
11. Favouring the right side or hand in things such as giving, taking, shaking hands, eating, drinking, walking, etc., and using the left hand for such things as cleaning oneself in the toilet, is recommended.

12. Eating, drinking and clothing oneself, etc., well, are allowed as long as the motive is not pride or arrogance. Life characterized by extravagance is abhorred.
13. Though extravagance is abhorred, this does not imply that a Muslim should not have money or not enjoy life. The effects of God's blessings upon him should be visible to others.
14. Being generous and not mean or avaricious is a virtue.
15. Gratitude to God should characterize a Muslim's life, whether He blesses or burdens him, and gratitude with patience and fortitude.
16. A Muslim must be always faithful.
17. In all aspects of life a Muslim must exercise moderation and be natural; unnaturalness and exaggeration are disapproved.
18. A Muslim should be self-sufficient and should seek the help of other Muslims only when it is urgent and necessary.
19. Copying or imitating other cultures and religions in any way is forbidden.
20. Obedience and carrying out another's orders or wishes may not contradict the teachings of Islam; if it does, the teachings of Islam must be given priority.
21. Maintaining sexual identity is most important. Imitation of men by women, or of women by men, in dress, manner of walking, etc. is forbidden.
22. One of the most pervasive characteristics of Islamic manners is discipline, leading to balance and harmony in the life of the individual and the community.
23. Flexibility and tolerance are also characteristics of adab al-Islam. Broadly speaking, any particular conduct is tolerated or accepted if it is civilized (i.e. considerate of others) and respectable (i.e. inoffensive to the individual and community) and provided it does not fall into the categories of the abhorred or forbidden.

Non-artificiality

Islam requires and demands moderation and naturalness in all aspects of life, worldly and religious. Extremism, exaggeration, eccentricity and affectation, caprice and complicatedness are rejected. The insistence on a certain informality in adab al-Islam is intended to ease their use by the vast majority of the members of the Muslim society.

Naturalness of manners is valued as a means of relieving social tension, of enabling and strengthening social relations.

Western 'etiquette' originated in the Royal courts of Europe, and was invented to meet 'the requirement of behaviour in courts and among aristocrats everywhere'. The meaning of etiquette was weakened when it spread to all classes. To this day Western etiquette varies from group to group. Members of so-called 'high society' observe more complicated and rigid forms of etiquette than the less well-to-do. This comes out of and helps sustain the class system.

Adab al-Islam, however, are different. They are not designed to divide society according to social classes. The rules, revealed through the Quran and the Sunnah, were not formulated by certain groups, i.e. the rich and powerful in order to subdue or distance other groups. Islam attaches great importance to the adherence of the whole of Muslim society to its adab. It does not consider these manners as the privilege or preserve of a certain group, but as a privilege open to every member of the Muslim society. A variety of etiquette levels is non-existent in Islam.

The function of adab al-Islam in unifying Muslim communities, as well as being an expression of their unity, is clear. But adab al-Islam are not just about coherence or consistency of behaviour; they are about coherence or consistency of right behaviour. The notion of 'proper' conduct may not, in Islam, be separated from the notion of 'good' deeds, nor from 'faith' and 'devotion'.

Faith and good deeds are both necessary in this world for a prosperous and ideal society in which there is mutual and shared responsibility. And in the Hereafter, faith and good deeds are the necessary conditions for forgiveness and salvation, for admission to Paradise. A large number of verses in the Quran link faith and good deeds as defining characteristics of a true Muslim.

Huge Network

In Islam, what is 'central' and 'essential' is determined by its broad relation to the goals of Islam, among which is the civilization or advancement of human society, the promotion of happiness and prosperity, material as well as moral. On examination, the prescriptions and prohibitions which form part of Islamic teachings will be seen to be not arbitrary decrees but an ordered system of commandments whose purpose (besides testing man's obedience and loyalty to God) is the advancement of man, according to a safe, proper and perfect course, at the individual, family and societal levels. The details of adab al-Islam are not meaningless formalities, unwelcome to the individual because they are unrelated to the actual needs of his personal or social life.

On the contrary, they directly address the different basic functions that concern all members of society at almost every moment of their lives. They are intended to concentrate attention on the central and essential, to rescue man from the peripheral and distracting. They distinguish means from ends and help individual and community to administer personal and collective resources effectively. It may be helpful to illustrate this general point by listing the basic human needs and functions as they are viewed within the perspective of adab al-Islam:

1. Clothes are primarily intended to protect the wearer against the climate, and to conceal parts of the body.
2. The purpose of housing is to provide shelter from the climate and to secure necessary privacy and safety.
3. Cleanliness, as well as protecting man from disease, expresses his humanity.
4. Adornment, make-up, etc. are a woman's means to look attractive and pleasant before her husband.
5. Speech is important as a means of communication, serving in the essential functions of exchange and relationship with other people, such as buying, selling, etc.
6. Humour reduces tension and relaxes people at a gathering.
7. Gifts are meant to express goodwill and to foster good relations with others.
8. Inviting others to eat, sharing food with others, makes and strengthens social bonds.
9. Social relations themselves are valued because they prevent or limit isolation of the individual. Social customs are valued because they create stability and harmony in social relations.
10. Graves are primarily for honouring the dead, but also to protect the living from the decaying corpse.
11. Animals, in direct relation to man, are intended to be used only for specific purposes such as provision of food, labour, transport. They are not meant to be used by man for his entertainment as, for instance, when animals are set against each other.

It will be immediately obvious that, without the restraint of adab al-Islam, all these means become ends, destroying a proper sense of values and priorities.

Clothes, houses, parties, gifts, drain the resources of individual and community, as people (having lost sight of the true function of these things) spend money in a fruitless endeavour to prove to others their greater purchasing power; in their world the ability to waste goods is a proof of personal success and of the success of the society to which they belong.

The consequences of self-adornment or amusement becoming ends in themselves can be measured in the fortunes devoted to these activities by the vast majority in Western countries and, by increasing numbers in Muslim countries. But the real cost of so defying the realities of human accountability under God's law, is the loss of the soul of each individual who hurries fretfully from one escapism to another, seeking to be always excited or distracted and, whenever he catches himself alone, feeling profoundly empty and wretched.

Adab al-Islam are designed to avoid such ungrateful waste of human potential, and encourage man to exercise that potential in full conformity with the true purposes and realities of his life. The rules of conduct for a Muslim life contain sound wisdom, whether viewed in religious, cultural, social, economic, psychological or even medical terms. It follows that, for a healthy, balanced life, individual and community should apply these rules comprehensively and conscientiously.

Wherever they are applied, two things must always be borne in mind, namely kindness and consideration. Among the root meanings of 'Islam' (besides surrender or submission) is peace; a 'Muslim' is one who has submitted to the decrees of God, who has sought to make peace with God and His creatures. Moreover, the Prophet defines a 'Muslim' as one who does not harm others by hand or tongue.

Kindness and Gentleness : According to a saying of the Prophet, kindness is required in every instance of Muslim conduct. One of the main ends of adab al-Islam is to train people to be kind and gentle in every matter and toward every thing. The following examples will illustrate:

1. Speaking should be loud enough to be audible to those addressed, never louder.
2. Bad or objectionable language should be avoided.
3. Laughter should not be characterized by loud or unpleasant sounds.
4. Weeping should be restrained and polite, not hysterically loud or abandoned.

5. Eating and drinking should be done at a gentle, dignified pace.
6. It is proper for a Muslim to restrain his anger, keeping himself within the bounds of courtesy.
7. Parents should give their children beautiful, meaningful names, and avoid names indicating difficulty and sadness.
8. Tenderness should be a most essential element in the love-making process.
9. Smiling at other people when meeting them is recommended.
10. Looking pleasantly at others while conversing with them is required as polite conduct.
11. It is necessary that a Muslim be gentle when criticizing others for something they might have done.

Consideration for Others : Inflicting any kind of harm or offence physically, psychologically or morally must be avoided. In the Words of the Prophet, 'There should be neither harming nor reciprocating harm.'

Anything done or said with disregard for others is not considered proper Muslim conduct. In fact, good behaviour in Islam depends to a large extent on showing consideration toward others. The contribution of adab al-Islam in this regard is enormous. Just a few examples will illustrate :

1. Disgracing or reviling others' beliefs, directly or indirectly, is forbidden.
2. The main principle governing one's behaviour on the road is to avoid harming, impeding or disturbing others, including such acts as spitting or making loud noises.
3. Reviling another or speaking of his mistakes is disapproved, even if a Muslim is reviled by him and even though his faults are spoken of by him.
4. Making jokes, using impolite or sarcastic terms at the expense of others, is prohibited. Character assassination through insinuation, backbiting and undesirable conjecture is also prohibited.
5. Distasteful expressions should be avoided while eating, as they might disturb or upset others.
6. In a group of three people, two should not talk privately as this might offend the third.
7. Reviling the dead is forbidden as this causes hurt to their living relatives.

8. In socializing with others, their comfort and well-being must be positively considered. For instance, neither a person's clothes nor mouth should smell badly; after eating onions or garlic, it is preferable that socializing is avoided.
9. To squeeze between two men in a mosque or to step on others while proceeding to a place, is forbidden, as this will annoy them.
10. To relieve oneself in still water, in the shade, on the road or in any public place, is forbidden, as this might prevent others from making normal use of such facilities and/or be a health hazard.
11. When shoes are taken off, they should be put in a place where they will not disturb others by their smell.
12. When sneezing, the mouth and nose should be covered; when yawning, the hand should cover the mouth; when speaking, one should not speak loudly, as this might annoy others. Even the sitting posture should be such as will not offend others, as does, for example, turning one's back to them.

Role of Adab al-Islam

Among the main aims of adab al-Islam is to help in establishing and maintaining healthy social relationships. As will be seen, among the necessary attributes of the ideal Muslim personality, are honesty, respect for others, honouring one's word, restraint of anger, patience, modesty, kindness, etc. These virtues eliminate mistrust and create trust, the necessary foundation upon which alone sound relations can be built and developed. In the Islamic view it is not enough simply to avoid doing harm to others, nor even to wish for others what you wish for yourself. What is required of Muslims toward each other is mutual responsibility and positive assistance.

As will be seen, formality in the manners of Islam is reduced to the barest possible minimum. This enables freer social intercourse, makes the social machinery run more smoothly and facilitates meetings and visits, for isolation is not recommended in Islam. Muslims are encouraged to meet each other, for that strengthens social bonds and defends the individual against the psychological consequences of social isolation. Moreover, Muslims are encouraged to meet frequently. It is the duty of the host to be hospitable and generous to his guest. Acceptance of an invitation to a meal is recommended and, in the case of an invitation to a wedding meal, acceptance becomes obligatory.

Visiting the sick, taking part in funeral processions, offering condolences to the bereaved, comforting and encouraging them, providing food for them, exchanging gifts with other members of the society, shaking hands when meeting or parting, sharing other happy occasions such as weddings and births, etc., are all ways to strengthen and develop social relations. Particular importance is attached to such exchanges between relatives and neighbours.

Islam has recommended Muslims to hold feasts from time to time and invite others to these occasions. It has also prescribed holding feasts on certain occasions such as weddings, births, the day of Sacrifice, etc. Eating together makes social ties stronger between members of a community irrespective of social status: this is why Islam disapproves of the feast to which the rich are invited and from which the poor are excluded and considers it the worst of feasts.

Loose Connections

Social relations should be quite free of personal interest, and engaged in wholly for the sake of God. Thus, a Muslim should not accept a gift presented by someone who intends thereby to influence him favourably. Invitations given out of some personal interest, e.g. in the hope of personal popularity or in expectation of some return, should be rejected. Social life is encouraged at a wider level, namely by meetings of the community as a whole. It is recommended that the five prayers prescribed in Islam be performed in congregation in the mosque. This provides the opportunity for a large number and variety of people to meet more than once each day. There is the weekly gathering on Friday to perform Friday prayer which, with certain exceptions, is obligatory upon every Muslim. Also, there are the two annual occasions to meet on the feast of Fitr (breaking the fast) and the feast of Adha (Sacrifice). Moreover, hundreds of thousands of Muslims from all over the world meet every year, for a few days during the pilgrimage season, in Mecca.

The mosque is an important centre where Muslims may discuss religious, social and political issues related to the community and the nation as a whole. Therefore personal matters (e.g. the announcement of lost articles, or other private business) should not be discussed in the mosque. As it is a place for public meeting it should be kept clean - that is the responsibility of every Muslim. Cleanliness and orderliness of the mosque contribute vitally to the success of social meetings held within it.

Personal cleanliness is an important factor when communicating with others, and Muslims are required to bath frequently and, where possible, use perfume, the more so when public occasions (the Friday congregation, for example, or the two Eid festivals, etc.) arise. Especially stressed are those areas of commonest contact, namely the face and hands, and above all the mouth, which deserves to be kept clean and pleasant-smelling because talking is so vital a factor in communication and contact with others. Islam is based upon *tauhid,* the absolute Oneness and Uniqueness of God, and rejects all kinds of polytheism whether primitive or evolved. The Shariah is, in fact, the embodiment of this concept, and its every detail springs from it. Adab al-Islam are consistent with tawhid, affirming and serving this most fundamental principle. Here are a few examples:

1. Names that mean being a slave of someone other than God, such as 'Abd al-Nabi (the slave of the Prophet), are forbidden.
2. Reviling natural phenomena, such as wind or rain, which are under God's command, is forbidden. So too is reviling one's fate, or the attribution of injustice to God.
3. Expressions or exclamations that contradict tawhid, that seem to ascribe partners to God, for example, 'What God wills and what so-and-so wills!' or 'I have no help except from God and you!', are strictly forbidden.
4. Slaughtering animals must be done only for the sake of God; if His name is not taken deliberately, or if some other name is taken instead, the meat of the animal becomes *Haram,* forbidden, the sacrifice void.
5. On the occasion of someone's death, expressions that contradict Islamic faith, such as, 'What will become of me now that our source of independence is gone' or 'He died a premature death', are forbidden.
6. Swearing by people or things other than God, His Names or Attributes, is forbidden.
7. A vow pledged for anything or anyone other than God, is null and void and should not be fulfilled.
8. A Muslim is required not to make absolute assertions without referring to God's will, and to say instead *Insha Allah* (If God wills).
9. To bow in respect to any person in not permitted, as bowing is reserved only for God in the act of prayer.
10. To refrain from travelling because some sort of supposed omen against it has been sighted, is forbidden, because this contradicts the principle of belief in destiny.

11. The purpose of visiting the cemetery, which is recommended in Islam, is to remind the living of death, thus influencing them to better their obedience to God and improve their conduct and behaviour in relation to others.
12. The Kaaba is the first house of God on earth. It was built by the Prophet Ibrahim and his son Ismail at Mecca in Arabia. Every Muslim faces the Qiblah in prayer the world over: it is a symbol of Muslim unity and of the unity of Islam. But it orients more than the Muslim's prayer. When animals are slaughtered they are made to face in the direction of the Qiblah; deceased Muslims are placed in the grave with their face towards the Qiblah. Even the design of the lavatory is connected with the Qiblah in that when relieving himself, a Muslim should avoid facing or turning his back to the Qiblah.

The contribution of Islamic manners to the unity and solidarity of Muslims will be discussed in greater detail in subsequent pages.

Adherence to the manners of normative Islam will result in the eradication of many bidah that have penetrated into Muslim life. Bidah can be defined as an innovated belief or practice added to the original and authentic Islamic belief or practice.

It has been rejected by the Prophet saying, 'He who innovates something in this matter of ours that is not of it will have it rejected.' And also, '. . . Beware of matters newly introduced (in religion), for every innovation is an error and every error will lead to Hell-fire.'

Anything added and introduced into Islam is considered as bidah and is therefore rejected. The effect of innovations upon the various aspects of Islamic life is tremendously negative.

They transform Islam from being a simple religion to one complicated and difficult to practise, which will lead gradually to the abandonment of at least certain aspects of Muslim life.

Bidah should not be confused with Ijtihad which is the use of individual reasoning to draw conclusions from the Quran or the Sunnah in conformity with the general principles of Islam, and exercised only by qualified scholars.

As mentioned above, many non-Islamic elements have been introduced into the behaviour and manners of Muslims. Here are some examples:

1. Certain religious occasions have been introduced into Islam, such as those of the Prophet's birthday (Maulid), his Ascension (Miraj), and his Emigration (Hijrah).

2. Mentioning God's name audibly and reading the Quran aloud during a funeral procession.
3. Shaking hands following every congregational prayer.
4. The practice that after a certain number of days a bereaved family should prepare food and serve others. The correct Islamic conduct is for friends and relatives to prepare food for the bereaved since they are over whelmed by sorrow.
5. The practice of plastering and ornamenting graves.

Psychological Aspect : One of the striking characteristics of adab al-Islam is that psychological factors are fully taken into consideration. A few examples are:

1. Divorce is highly discouraged during the woman's monthly period, as she is usually passing through a period of psychological tension.
2. Apart from the benefits of hygiene, cleanliness is prescribed in Islam because it refreshes and re-orientates body and mind. This is true in the case of performing ablution before prayer and washing the whole body after sexual intercourse and at the end of childbirth and menstruation. Those who have washed the body of a deceased person are recommended to bathe afterwards. The significance of this advice is that taking a bath in such situations helps to rid people of the psychological effects of those situations.

Medical and Hygienic Aspects : Islam teaches Muslims to be always clean and pure. The daily manners of cleanliness and purity of body, place, clothes, etc., contribute enormously to the soundness of bodily health, as reliable medical evidence confirms, for cleanliness prevents the transmission of microbial diseases.

'Wudu' (the ablution) demanded of Muslims several times every day, as a necessary condition before prayer, requires washing those parts of the body that are generally exposed to dirt and dust.

Paring the nails (ordered by Islam) is to prevent the accumulation of dirt and impurities on fingers which are in constant use for eating and drinking, as well as shaking hands.

Cleaning the axillary and pubic regions from growing hair is also prescribed by Islam. It helps to keep the sweat glands functioning well and prevents the multiplication of the bacteria that would otherwise affect those sweat glands.

Among the impurities from which a Muslim should keep away and purify himself, his clothes, etc. are faeces and urine. The urine contains urea and other nitrogenous compounds which disintegrate into ammonia through the effect of bacteria, giving rise to unpleasant odour. Pinworms (oxyuriasis), viral hepatitis, ascariasis and taeniasisi are among the diseases transmitted mainly through swallowing the infective stage present in faeces.

The fact that the Muslim should not overeat, but should rather stop before his stomach is full, has medical as well as social and moral benefits. The stomach contains stretch receptors; when distended it can give rise to pain and discomfort, as well as more disabling ailments.

When drinking, the Muslim is advised not to breathe into the vessel, for carbon dioxide is present in the expired air in a higher percentage than in the inspired air, and high concentrations of carbon dioxide in the circulation negatively influence several physiological functions.

After drinking milk, the Muslim owes special thanks to God, for the benefit contained in it. Milk is considered adequate nourishment, a complete diet. It contains all the essential nutritional components: carbohydrates, fats, and proteins, in addition to many vitamins and minerals, mainly vitamin D, calcium, phosphate, deficiencies of which cause rickets in children and osteomalacia in adults.

Slaughtering according to Islamic law provides meat that is clean of blood. Blood is known to be a good breeding ground for micro-organisms which can be the source of many diseases. Besides the health aspect, there is the cultural fact that many people feel disgusted, even ill, when they see meat with blood clotted or oozing amidst the meat fibres. Eating or drinking blood is forbidden in Islam.

Pork is also forbidden in Islam. Pigs are not selective about what they eat and can be fed on garbage, on food remnants. On this subject, Sake has observed: 'There are a good number of germs, parasites and bacteria that infest swine and live in its flesh which, when it is eaten, transmit diseases to man. Among these parasites are tapeworms, round worms, hook worms, fasciolopsis buski, paragonimus, clonorchis senesis and erysipelothrix rhnsiphathiac.' He goes on: 'In short, the pig, the supreme germ carrier, is the cause of many serious and fatal diseases, among them dysentery trichinosis, tape worm, round worm, hook worm, jaundice, pneumonia, suffocation, intestinal obstruction, acute pancreatitis, enlargement of the liver, diarrhea, emaciation, high fever, hindering the growth development in children, typhoid, lameness, heart trouble, abortion, sterility and sudden death.'

Drinking alcohol is prohibited by Islam. Although it has some beneficial effects, it leads to addiction with all its moral and physiological problems. Further, ingestion of large amounts causes irritation of the stomach and peptic ulcer formation. It also affects the liver and causes its inflammation, cirrhosis and ultimately liver failure.

The Muslim is required not to restrain a sneeze, rather to thank God for this blessing. Sneezing results from irritation of the mucous membrane of the upper respiratory tract and it leads to the expulsion of the irritating substance. Prevention of sneezing will retain the irritant which may then cause inflammation where it lodges. Covering the mouth when sneezing is recommended in order to prevent the transmission to other persons of bacteria which may be present in the upper respiratory tract of some individuals.

Circumcision, required of every male Muslim, has been increasingly carried out in some parts of the Western world on medical grounds. The prepuce (a quite redundant piece of skin), if not cut off, can accumulate dirt and organisms which encourage the growth of bacteria. This may be one of the factors causing cancerous changes in the female genital tract.

Sexual intercourse during menses, which is completely forbidden in Islam, is harmful for two reasons:

1. The cervix is opened during menses, and intercourse will facilitate the entry of bacteria into the uterus and the fallopian tubes leading to inflammation and formation of adhesions which can cause sterility.
2. The negative psychological effect on the man when he discovers blood on his sexual organ. This may create a sensation of disgust such as to inhibit proper sexual relations with his wife.

The wisdom behind the prohibition of anal intercourse is that it is a painful process and it stimulates the defecation reflex. In addition, the male sexual organ may be soiled with some faeces which may contain pathogenic micro-organisms, in turn causing urinary tract infection in the male.

During the menstrual period the female sexual hormones are disturbed, leading to psychological upset, mainly in the form of nervous tension and depression, and this may explain the changes observed in the behaviour of women during the menstrual period. It partly explains the wisdom of the exemption of women from prayer and fasting. The fact that, according to Islamic injunctions, the corpse must be buried without delay, shows proper understanding of the dangers of putrefaction: dangers much greater in hot climates where no cooling facilities are available.

The wisdom behind forbidding Muslims to own dogs, except watch and hunt dogs whose place must be outside the house, is clearly seen in the fact that the saliva of dogs contain rabies virus which can be transmitted to man by biting or by contact with the dog's saliva through any cut in the skin. Echinococcus worm is found in the intestine of dogs; transmitted to man through food contaminated with dogs' excreta, it can lead to the formation of cysts primarily in the liver and lungs.

The observance of adab al-Islam is also essential to a healthy economy; extravagance is forbidden, thriftiness encouraged, even required. Money plays an important role in the life of a nation, both in times of peace and of war. As a store of value it serves as a reserve of ready purchasing power and medium of exchange. Money power is essential for the nation as a whole.

The private individual is not absolutely free to spend any amount of money in any way he likes, as this leads to the destruction of this national power. Adab al-Islam give Muslims a religious motive for saving. In other words, it is the religious duty of every Muslim to abstain from extravagance, for Allah says in the Quran: 'Lo! the squanderers were ever brothers of the devil, and the devil was ever an ingrate to his Lord.'

Here are different aspects of Islamic life which demonstrate the importance that Islam attaches to a healthy economy:

1. Moderation in eating and drinking is required. No food, however little, should be wasted. Forbidding wastefulness saves a large amount of the national wealth, and directs it to more useful investments.
2. Moderation in dress is required. Clothes should not become an end in themselves, and spending large sums of money on clothes should be avoided.
3. Furniture and other household items should be of moderate price. Silver or gold should not be used in domestic furniture or for utensils, or in any other items. Also silk or silk brocade should not be used in furniture or in men's clothes.
4. Large sums of money should not be spent on building lavish houses. Even extravagance in mosque buildings is forbidden. Ornamentation in both cases should also be avoided.
5. In Islam, the ideal wedding is that which involves the least expense and avoids the unnecessary things.
6. Funerals should also be inexpensive. Extravagance is forbidden. Coffins should not be used, unless to comply with special regulations or for health reasons.

7. Though generosity and hospitality toward guests is highly recommended in Islam, extravagance is forbidden.
8. Suspending work on Friday is not specifically prescribed in Islam except for about an hour to say the Friday prayers. Useful work should be continued, for to stop working for even a day may cause a loss to the national economy as a whole. Abandoning work on Friday is not encouraged, for the concept of the Sabbath does not exist in Islam. However, if Muslims have to have a day off, it should be Friday and not Saturday or Sunday.
9. Skill and thoroughness in every task entrusted to a Muslim is considered as his duty in Islam: according to the Hadith, 'Verily Allah has prescribed proficiency in all things.' A successful economy is obvious when industry and quality combine.

The family 'provides the environment within which human values and morals develop and grow in the new generation; these values and morals cannot exist apart from the family unit. The family system and the relationship between the sexes determines the whole character of a society and whether it is backward or civilised.'

Because marriage and family are so important, it is not surprising that so large a number of Quranic verses and Prophetic Traditions are devoted to these two areas; these sources provide the basis and the details necessary for successful marriage and a morally sound, stable society.

1. A Muslim is recommended to marry at an early age. Marriage enlarges the circle of relatives by adding new ones through the marriage tie. Breast-feeding by foster nurses is permitted in Islam for it too enlarges the circle of the family with new-found relatives, called 'relatives in breast-feeding'.
2. Muslims are encouraged to make marriage an easy task. According to the Islamic view, the most blessed marriage is that which involves the least burden upon the bride and bridegroom.
3. Celebrating marriage has been made commendatory in Islam, for marriage is a social event.
4. Although singing is generally forbidden in Islam, it is allowed on the occasion of marriage.
5. Holding a wedding feast is recommended and rejection of the invitation, when it is possible to accept, is not allowed on this very special occasion.

Islam is concerned that marriages should succeed. They cannot do so unless properly founded.

The conditions and recommendations for success are:

1. Full mutual agreement by the man and the woman to marry one another.
2. Common ground and understanding between the man and the woman are obviously necessary. A common conception of life, way of living and common ways of overcoming disagreements is needed, and all these are provided by the Islamic faith and Shariah. Therefore, the ideal husband and wife are those who adhere most to Islam.
3. As preparatory steps towards marriage, Islam recommends that the man and the woman should have sufficient information about each other's knowledge and practice of Islam and that they should also see each other.
4. There is no room for any intent on either side to have a temporary marriage. Islam recognizes only the intention to have a lasting marriage.
5. To fulfil all the conditions in any marriage contract is considered by Islam as among the best of deeds and the highest of moral virtues. According to the Prophet: 'The most worthy conditions to be fulfilled by Muslims are those included in a marriage contract.'
6. Husband and wife are advised, in case of disagreements, to try to solve their problems without the interference of anyone else.
7. The husband-wife relationship if it is to succeed must be based upon mutual respect, understanding, cooperation, love and mercy.

A study of adab al-Islam shows the importance of marriage in Islam. The special relationship of husband and wife is recognized in adab al-Islam in the following ways:

1. Men are not allowed to wash the bodies of dead women, nor vice versa unless they are married to one another. In the case of a deceased wife the husband has the right to place her body in the grave.
2. Men and women are not allowed to see each other's private parts - even though they are related to each other by blood as brother and sister, or mother and children - except in the case of husband and wife.

3. Women are forbidden to mourn a deceased relative including even a brother or father for a period exceeding three days; but a widow may mourn for her dead husband for a period of four months and ten days.

The parent-child relationship also has an important place in the manners of Islam. According to the Prophet of Islam, Paradise lies at the feet of mothers. If good manners toward others are a form of politeness, they are an obligatory religious duty in the case of parents. Strong kinship, affection, responsibility should not be confined to children and parents, but extended to all relatives. There is, first, the moral responsibility to visit relatives from time to time, to ensure that they do not feel neglected and ignored. Second, there is the financial responsibility upon those more able to assist their needy relatives. If a Muslim dies in debt, his relatives are recommended to discharge the debt as soon as they can.

Allowing breast-feeding by a woman other than the mother, as mentioned earlier, enlarges the circle of relatives, and must be recognized and welcomed in mutual responsibility. Family feeling and responsibility are so stressed in adab al-Islam because the family is the formative ground of the whole range of human sentiments, and therefore the best foundation for a healthy, stable society is a healthy, stable family life.

Norms of Sexual Behaviour: Islam recognizes sex as a portion of nature created by God, and nothing created by Him is evil or wrong if used and practised according to His commands.

There is no doubt that sex is necessary for the development of the individual's personality, and for the society as a whole. Sexual development is intimately connected with feelings of personal worth and the assurance of being loved. Sexual deprivation endangers mental health, hinders good relationships and creates inefficiency in the society. But sex can be a destructive force if not controlled and channelled through marriage. It will then be a force working against the individual, the institution of marriage and family, and the society as a whole. In fact, 'sex is capable of impelling individuals, reckless of the consequences while under its spell, towards behaviour which may imperil or disrupt the cooperative relationships upon which social life depends'.

Sexual behaviour, therefore, must be controlled. This, however, seems difficult, and may indeed be impossible in any society without the assistance of other elements and factors that help the individual to keep sexual desires in check. Islam provides a solution to this problem through the observance of the following rules of conduct:

1. Marriage should be made easy for every member of the society and opportunities for early marriage enhanced.
2. All factors and conditions that incite the individual to indulge his sexual desires outside marriage should be blocked.

   Adab al-Islam are vital here:

(a) The body of the woman is of such a nature that it causes sexual excitement among men. Because this is so and not the other way about, Islam has forbidden all forms of nudity and exploitation of the female form. It prescribes a form of dress designed to cover the whole body except face and hands so as to protect the woman from the gaze of men and to protect men from exposure to her charms. There is no doubt that clothes convey inter-personal attitudes among which is that of sexuality.

(b) The separation of the sexes is necessary in Islam. This helps to ease sexual tension.

(c) A Muslim woman should not adorn her face with cosmetics nor use perfume outside the home. Such actions should be confined to her home and for her husband.

(d) Women are not allowed to bathe in a public bath used by men.

(e) When a woman speaks to a man other than her husband or relatives whom she is forbidden to marry (mahram), her speech should not be inviting, but should remain objective and crisp.

(f) Showing decorous shyness is also required of men, both in dress and personal conduct. If, by chance, a Muslim's gaze falls upon a woman, he should turn away his eyes: a second look is forbidden.

(g) Privacy in sexual relations is of the utmost importance in the Islamic view. Husband and wife are a mercy to each other, a garment and veil. It is forbidden for either husband or wife to discuss their sexual relations with others.

All the rules given above and others concerning sexual conduct are intended to enable men and women to benefit from the blessings of sex within marriage, and to enable the society to benefit from the blessings of marriage and secure family relations.

Chapter 3

Scientific Vision in Islam

Knowing Different Tongues

Learning of other languages is among the things recommended in the traditions of the Prophet for every Muslim to achieve. Allah's Prophet stole a march towards achieving knowledge from this aspect. He commanded his copyist, Zaid bin Sabit, to attain proficiency in the Suryani language. Zaid says that he was commanded by the Prophet (S.A.W.) to learn it and accordingly he learnt to correspond with the Jews in the Suryani language. The Prophet (S.A.W.) said:

> *"By God, I am not satisfied with the Jews that they would correctly copy my letter." Zaid says that before half a month passed he attained proficiency in the Suryani language and then he started writing letters to the Jews on behalf of the Prophet and replying to them on his behalf."* *(Bukhari)*

To learn the different languages is among the needs of Islam, because the message of Islam is for all the peoples of the world, and it is impossible for all the peoples to learn any one single language, when the difference of languages is among the signs of Allah. "Therefore, it is easier and more reasonable to translate the Islamic teachings in all those languages which the people speak and understand than to teach the Arabic language to all the peoples. Allah has said:

> *"And We never sent a messenger save with the language of his folk, that he might make (the message) clear to them."* *(Ibrahim : 4)*

The commentators in explaining this verse write that the Prophet of Allah was born in Arabia, speaking the Arabic language, but the representatives that he sent to the places around his country were asked to translate his message in other languages and they conveyed his message in the language of the people concerned. The commentators write that either the Quran should have been sent in all the languages of the world, or only in one language. The first thing is useless because by translation that purpose can be achieved, but the Arabic language was selected because at that time many were conversant with it and the fear of changes of the message in that language was much less.

From this discussion, one thing that comes out very clearly is that it is enjoined upon Muslims that they should learn other languages, otherwise they will be considered to have been dishonest with the treasure (message) of which they have been made the trustees, and they will be held responsible for keeping the people unaware of and unaquainted with that message knowingly. This fact also should not be lost sight of that knowledge or learning has no native place, nor is limited to any race. If we study the sources of the learning of the ancient and the present times, then we will be able to drink from the springs of knowledge. There had been many nations that had remained unlettered and uneducated, and paradoxically it has also happened that uneducated forefathers brought up a generation full of researchers, scientists and learned men. Europe itself was in the darkness a few centuries ago. It was ignorant. But today it is the protector of the heritage of ancient civilizations. Muslims are enjoined to travel far and wide for seeking knowledge, from whatever source it may be obtained or in any city it may be available.

Allah's Messenger has said: "A Momin cannot be content with good (knowledge) which he hears, until he goes to Paradise." (Tirmidhi)

> *"Wisdom is a Momin's lost property; he is the most deserving to obtain it wherever he may find it."*
>
> *(Tirmidhi)*

> *"Any man who sets out to seek knowledge is in the path of Allah till he returns home." (Tirmidhi)*

To learn and to teach is the spirit of Islam. Without it neither its essence can remain nor can a guarantee be given about its future. In the eyes of Islam the position of the individual is that either they are students, seekers of righteousness and guidance, or they are learned men, but seeking further knowledge. Besides this there is no value of other kind of individuals in its eyes. Allah's Messenger (S.A.W.) has said:

> *"The learned teacher and the taught are both participants in righteousness, and in the remaining people there is no aspect of righteousness." (Ibn Majah)*

Sweeping Power

A firm and strong faith is such a never-drying spring, from which flow the strength for the desired activities, coveted courage and forbearance to tolerate adversities and to face dangers. It creates in man such a restless feeling and deep attachment to his ideal that if he is unable to achieve his coveted objective, he does not hesitate to partake of the drink of death.

When faith finds a place in a man's heart and takes deep roots in it, brings out these results only. It fills a man's heart and mind with such power and strength that cover and influence all his dealings. Accordingly, when he opens his mouth, he talks with confidence and certainty.

When he undertakes a work, he attends to it with full interest and sincerity. When he starts on a journey, his destination is before his eyes. If he enjoys the wealth of the correct and firm thinking, the world of the heart too is inhabited by the enthusiasm and restless courage. Hesitation and ambivalence do not find a place in his heart, and high-velocity winds do not move him from his path or make him deviate from his objective. It will not be surprising if he says to every one, in the words of an Urdu poet:

> *"Come here O tyrant ! we will try our art,*
>
> *"You try your arrow, and I will try my liver (courage)."*

And he may challenge the people around him thus:

> *"You work in your manner, I too an acting. Soon you will know who will get disgraceful punishment and who will get the everlasting punishment."* *(Zumar: 39-40)*

This challenging accent, this independent spirit in action and deeds, this self-confidence in understanding truth and tradition are the qualities which make him a distinguished personality in life. He deals with the people in the light of the facts seen and experienced by him. If he finds the people on a policy which is right and truthful, he extends his hand for cooperation, and if he finds them committing errors, he withdraws himself, and leaves his conscience alive and wakeful.

> *Allah's Messenger has said: 'Every one of you should desist from walking with every traveller. He should not say that he is with the people, and that if people would do good deed, he would also do the good deeds ; and that if they would do wicked deeds then he would cooperate with them. You should prepare yourself to cooperate with them if they do righteous deeds and to keep away if they do wicked deeds."* *(Tirmidhi)*

But one who is weak, the current customs and habits make one their slave. On such a man's conduct rule the things which are current in the society. If these customs and practices are wrong and destructive, then he carries the burden of the troubles of this world as well as of the next.

Among the people, various kinds of innovations have become customary on the occasions of celebrations and mourning. They pay more attention to performing these innovative acts than on the realities of the religion.

But a straight-going Momin does not take any interest in these things, for which there is no supportive proof in religion. He is confronted with opposition and experiences difficulties in opposing the popular and customary rituals, but it is obvious that he need not care for any condemnation from anybody in the affairs of Allah. He has to achieve his ideal. No weapon of criticism and fault-finding and no injuries from tongue can obstruct his way.

Falsehood which sometimes is successful is subsequently ruled by powerful individuals. They then destroy its position and rank. This also cannot stay for a long time with the help and support of its allies, because many enemies who are today with it, having been deceived by falsehood, tomorrow they would become the supporters of the other enemies; they approve of their aims and objects after knowing their character and pledge their support after severe hostility and spite.

Ibn Abbas has narrated that Allah's Messenger has said:

> *"He who has displeased Allah for seeking the pleasure of the people, Allah is displeased with him and those people are also displeased for pleasing whom he had earned Allah's displeasure. And he who pleases Allah by displeasing the people, Allah is also pleased with him and also those people whom he had displeased for pleasing Allah, so much so that He made him splendid and his speech and acts in the eyes of others beautiful."*
>
> *(Tibrani)*

A Muslim should stick to what he believes to be true, and he should ignore all the insults, fun-making, and difficulties with which he is confronted. He should adopt for himself such a policy through following which he should always try to get rewards (sawab) from Allah. If those, who believe in superstitions and absurd things, make fun of the faithful people and laugh at them, then it is necessary for a Momin to be strong and to stand his ground with firmness.

> *"When they see you, (O Muhammad !) they treat you only as a jest (saying): Is this he whom Allah sends as a messenger ? He would have led us far away from our gods if we had not been staunch to them. They will know, when they behold the doom, who is more astray as to the road."* *(Furqan : 42-43)*

No doubt, a Muslim must feel in his personality the strength of belief and in his heart the pressure and awe of faith. If the things around him do not influence him, then he is like a rock which is not moved by the lashing of the waves of the sea. What harm these men can inflict on a man who feels in his heart the strength of faith and belief, and on account of his relation with his Lord and steadfastness in his religion feels in himself a new determination and a fresh courage ? If all these rush and attack, they will not be able to harm him a bit. Ibn Abbas says that he was sitting on a mount behind the Prophet. The Prophet said : "O child! remember Allah, He will take care of you. Remember Allah, you will find Him everywhere. Recognise Allah's rights in your prosperity, He will recognise you in your adversity. If you want to ask anything, ask from Allah. If you need help, seek help from Allah, for if all the men together decide to help, they will not be able to do so, if Allah has not written that for you and they have no control over it. And if all of them decide to inflict some harm on you which Allah has not meant for you, they cannot harm you a bit. The ink of the pen has been dried and the sheets have been collected." The fact is that in a Muslim the basis of strength and power is the belief in the oneness of Allah. Similarly other virtues prevent him from accepting any disgrace and insult in this world, because a Muslim is most honoured and of high rank on account of his relationship with the heavens. In his own sphere of faith he has the power to become a whole community. These are Allah's words, speaking for him

> *"Say: 'Shall I choose for a protecting friend other than Allah, the Originator of the heavens and the earth, who feeds and is never fed ?' Say : 'I am ordered to be the first to surrender (to Him). And be not you (O Muhammad!) of the idolaters'."* *(Anam: 14)*

Best Manifestation : Islam has declared achievement of strength and power essential. Its one characteristic and manifestation is that you make a firm determination and a strong resolve to achieve, with the help of your nearest available means and resources, your objective. Try your utmost in achieving your goal. You should leave no stone unturned and no room for chance, and thereafter leave the outcome in the hands of destiny. There are many individuals who take Allah's shelter in order to cover their objectionable defects reprehensible negligence, inability and laziness, and grumble against luck. Islam has disapproved of this tendency.

> *Auf bin Malik says that Allah's Messenger once gave a decision in a dispute of two people. When the man against whom the Prophet's decision was given was returning, said : "For me Allah is sufficient, and He is the best support." The Prophet said: "Allah sends curses on helplessness and weakness. You should give proof of your wisdom. When you are overpowered in any matter say : `For me Allah is sufficient, and He is the best support'."*
> *(Abu Daud)*

It is the duty of everybody that he should make full efforts and try to the best of his ability to overcome his difficulty, till the time he achieves his objective. If he overpowers his difficulties then he has fulfilled his responsibility. However, if after making all the efforts he fails, then at such a time the support of Allah is the best shelter for him, which would help him to overcome the sense of defeatism and frustration. In both the states he is strong and powerful. First by making efforts and working, and in the second case by relying on God he receives strength. Islam does not like that in your affairs you should be a prey to vagueness and hesitation. You should not be undecided in the matter of selecting the advantageous alternative. Your head should not be filled up with doubts and misgivings, resulting in an atmosphere of indetermination and indecision, making it difficult for you to come to a decision.

It does not like that due to your weakness you may not be able to strongly hold the advantageous things in your firm grip, and they should slip through your fingers and may be wasted. This restlessness and indecision does not become a Muslim.

> *Allah's Prophet has said : "A strong Momin is better than a weak Momin and is more liked by Allah, and there is good in each one. Desire profitable things and seek Allah's help and be humble. If you are harmed then do not say that had you done in this way the result would have been different, but say Allah is Controller, whatever He likes He may decide, because the botheration of ifs and buts opens the door of the devil's workshop."* *(Muslim)*

What is the work of Satan to remind of the troubles and the difficulties of the past, which would create a sense of heart-breaking disappointment and deprivation. Man thinks about the prospects of his present and future. As regards shedding tears on the defeats of the past, to bring back the memory of the past sadness, to think of old enmities and to be entangled in the net of ifs and buts, are inclinations which do not suit the conduct of a Muslim. Quran has listed them with sorrow and frustration in those manifestations which are generated in the hearts of the infidels:

> *"O you who believe! Be not as those who disbelieved and said of their brethren who went abroad in the land or were fighting in the field: If they had been (here) with us they would not have died or been killed; that Allah may make it anguish in their hearts. Allah gives life and causes death and Allah is Observer of what you do."*
>
> *(Ale Imran: 156)*

One Hadith has it: "One who wants to be strong among men, should rely on Allah."

Trust in Allah which makes a man powerful is a kind of confidence in Allah, which saves a man from destruction at a time when he is surrounded on all sides by harrowing difficulties, and when he is unable to get help from any one else, nor is there any hope of getting it from elsewhere.

Accordingly he becomes a mountain of strength at the time of confrontation with the enemy. If the reliance is on Allah, then inspite of the shortage of weapons and war-equipment and insufficient number of supporters, he feels that he has a strong support. From this trust in Allah he .receives encouragement and support to be steadfast. He sticks to his job till in the dark and frightening atmosphere the glad tidings of victory are heard by him. The holy Quran says that trust is such an eternal food for war that with its help Prophets and their followers have bravely and successfully faced the tyrants of their time:

> *"How should we not put our trust in Allah when He has shown us our ways ? We surely will endure that hurt you do us. In Allah let the trusting put their trust."*
>
> *(Ibrahim : 12)*

The faithful and their supporters stand their ground, sticking to their mandate. They have expectations of well-being in the future. They have full confidence that their present weakness will be converted into a powerful victorious force, but the wicked and evil rulers and their disciples term this determination and trust of the faithful their pride and madness:

> *"When the hypocrites and those in whose hearts is a disease said: `Their religion has deluded these. Whosoever puts his trust in Allah (will find that) surely, Allah is Mighty, Wise."* (Al-Anfal : 49)

For becoming strong and powerful a Muslim should take care that he keeps away from the life of wickedness and evil, loves the policy of cleanness and steadfastness. A man who is ill-mannered, and bereft of decency and consideration, cannot attain strength. He should put on the hide of the beasts and walk in the wake of the kings as a servant.

Allah informed the nation of Hud, that was tyrant and rebellious against Allah, the correct and profitable causes of strength:

> *"Ask forgiveness of your Lord, then turn to Him repentant; He will cause the sky to rain abundance on you and will add to you strength. Turn not away, guilty.* (Hud : 52)

The kind Prophet wanted to present the worship to the people in a beautiful form and to persuade them to perform it. When a man performs a righteous deed, he opposes the Satan and tries to rise towards the angels. At that time how great becomes his sanctity and magnificence! To focus attention on this the Prophet has explained it by giving an example:

> *"When Allah created the earth, it tilted and was unsteady. Accordingly Allah put the stakes (nails) of mountains in it, and it became steady, and stood in one position. The angels were amazed by the strength of the mountains. They asked the Creator : `Our Lord ! Have you created anything harder than the mountains ?' He replied: 'Yes, Iron is harder than this.' The angels again asked 'Is anything harder than iron ?' He said : 'Yes, Fire has more power.' They asked : 'Is there anything more powerful created by you than fire ?' He said : 'Yes, Water is more powerful than this.' The angels asked : 'Does anything among your created things exist more powerful than water?' He said 'Yes, air has more power than this.' They asked 'Have you created anything more powerful than air?' He said : 'Yes, Adam's sin is more powerful, provided he gives charity from his right hand without letting his left hand know it."* (Tirmidhi)

Man is the strangest creature of the universe. The day his personality attains greatness and excellence of moral character he becomes the hunter of the universe. He brings under his control the hardest and the most powerful things of the universe, and derives benefit from it. But the day when his personality declines, he earns the curses of the inhabitants of the heavens and the earth, and the particles of dust carry him with them in their flight.

In the *Hadith* quoted above the value and importance of such a virtuous man has been mentioned who tries to forge ahead in the field of righteousness and who tries to touch the heights of excellence and decency. One factor of strength is that a Muslim should be in the habit of stating the truth unhesitatingly. He should meet people with an open heart, and on the basis of righteous values and principles. He should not compromise in the matter of truth, so that his decency and his companions' character may not be tarnished. He should consider his strength a direct outcome of his belief which he represents and for which he is alive. He should never waver in unhesitatingly and courageously proving a reality.

It is reported that when the Prophet's son Ibrahim died, the sun went into an eclipse. The people said that the eclipse was due to the death of Ibrahim. Allah's Messenger gave a sermon to the people, and said:

> *"The eclipse of the sun and the moon are not on account of the death or life of some person, but they both are the signs of Allah, which He shows to His slaves. So when you see the eclipse of the sun or the moon, you run for offering salat."* *(Bukhari)*

A man who breathes in the atmosphere of realities, does not compromise with falsehood and absurdities. He is always indifferent to such things, and his uncompromising words point to the vast treasure of greatness and nobility, whose owner does not derive any benefit from deception and his character stands on the rock of excellent moral character.

The performance of the duty of ordering the righteous thing and preventing the commitment of the forbidden thing comes from the personal excellence, because it results from the courageous talk of the sincere people who want to earn Allah's reward by ending their own egoist leanings.

In our other books we have explained the social and political objectives which is related to the performance of the righteous and the forbidding of the forbidden. (Author's Arabic book)

Here what we want to emphasise is that a Muslim must necessarily straight away criticise the general evils, should be courageous in attacking them, neither the fear of a big man nor the consideration for a relative should prevent him from doing the right thing, and in the path of Allah no condemnation from any source should block his way.

Islam has disliked that a man should feel weak in the presence of wicked and evil persons, and should address them in a respectable way. Allah's Messenger has said: "When a man addresses a hypocrite as 'Ya Sayyedi' (My master), he makes Allah very wrathful."

This is a double crime that a man should not respect Allah's commands about forbidden things, and then he should only listen to those who think him respectable and should not care for those who consider him mean and humble:

> *"He whom Allah scorns, there is none to give him honour. Surely, Allah does what He wills."* *(Hajj: 18)*

Islam has declared backbiting as Haram, so that man's life may continue and the factors of strength may remain in it, for the man who states the defects of a person in his absence and derives satisfaction from it, is undoubtedly very mean and low.

But the man who has the strength to respond to the motivation and call of truth, he stops those whom he likes, in whatever manner and words he thinks proper he criticises them. He does not keep anything hidden in his heart for condemning anybody behind the scene. However it does not mean that we may address anybody whom we like in an insulting way. If we find any defects in persons, we may fix up certain norms about dealing with them.

If his defect is limited to his own person or if it is not in consonance with his position, then it would be foolish to castigate him in his presence or in his absence. And if his steps are slipping towards a sin, and he does not seem to be in a mood to give it up-like a horse who flounders and falls on his face-then to defame such a person among the people is meanness.

However, if he is a blatant sinner, and he openly breaks the rights of Allah and usurps the rights of his fellow men, then it is necessary that he should be opposed with the words of truth and without caring for anybody he should be properly warned.

Since this dialogue has to be straight, it is necessary that curses and abuses should be avoided and physical hurt should be averted. The purpose should be to change the bad habit and to reform the individual and the society. It does not mean that his mention before his enemies should be in demeaning words, so that you may get closer to their hearts, or may derive some benefits or may claim yourself to be innocent of those sins.

> *Allah's Messenger has said : "He who has eaten food in exchange for the honour of a Muslim, Allah will feed him fire of hell in compensation on the Doomsday ; and he who put on clothes in exchange for dishonouring a Muslim, Allah will clothe him in compensation with the cloth of hell fire: and if he who earned respect and fame by playing with the chastity of a Muslim, Allah will make him taste fully for this on the Doomsday." (Abu Daud)*

Backbiting is the policy of the weak persons, and "only those people try to indulge in backbiting who are unable to strive for themselves."

Sycophants Disliked : Islam dislikes those persons who become merely supplement of other people, those persons who live on the charity of others, those who want to live like foxes that is content with eating the remnants of a Lion's prey.

> *"O Allah ! I seek shelter through you from sorrow and hardship. I seek shelter from humility and laziness, and through you seek shelter from cowardice and miserliness, from the defeat of the religion and from the cruelty and tyranny of oppressors. (Abu Daud)*

Patience and hope are the weapons of the present and the future. In their company man is able to bear the severest of the hardships and is not disgraced, and all sides of his life become more safe from evils, and he rises above the mischief and trials, because he is a Momin-a faithful slave who begs and supplicates in humbleness before Allah only.

Non-Religious Education

The learning, to which a Muslim turns and to open the gates of which he tries his utmost, is not confined to 'Albidya' and 'Qaduri' (religious books), but every branch of learning which widens 'the thought and opens the closed windows of the intellect, may guide him to real knowledge, which may open the new avenues of discoveries and inventions, and which may teach him the secrets of the world leadership, which may give him a control over the hidden secrets of energies, are all included in the list of learnings, the achieving of which is the duty of a Muslim. It is the responsibility of every Muslim that he should take away his share of knowledge from this treasure. A number of verses and traditions are witnesses to this wide sense.

The traditions which encourage the tendency of deriving benefits from every kind of learning are innumerable, but a few are quoted here:

> *"He who walks for achieving and in search of knowledge, for him Allah makes the path to Paradise easy."*
> *(Muslim)*

> *"No earner can earn anything better than that knowledge the superiority of which guides a learned man of religion towards the right guidance or turns him away from waywardness ; and no man's piety can be right unless his intellect is right."* *(Tibrani)*

> *"It is not permissible to envy anybody except two men, first that man whom Allah gave wealth and he distributed it in the cause of Truth and second that man whom Allah blessed with wisdom, with which he gives his decisions and teaches it."* *(Bukhari)*

> *"Allah, His angels, and all the creatures of the earth and the skies, even the ant in its hole and the fish in the sea, pray for the man who teaches righteousness to the people."*
> *(Tirmidhi)*

In these holy traditions the words knowledge and learning have been used for every art, science or technique which can be the cause of good and by wisdom is meant that learning which protects from harmful things and encourages turning to useful things. It is not necessary to confine learning to any special culture. It is like saying a particular portion of property as wealth and to refuse to call the remaining portion as wealth, for no food reason. There is no doubt that at the head of the list there should be that learning which teaches Allah's rights over humans and the knowledge of mutual rights and duties among humans themselves, because even today the teaching of right guidance and virtuousness play an important role in the formation and organization of societies and in guiding a country's politics. But it would be very imprudent if we would think that the learning has been exhorted to be achieved in the Quran and a Hadith is merely *Fiqh* and *Hadith* and the branches of learning allied to these, and that the position of the other worldly learning is unimportant, the achieving of which or otherwise is left to the individual's sweet will, and for which there is no responsibility on him. This is a very serious misunderstanding, for the learning or the sciences about the universe and life, the discussions about the control over the earth and the heavens and their effects are not less important than the pure worldly branches of learning. And sometimes the outcome of the study of the modern sciences proves, in connection with the understanding of Divine nature and understanding of the self, to be more effective than diving into the religious learning. In this connection the guidance of the holy Quran is sufficient for us. When it describes the greatness of learning and the superiority of the learned men, its allusion by this knowledge is the understanding which is the outcome of thinking about and contemplating over the vegetable and the animal worlds and other physical things, and by Ulama or the learned men are meant those persons who comprehend the greatness of the Creator by understanding the greatness of the creatures and the creation.

> *Do you not see that Allah sends down rain from the sky ? With it We then bring out produce of various colours. And in the mountains are tracts white and red, of various shades of colour, and black intense in hue. And so amongst men and crawling creatures and cattle, are they of various colours. Those truly fear Allah, among His servants, who have knowledge; for Allah is Exalted in Might, Forgiving.* *(Fatir: 27-28)*

> *And of His signs is the creation of the heavens and the earth, and the difference of your languages and colours. Verily, herein indeed are portents for men of knowledge.* *(Rum: 22)*

In order to serve the religion and to disclose the secrets of the realities of the life, the learning of the worldly sciences and knowledge is not less important than the learning of the religious teachings. The difference is only this that learning of the physical sciences requires a lot of time and labour, while learning of the religious instruction is comparatively easier, provided a few months are earmarked for that. However for learning minor details of religious teachings and its branches more time and study would be needed, but this long period and time depends, like other collective and social interests and advantages, on the needs of the government. It is for the government to decide whether the required time and labour be spent on that project or not.

The study of the rights and the law according to religion, in itself, is not more important than the learning of the worldly sciences, like medicine, etc., even if a person attains the prominence attained by Imam Abu Hanifa (R.A.). The person will gain importance and superiority only on the ground that he had attained that knowledge for the sake of Allah and how much he is successful in imparting it to the people and making it beneficial for them for the purpose of Allah's pleasure only.

Worth of the Objective

The difference between the pure religion and specific world is very ordinary, and also very big, but as we have stated we will have to make the purity of purpose and the ideal as the real deciding factor, because a thing, which becomes a major sin on account of the carnal desires, is considered as a Jihad (striving) in the cause of Allah, if it is performed with the sincerity and purity needed.

In the Quran, it is stated:

> *The wealth and children are an ornament of the worldly life.* *(Kahaf : 46)*

It is so, if they are exclusively treated as such, but these resources also help in helping the cause of Jihad and Allah has called the abundance of wealth and progeny as sources of his assistance:

> *Then We gave you superiority over them, and helped you with wealth and children, and increased your numbers.*
> *(Bani Israil)*

Abundance of wealth and children only helped this Ummah to revive after a collapse. After its downfall, it has stood up to rise to the heights destined for it. It has attained the pleasure of Allah after having lost it earlier.

Same is the case with learning. If a man obtains proficiency in the science of fertilisation and with its help makes Allah's land more fertile and greener, then his reward will not be any less, and it is quite likely that if he believes in Allah and follows the righteous path, he will probably get better rewards from Allah than the worshipper who pays during the night and is very keen to offer prayers regularly.

Islam has given a very honourable position to the men of learning, and has always been appreciating their efforts. It has given them the glad tidings of countless rewards.

Maaz bin Jabal (R.A.A.) says:

> *"Seek knowledge, because to seek knowledge for the sake of Allah is righteousness, to pursue knowledge is worship, to hold discussions on it is remembering God. Research and striving for it is* Jihad. *To impart education to those who are ignorant is charity. To spend it on the deserving people is the means of nearness to God, for it teaches one about what it is* halal *and* Haram. *It sheds light on the*

paths of the people of the Paradise. Knowledge is the companion of the loneliness, a friend of the stranger; it converses in the privacy and points out good and bad conditions. It is a weapon against the enemies, and a means of ornamentation in the gathering of the friends. Through it Allah raises nations and makes them leader and guide, that are followed and are obeyed, and whose advice is sought. The angels wish to have them as friends, and pass their wings lovingly over them. All the creatures of the land and the sea pray for their salvation. The fishes in the sea and the insects, the beasts of the forests and the animals pray for them, because knowledge revives the hearts from the death of ignorance, it is a tower of light in the darknesses. A man reaches to the high rank of the noble persons, and achieves glory in this world and the next. Thinking and contemplation in the cause of knowledge is equivalent to observing fasts. The duty of learning and teaching is equivalent to offering prayers during the night. Through this, relationships are united; through it, a distinction between halal and Haram is made. It is the leader of the activity and controller. Fortunate people attain it and unfortunate ones are deprived of it."

Power of the Reason

Learning is as much necessary for Islam as it is for the human life. And this religion can find a place in the hearts of only those people who have solid learning and possess a healthy intellect. That is why Allah says:

> *This is a clear message for mankind in order that they may be warned thereby; and that they may know that He is only One God, and that man of understanding may take heed.* *(Ibrahim : 52)*

Quoting the talk of the people of hell, the Quran says:

> *Had we been wont to listen or have sense, we had not been among the dwellers in the flames.* *(Mulk : 10)*

Describing the example of those whose sensitivities are dead, the windows of whose mind are closed and whose abilities are frozen, the Quran says:

> *Those who disbelieved are like the cattle which hear nothing, except a shout and a cry, when they are called.*

They are deaf, dumb and blind, and therefore they do not understand anything. *(Baqarah: 171)*

When a person reaches the age of understanding and maturity, and his abilities and energies are developed, and when he becomes capable of absorbing the best teachings and the progressive civilization, Allah blesses him with the knowledge about Islam. This helps him to shape his life in such a way as to achieve progress and perfection, and by following the path of Islam the venues for achieving success in the material world are also thrown open for him.

Take the example of salat (prayer), which is the first form of worship in Islam. If you think over it, you will find that its performance and its announcement are such that appeal to the intellect. The call for the prayer (Adaan) taps the intellect, awakens the heart, declares Allah's greatness and His Oneness, and invites men for attaining success.

It is not the sound of the bell that rings and creates some vibrations in the atmosphere, and which probably stirs some vague feelings. Similarly the prayer consists of the verses and prayers that have come from a Book which is full of righteous teachings virtuous lessons and best of guidance. The prayer is accepted by God only when it is performed in the correct way, and when its real meaning and sense is understood by man's intellect.

The fact is that a man attains high position owing to his intelligence, ability to derive benefit from his experience, and the consistency of his nature, in the same proportion in which these qualities are found in him, and he achieves distinction among Muslims. But those who lack this gift from God, i.e. intelligence and whose mentality is sick, they cannot hope to achieve any distinction in this religion.

Consider the first verse of the holy Quran:

Recite, (O Prophet!) in the name of your Lord, who created; created man from the clot of congealed blood. Recite and your Lord is very Gracious, Who taught knowledge with pen, taught that knowledge to man which he did not know. *(Alaq : 1-5)*

This is the first voice which tells about the value of the pen and declares a war against ignorance and negligence. It considers reading and learning as the first brick for the making of a great human. Allah has elevated the position of the Ulama (learned men) to such a high degree that for giving a witness to His oneness and to affirm His justice he has placed Himself, the angels and the learned men in the same category:

> *Allah (Himself) is a witness that there is no God, save Him. And the angels, and the men of learning too are witness. Maintaining His creation in justice, there is no God save Him, the Almighty, the Wise.(Al-i-Imran : 18)*

It is not surprising because how can foolish and narrow-minded people absorb the light of the Brightest Being? How can a man, who loses himself in the pleasures and luxuries of the world, find a way to understand anything about the Wisest Ruler? Or how can he see His great attributes and great signs? That is why Allah has declared the learned men to be respectable and honoured men, and has given them preference on account of their knowledge and learning. Allah's Messenger has said: "On the Day of the Judgment, when Allah will sit on judgment, He will address the Ulama and say:

> *"I had placed My learning and forbearance at your disposal because I wanted to forgive your lapses, I have no care about any thing except this."* *(Tibrani)*

Hafiz Manzari (R.A.A.) says that Allah's words 'learning and forbearance' merit consideration. "If you ponder over these two attributes, you will realise that here the learning of our times which is bereft of sincerity and forbearance is not meant." By mentioning forbearance the idea is to point out that the learning should be such which should not encourage internal differences and it should be able to control the carnal desires of man.

Learning Superior to Worship : For Allah the best knowledge is better than that act which is performed with hesitation and confirmed learning is better than that worship which is performed with ignorance and lack of understanding.

Allah's Messenger (S.A.W.) has said:

> *"The superiority of knowledge is greater than the superiority of worship."* *(Bazaar)*
>
> *"Less knowledge is better than much worship which is performed with ignorance."* *(Tibrani)*
>
> *"Systematic religious thinking is the best worship."* *(Tibrani)*
>
> *O Abu zar! As soon as it is morning, learn a verse from Allah's Book. It is better than performing hundred rakat of prayer, and that you should learn a chapter of*

knowledge daily, whether you may or may not act. It is better than your saying one thousand rakat of prayer.
(Ibn Majah)

The secret of this command is that the worship performed by the ignorant people is as useless as their friendship, on the contrary they put themselves to a loss but they think that they are doing some useful work, as they become a source of loss to their friends due to their ignorance while their intention is to benefit them. Ignorant worshippers very vigorously perform the external manifestations of the religious worship, and they have very strong feelings about that, but on account of conceit and false pride their attitude is so harsh that it many times causes a loss. But for the men of learning their light of knowledge paves the way for them and guides them to the good of all concerned, although their acts maybe less, but there is abundance of light and straightness in their acts.

For this reason, Allah's Prophet (S.A.W.) has said:

"One Faqih *is more over-powering for Satan compared to a thousand worshippers."*

Another *Hadith* is:

"A learned man has the same superiority over a worshipper which I have over an ordinary man from amongst you." *(Tirmidhi)*

In another tradition, it is mentioned:

"A learned man has a superiority of seventy degrees over a worshipper, and between every two degrees is the distance equal to the running of fast horses for seventy years, because Satan puts into circulation innovations among the people and a learned man sees it and tries to stop it, when the worshipper is busy in the worship of his Lord, and he cannot turn his attention to that innovation nor can he know about it. *(Isbahan)*

The Importance of learning can be seen from this verse of the holy Book:

As for these examples, We coin them for mankind, but none can grasp their meaning save the men of learning.
(Ankabut : 43)

Chapter 4

Reforms Under Islam

Status of Women

Women, in Islam, are considered equal with men in their rights to enter into contracts and to hold property and dispose of it as they wish. They enjoy economic independence and possess all such rights a give them an equal human status with men but they are required to observe certain-rules of morality so that promiscuity may not lead to corruption. The fundamental principle, with regard to women, is that they should be held in honour; the mother that bore us must ever have reverence, the wife who is our best companion should be treated well.. Men and women are quite equal to each other in their origin:

> *'O yet mankind! fear your Lord, Who created you of a single soul and He created thereof its spouse and from the pair of them spread abroad many men and women'* *(4:1).*

Surah IV (Nisa or the Women), in the Quran, deals with women. It begins with an appeal to the solidarity of mankind, the rights of women and orphans, and the multiplications of family relationship. It recognizes the rights of women pertaining to marriage, property and inheritance. Women as human beings, are entitled to similar rights to life, honour and property-Sex distinction which is a distinction in nature does not count in spiritual matters. The reward for both sexes for their good deeds is similar, both male and female, men and women are considered as members of a family.

Says God :

> *I will not let go waste the deed of a worker amongst you— male or female, one of you being from the other'* *(3 : 195).*

The equal status of sex is thus recognized in spiritual matters and they are also equal in their rights to live an honourable life. The position of women as mother is highly exalted and, according to the Prophet, 'Paradise lies underneath the feet of mothers' and man is enjoined to be kind to his parents and particularly to the mother who bore him in pain and in plain did she give him birth (46 : 15).

As reported by both Bukhari and Muslim, when a man asked the Prophet as to who had the first claim to his good treatment, mother was the answer, the same answer was repeated three times and he thereafter said 'then your father'.

So far as wife is concerned the Quran says: 'Live with them on a footing of kindness and equity (4 : 19), and as reported by Tirmidhi the Prophet said: 'Best among you is he who is good to his wife.' In his memorable address on the occasion of Farewell Pilgrimage or Hajj, the Prophet called upon men to be kind to women and pay heed to their rights:

> *'Ye people! Ye have rights over your wives, and your wives have rights over you. Treat your women with kindness—verily, ye have taken them on security of God, and made them lawful unto-you by the words of God'.*

How to be Practical ?

Islam is just a practical system of life. While giving to women their rights it does not lose sight of their nature, and differentiates between man and woman when such differentiation becomes necessary according to their nature and the functions which they have to perform in life. 'Men are the maintainers of women because of what Allah has made some of them excel others and by reason of what they spend out of their wealth (4 : 34). This points to the duties of wives, foremost among them is to guard their virtues and remain obedient to their husbands and also to protect their interests in their absence as ordained by God.

The duties of a wife as above are in response to the duties of her husband towards her as he is responsible for food, clothing and other needs. In some of the cases it seems that the husband enjoys some authority over his wife but she has the right to demand divorce of him if she fears ill-treatment of her husband.

In this case she should give back to her husband the dowry she received from him as the husband too, in the event of divorcing his wife, has to forego all that he gave her. The marriage may be dissolved if she proves before the court that she has been ill-treated by the husband or he failed to give sustenance allowance agreed upon between them. The most effective weapon is to secure the right to divorce from her husband at the time of entering into marriage contract with him. It must be borne in mind that woman is created by God as a mate for man:

> *'And one of the signs is that He hath created for you mates of your own species that ye find comfort in their company; and (with that end in view) hath put between you love and tenderness'* *(30 : 21).*

Man and wife are so closely attached to each other that they are treated each other's garments (2 : 187). In other words, they are for mutual support, mutual comfort, and mutual protection, fitting into each other is garment fits the body. Woman, as such, is allowed to have husband of her own choice and cannot be given in marriage without her consent. The Prophet, as reported by both Bukhari and Muslim, has said:

> *'No widow should be married without consulting her; and no virgin without her consent and her consent is her silence.' The marriage is dissolved if she declared that it was without her consent.'*

Unlimited number of wives of the pre-Islamic period was limited to four only and that too under strict condition. The door for polygamy is left open to meet emergencies. War, for instance, takes a heavy toll of men and the balance between the sexes is seriously shaken, or the wife falls sick for an unlimited period and sometimes the disease becomes incurable so as to render the sexual union impossible and it is in such cases that polygamy becomes a social necessity.

With regard to the right of women to work and move in public, it may be said that Islam does not forbid them but they are not supposed to abandon themselves to promiscuity and make a display of their figure or appear in undress. History bears witness to the fact that in the days of the Holy Prophet and those of the rightly-guided Caliphs women took an active part in life. They worked as nurses, teachers, and engaged themselves in such professions as suited them but they were, at the same time, bound to observe strictly the rules of morality and never to mix with men indiscriminately.

Modesty, according to the Prophet is the branch of faith, hence the need for modesty is the same in both men and women. But on account of the differentiation of the sexes in nature, temperaments, and social life, a greater amount of privacy is required for women than men:

> *'Say to the believing men that they should lower their gaze (before women) and guard their modesty; that shall make for greater purity for them; and God is well-acquainted with all that they do' (24 : 30).*
>
> *'And say to the believing women that they should lower their gaze (before men) and guard their modesty; that they should not display their beauty and ornaments except what (must ordinarily) appear thereof and draw their veils over their bosoms' (24 : 31).*

The chastity of women is, therefore, greatly stressed in Islam. The more so, because women are the sole breeders of the offspring and their character has a direct effect upon them. The respect, in which women are held in Islam, is manifest in the fact, that one who accuses them of immorality and does not prove it is liable to the punishment of eighty lashes and also declared unworthy of giving evidence before a court of justice (in addition to Divine punishment in the Hereafter). There may be a question : Why should woman be treated as inferior to man with regard to inheritance and evidence? So far as the law of inheritance is concerned the shares of different heirs vary, according to individual circumstances but it cannot be denied that there is a principle according to which the male gets twice the share of the female:

> *A male shall have as much as the share of two females (4 : 11).*

The inequality between male and female is due to the fact that the female, in addition to what she inherits, is entitled to dowry from her husband over and above her maintenance allowance. Further, she has lesser obligations to fulfil than those of man. Man is of the stronger sex and, as such, has to struggle for life, earn livelihood and maintain his family. It is here that there is a distinction between man and woman. They are, no doubt, equally important component parts of society; but their functions in life differ which make a difference between them. The physical constitution which befits a woman for her specialized functions of conceiving and suckling is not the same for man. Man is tough and hardy, while woman is weak and emotional. She is often overcome by emotions and cannot maintain the balance of mind. The evidence of two women is therefore equivalent to that of one man, for if the one (of the two women) erreth the other will remember (2 : 282).

In the end we have to say that Islam takes into consideration the rights of even a non-Muslim wife of a Muslim. Muslims are allowed to marry such women as belong to the people of the Book (e.g. Christian and Jewess). Such wives are allowed to retain their religion throughout their life :

> *'There being no compulsion in religion'* (2 : 256).

The economic and political systems, as specified above point to the fact that they are free from extremes and possess all the qualities of a morally good life which discards everything that is evil and follows the principles of justice.

Three steps are mentioned so far as family disputes are concerned:

> *'As for those (women) on whose part ye fear rebellious attitude, admonish them, and keep away from them in their beds and chastise them; but if they obey you, seek not a way against them. Verily Allah is High, Great'* (4 : 34).

Here it may be noted that according to Shafii some slight physical correction may be administered if suspension of sex relations is not sufficient to correct the wife, while all authorities are unanimous in depreciating all sorts of cruelty. According to Bukhari, the Prophet said:

> *'Let none of you scourge his wife the scourge of camel and then towards the end of the day have intercourse with her.'*

Men are ordained to live all their life in the presence of God, never seeking occasion to annoy their wives if they are obedient. An excellent plan to settle family disputes is given in the very following verse:

> *'And if you fear a breach between them (the couple) set up an arbiter from his household and an arbiter from her household; (then) if they desire reconciliation, Allah will effect harmony between them. Verily Allah is All-Knowing, All-Aware'* (4 : 35).

In its capacity to absorb all that is good in life and foster good human relations, Islamic social system is par excellence and unparalleled in human history.

Ideal Life

Good character is the sum of personal virtues which guarantees correct and agreeable behaviour in daily social interaction. A person of good character will invariably conform in his behaviour to a strict code of ethics.

What should be the underlying principle of this code of ethics? According to a hadith it is simply this: you should like for others what you like for yourself, that is, you should treat others just as you want to be treated by others.

Everyone likes to be addressed with good manners and pleasing words. So everyone should speak gently to others. Everyone wants his existence to be problem-free, so he should avoid creating problems for others.

Everyone wants others to deal with him in a sympathetic and cooperative manner. So what everyone ought to do while dealing with others is to give them his full sympathy and cooperation.

This standard of ethics is very simple and natural. It is so simple that anyone may easily learn it, be he literate or illiterate, able bodied or disabled, and regardless of his likes and dislikes. This hadith has given such a criterion for human ethics that no one can find difficult to understand. In this way Islam has set forth, in the light of everyone's personal experience, what behaviour may be indulged in and what behaviour has to be refrained from.

According to another hadith, the best of us is one who is best in moral character. Accordingly, becoming a good human being has nothing ambiguous about it. Its simple formula is that of avoidance of double standards. One who lives his life by this formula is indubitably a person of the highest moral character.

The Determination

Islam attaches the utmost importance to intentions (*Niyyat*). No action is acceptable to God purely on the basis of its outer appearance. He accepts only such actions as are performed with proper intention, and rejects those performed with ill intention. Right intention is the moral purposiveness which underlies all actions performed solely for God's pleasure. One who acts on such feelings will be rewarded by God in the Hereafter.

An ill-intention, on the other hand, is a negative spur to worldly attainment. Ostensibly religious acts, if performed for worldly gain or public commendation, are in this sense ill-intentioned. Any fame, honour or popularity which ensues from an ill-intentioned act is a hollow triumph and is looked upon by the Almighty with extreme disfavour.

Intention is rooted in man's inner thinking and feelings. A common man is unable to penetrate the inner recesses of a person's mind but God knows full well what a man's thought processes and feelings are. People can be deluded by appearances, but God has complete knowledge of everything. He will deal with people according to His knowledge and will reward everyone exactly as he or she deserves.

Intention has to do with the inner reality. A thing which loses its reality or its meaningfulness is valueless. Similarly, an act which is performed with ill intention or with no good intention, has no value-neither in the eyes of man, nor of God.

Things are of value only when they are pure, without any adulteration. An act done with right intention is a pure act, and an act performed without right intention is an impure act.

Facts of Life

A believer in God is also necessarily a truth-loving person. He always speaks the truth. In all matters he says just what is in accordance with reality. A true believer cannot afford to tell lies, or hide facts. What does it mean to speak the truth? It is to have no contradiction between man's knowledge and the words that he utters and for that matter, whatever he says should be what has come to his knowledge. Falsehood, by contrast, is the utterance of statements which do not tally with knowledge.

Truth is the highest virtue of a believer's character. A believer is a man of principle. And for such a person telling the truth is paramount. For him no other behaviour is possible, for he finds it impossible to deny the truth.

The world of God is based wholly on truth. Here everything expresses itself in its real form. The sun, the moon, rivers, mountains, stars and planets are all based on truth. They appear just as they really are. In this unfathomably vast universe of God nothing is based on untruth. There is nothing which shows itself in any form other than its real form. This is the character of nature, which is spread out on a universal scale. A believer too has exactly the same character. He is totally free from falsehood or double standards. A believer is all truth. His whole existence is moulded to truth. From the very first he appears to be a true person both inside and out.

Speaking the truth is not only a matter of policy for the believer it is his very religion. Compromising in the matter of truth is not possible for him. He speaks the truth as he cannot live without doing so. He speaks the truth because he knows that not speaking the truth is the negation of his own personality and commitment to something which is the negation of the self is not possible for any worthy person.

The Forgiveness

Once at the time of Asr (Middle prayer) in his speech to the people he said:

> *"Adam's sons have been created of different types. There are some who get angry late and very soon return to*

> *normal. Some people become wrathful soon and soon they return to normal, and some people become angry late and are also late in returning to normal, that is the return to normalcy is according to the speed of getting angry. Be careful. Some people get angry soon and they return to normal late. Listen, the best people among these are those who get angry late and immediately repent, and the worst among these are those who get angry soon, but are very late in coming to normal. Listen, among these there arc some who repay the loan in a better way, and also demand in a good way. Some people are lazy in repaying, but good in demanding. Some demand in a bad way and repay in a good way, i.e., they have one good quality and one bad quality. Some people prove to be bad in demanding and in repaying too. Listen carefully, the best among these are those who are good in demanding and also good in repaying, and the worst are those who are bad in both the things.*
>
> *"Keep in mind, anger becomes a spark in the heart of Adam's son. Do you not see that at the time of anger a man's eyes become red, and his nostrils become enlarged. If any one sees these sign in a man, he should be glued to the earth."* (Tirmidhi)

That is, he should sit in his place, he should not move so that the matter may not get worsened.

Because the flames of anger and wrath burn all matters. Intelligence and consciousness disappear from it, and man is imprisoned in the magic of passions. Then these affairs do not improve. The above-quoted Hadith explains the kinds of men and their achievements and value in greatness and morality. Wherever necessary, a faithful bends himself.

An angry man indulges into various kinds of foolishness. Sometimes he abuses the door if it does not open immediately for him. In his anger he breaks whatever machine or its part may be in his hand, and abuses the animal that is not brought under control.

> *A man's sheet was flown away by the wind and he cursed it. Allah's Messenger said : "Do not curse it, because it is bound by the commands of God and it is under His control. He who curses a thing which did not deserve it then the curse returns on him."* (Tirmidhi)

There are many evils of anger, and their results are more devastating. It is therefore said that to keep the self in control at the time of anger is the proof of the praiseworthy power of control and the noble strength of toleration.

Ibn Masood has narrated that Allah's Messenger had asked:

> *"Whom do you call a sandow ?" People replied : "One who is not knocked down by anybody is called a sandow among us." He said : "No, sandow is one who controls his self in his anger."* *(Muslim)*

One man requested the Prophet: "Give me some advice, out not such a lengthy one that I may forget. The Prophet said : "Do not be angry." (Malik). What reply could b better and shorter than this one? Allah's Messenger always gave importance to the temperament and the environment of the individuals and groups in giving them instructions and training. He used to lengthen or shorten his speech according to the demands of the occasion.

The efforts which were made to remove the jahiliya had two foundations : One was ignorance against learning and the second against tolerance. The first ignorance he removed with the help of knowledge, understanding, sermons and advice, while the second was removed with the help of suppressing the rebellious desires and preventing mischief, etc. The Arabs of the pre-Islamic days were proud of their ignorance and wickedness. As an Arab Poet of the time says:

> *"Beware! None should show any ignorance and wickedness before us, else we will prove to be more ignorant and wicked than all"*

When Islam came, it removed this intensity of feeling and emotionalism, and introduced the practice of pardon and forgiveness in the society. If one could not pardon, then one was given the command to act justly. This objective could be achieved only when anger and wrath could be kept under the control of the intellect.

There are a number of sayings in which the Prophet has given directions to the Arabs leading them to this ideal, so much so that the manifestations of tyranny, aggression, anger and wrath have been declared out of the circle of Islam. The things which unite a group and do not allow it to be disturbed, abuse, etc., has been declared to be the agent which breaks this unity:

> *"Abusing a Muslim is wickedness, and his quarrelling and fighting is infidelity."* *(Bukhari)*

"When two Muslims meet, a curtain from Allah is hung between them. When one of the two says obscene things to the other he tears this curtain of Allah." (Baihaqi)

One Arab came to the Prophet to learn the teachings of Islam. Before this he had neither seen the Prophet nor did he know about his message. His name was Jabir bin Salim. He narrates : "I saw a man whose opinions are being copied by the people. If he says anything people convey it to others. I asked them who this man was. They said that he is Allah's Messenger. I said to him : 'On you be peace (Alaik-as-Salam) O Messenger of Allah !' He said : `Do not salute like this. This is the salute of the dead ; but say Peace be on you. (Assalamu Alaik)'.

That Arab says : "I asked : 'Are you Allah's Messenger?' He replied : `I am the messenger of that Being whom you call in adversities, and he removes your adversities, and if famine catches you and you call Him, He grows grass for you; and if you lose your mount in the arid ground, then you call Him and He causes your mount to be returned to you."

He says that I told him : "Advise me." The Prophet said: "Do not abuse anybody." Accordingly, thereafter I did not abuse any free man, slave, camel, goat. Then he said: 'Do not consider any virtue as mean, even if it is your brother's talking to you with a smile. This is also a virtuous act.' Then he said: 'If somebody reproaches you and makes you feel ashamed on any of your defects, do not make him feel ashamed on any of his defects, because this act of his will prove troublesome for him."

(Abu Daud)

Rebuking and Reproaching : There are also some people whose anger does not cool down. They are always in a turmoil, and this wrathfulness imprints a stamp of stone-heartedness and harshness on their face. If anybody clashes with them they spit fire like an oven. Anger, wrath, squeezing of the nostrils and reddening of the eyes, and then there starts a series of abusing and cursing. Islam is innocent of all these dirty qualities.

Allah's Messenger has said: "A Momin does not taunt, does not curse and reproach, does not indulge in obscene talking and obscene acts." (Tirmidhi)

Cursing and reproaching are the signs of meanness, and it is a quality of lowliness. Those who curse others far ordinary things, they put themselves to great ruin. It is the duty of a man that he should avoid this unseemly act, even if he is harmed considerably by his opponent.

As faith will be nourished in the heart, along with it will grow generosity, broad-mindedness, tolerance and forbearance, and there will grow hatred of anger for the usurpers of our rights and dislike for the desire for their destruction.

The Prophet was requested to invoke God's wrath against the polytheists and to curse them. He said:

> *"I have been sent as a blessing (Rahmat). 1 have not been sent as a rebuker and reproached."* *(Muslim)*

A Muslim however much he would control his self, however much he would control his anger, would pardon others' errors, and however much would sympathise with others on their mistakes, in the same proportion his rank will be raised before Allah.

For this reason, the Prophet disapproved of Hadrat Abu Bakr when he cursed his slave, and said:

> *"How can it be proper for a truthful man that he should rebuke and reproach."* *(Muslim)*
>
> *In another tradition it is mentioned that the Prophet has said: "It is not possible that you indulge in rebuking and reproaching and at the same time remain* siddiqi *(truthful) and straight."* *(Hakim)*

Hadrat Abu Bakr, to atone for his error, freed his slave and went to the Prophet for apologising and said that he would not do such a thing again.

The reason for this is that rebuking and reproaching is such an evil as is more expressive of one's blind rage than the idea of punishing others. It is not at all proper to insult others by yelling at them.

> *Allah's Messenger has said : "When a man curses somebody, then that curse rises up to the sky, but the gates of the sky shut. Then it turns to the earth. Here also the gates are found shut. Therefore it wanders to the right and to the left, and if it does not find a proper place it goes to the man who was cursed. If he deserved well and good, otherwise it returns to the man who cursed."* *(Abu Daud)*

Cursing and Abusing : Islam has declared cursing and abusing, exchange of vulgar and obscene words and acts as Haram (forbidden).

Many clashes occur in which people's honour is attacked and a series of exchange of accusations and fault-finding ensues. The reputation of the relatives, and the female folk of the household is damaged and attempts are made to rake up the dust of centuries. There is only one cause of all this dirty sinning, and that is man is overcome by anger and he washes his hands off all decency and good manners.

The entire responsibility for committing this low and mean type of sin goes to the head of the man who first put the spark to the combustible material. It is written in the Hadith :

> *"The entire sin for mutual abusing and cursing will be on the man who first started it, except when the oppressed crosses the limit."* *(Muslim)*

There is only one way of escaping these intense sins, and that is that tolerance and forbearance may be allowed to have an upper hand over anger and rage, and pardon and forgiveness may be allowed to rule over the passion of taking revenge.

There is no doubt that when a man's own personative or that of his relative or friends is attacked and when he is made to suffer, and he has the means and sources for taking revenge, then he wants to avenge himself immediately and does not rest till he satisfies his passion for revenge.

Hardness be Replied with Softness : But in such cases another policy can be adopted which is much nobler and is liked by Allah, which shows man's greatness and his regard for relationship and that is that he should control his anger, and should not indulge in abusing and cursing. He should restrain himself and should not be bent on taking revenge. He should consider the overlooking of the errors of the wrong-doers as a kind of gratitude to Allah, who has given him such a position that whenever he may want may take back his right.

Ibn Abbas narrates that when Ainia bin Hasn came, stayed in the house of his nephew Hur bin Qais, who was greatly respected by Hadrat Umar, because the readers of the Quran were the members of the Consultative Committee of Hadrat Umar, whether they were old or young.

The uncle asked the nephew to take him to the Amir-ul-Mominin, Umar bin At-Khattab. Accordingly permission was sought, and when both of them went in the presence of Umar, he very harshly said to the Khalifah:

> *"A pity on you, O son of Khattab! because you neither give us gifts nor do you deal with us justly." Hadrat Umar was enraged on this and wanted to punish him.*

The nephew, Hur, immediately intervened and said : "Amirul Mominin! Allah says to his Prophet : `Adopt the method of softness and forgiveness, advise for doing righteous deeds and do not clash with uneducated. This man is uneducated, he may be forgiven.'

> *Accordingly, the Amir of the Faithfuls forgave him and did not deviate slightly from the teachings of those verses when it were recited before him and he was the true follower of the Book of Allah."* *(Bukhari)*

Hadrat Umar was enraged because that Arab had come merely to provoke him. The idea of punishing him came to his mind because he had not gone there with the intention of giving right advice or reform. The only purpose of his going there was to rebuke the Amirul Mominin and to receive rich gifts without working for them. But when he was told that the man was uneducated, he controlled his anger and allowed him to go scot free.

> *It is written in a* Hadith *: "He who controls his anger though he had the power to act on it, Allah will call him first of all on the Day of Judgment and will give him the authority to select whatever houri he likes."(Abu Daud)*

Ibada bin Samit says that the Prophet has said:

> *"May I not tell you those qualities for which Allah will give you tall buildings in the Paradise and He may raise your rank?" The people said: "Certainly, tell us O Messenger of Allah!" He said : "He who behaves with you in the manner of an uneducated person, you behave with him with tolerance, forgive the oppressors, and give to those who deprive you, and he who cuts away from you, try to join him."* *(Tibrani)*

Quran has declared these decent habits and qualities as the path of welfare by which a man can enter the Paradise.

> *"Be quick in the race for forgiveness from your Lord, and for a Paradise whose width is that (of the whole) of the heavens and of the earth, prepared for the righteous,- those who spend (freely) whether in prosperity or in adversity; who restrain anger, and pardon (all) men ; for Allah loves those who do good."*
>
> *(Al-i-Imran : 133-134)*

The Excellent Example : The way in which the Prophet ignored Abdullah bin Ubay, the leniency which he showed him, and the manner in which he overlooked his crimes, are instances whose example cannot be found in the entire human history. Abdullah bin Ubay was the worst enemy of the Muslims. He used to be always in search for finding out ways of inflicting injuries and damages to Muslims and he was in league with the devil against the Muslims. He never let slip any opportunity of harming Muslims, of defeating them and spreading a network of conspiracies against them. He cast aspersions on the chastity of the Mother of the Faithfuls, Hadrat Aishah, and he incited some people to indulge in the whispering campaign against her and thus weaken the foundation of the Islamic society, as from the ancient times the eastern traditions had given a very high position of decency and nobility to women.

For this reason the Messenger of Allah and his dear companions were terribly distressed and were in great mental anguish. They were in a great dilemma on account of this blatant false accusation, till at last the verses of Surah Noor were revealed which refuted the charges of the hypocrites, vouchsafed the chastity and purity of Hadrat Aishah and exposed the machinations of the enemies :

> *"Those who brought forward the lie are a body among yourselves ; think it not to be an evil to you ; on the contrary it is good for you ; to every man among them (will come the punishment) of the sin that he earned and to him who took on himself the lead among them, will be penalty grievous."* *(Noor : 11)*

In this tragedy, those who had openly accused the Ummul Mominin were punished, but the germ which had spread this disease was not touched, so that he might further go on with his nefarious activities of harming Muslims.

Allah blesses His Prophet and his armies with victory and glory. Islam refined the disorderly government of the centuries and reformed the corrupt society. The enemies of Islam were then found within the limits of the Islamic society. Abdullah bin Ubay was pining within himself till he fell ill and died, after leaving the bad and deadly odour of disruption behind him. His sons went to Prophet seeking his pardon for their father. He forgave him. Then the son requested for the Prophet's shirt for the shroud of his father. He gave it to them. Then they requested him to lead his funeral prayer and to pray for their father. The gracious Prophet did not refuse even this request of theirs. He stood up to pray for the salvation of the person who in the past had attacked his honour and reputation.

But Allah denied to grant all these concessions, and this verse was revealed:

> *"Whether you ask for their forgiveness or tot, (their sin is unforgivable); if you ask seventy times for their forgiveness, Allah will not forgive them ; because they have rejected Allah and His Prophet; and Allah guides not those who are perversely rebellions. (Tauba : 80)*

In this tragic event of false accusation was also involved a near relative of Hadrat Abu Bakr, who was living on his help. This man did not hesitate to falsely muse the pure and chaste lady, whose father was giving him help and was sustaining him. He forgot the right of Islam, and did not care for the relationship, and tore to pieces the old custom. Hadrat Abu Bakr was deeply stirred and he swore that he would not give anything to this near relative of his and would not show any kindness to him as in the past. Thereupon the following command from Allah was revealed

> *"Let not those among you who are endued with grace and amplitude of means resolve by oath against helping their kinsmen, those in want, and those who have left their homes in Allah's cause ; let them forgive and overlook; do you not wish that Allah should Forgive you ? For Allah is Oft-Forgiving, Most Merciful."(Noor: 22)*

Accordingly, Abu Bakr restarted helping his relative saying: "I like that Allah may pardon me."

The Humility

Modesty is the true symbol which indicates human nature. It gives an idea of a man's faith, virtue, etiquette and morals. If you see a man hesitating or restive at the time of performing some improper act, or he is sorry on doing some wrong work and the colour of his face is changing, then you can consider him to be a man with a living conscience. He is a man of simple nature and right temperament. But if his face does not show any colour, no trace of modesty or shame is seen on it, his mind does not take any notice of the wrong act being performed by him, he is totally careless about what he is taking up and what he is leaving, then there is no virtue in him, there is not an iota of modesty and shame in him which can prevent him from committing sin and from living a sinful life.

Islam has taught its children modesty, and it has considered it its most distinguishing quality. Allah's Prophet (S.A.W.) has said:

> *Every religion has its moral, and the moral of Islam is modesty. (Malik)*

In the time of Prophet Moosa (Moses) (A.S.) the special element of the Jewish teachings was courage and bravery. In the time of Isa (Jesus) (A.S.) the Christian teachings gave a special place to charity and generosity. And the distinguishing feature of Islam is modesty and sense of shame, when all religions and nations give importance to all the good qualities and take a reckoning of them.

The sense of loving virtue and hating wickedness found in a Muslim has been said by the Prophet (S.A.W.) to be the foundation of adopting virtues and rejecting evils, in order that before the final requital the feeling of love for the good and hate for the evil should be generated in every man. How truly Ibn Qayim has said:

> *"Suppose the Messenger of Allah (S.A.W.) had not brought Allah's Message and the fire of Hell had not been kindled, then was it not incumbent upon the slaves to display modesty before their Benefactor."*

The Prophet (S.A.W.) was the softest of men, most virtuous, decent and the most considerate for giving the dues of Allah and others. He was the farthest away from evil.

> *Abu Saeed Khudri (R.A.A.) says : "Allah's Messenger was (S.A.W.) more modest than the maiden staying behind the veil. If he saw any unpleasant thing, we could see its sign on his face." (Muslim)*

Modesty and Faith

Faith, in fact, is the name of the best relationship between the slave and his Lord. It affects the human life primarily in this way that it purifies the self, morals are improved, and actions are corrected. This so happens when there is an awakening in the self which would keep it away from errors and induce man to hate even the smallest of sins.

If a man does not keep away from small errors and goes on committing them without any care, then it is the symbol of the fact that there is no modesty in him and his faith has been shaken.

> *Allah's Messenger (S.A.W.) has said : "Modesty and Faith are one another's companion. If one goes, the other will also not remain." (Hakim)*

The reason for this is that when a man gives up modesty, he gradually moves from a smaller coil to a deadly evil and from a smaller sin to a bigger sin, till he reaches the lowest of the low. One Hadith of the Prophet (S.A.W.) takes off the veil from this fall of man. It begins with lack of modesty and consequently reaches the worst of the sins.

> *"When Allah wants to destroy a man, He takes away modesty from him. When he is deprived of modesty, he becomes the most detestable man. And when he becomes detestable, he loses trust. When he loses trust and honesty, he becomes extremely fraudulent. Allah's blessing is snatched away from him. He becomes extremely cursed, and when he becomes reproachable, then the yoke of Islam comes out from his neck."* *(Ibn Majah)*

The explanation of the psychological sickness and how it advances, stage by stage, has been very dexterously shown. It has been explained how an evil progressively leads to the commitment of the worst sin. When a man tears the raiment of modesty and does not keep an account of his acts, nor does he care for she reproaches of others, then he extends his hand of aggression to others, he subjects his subordinates to tyrannies. A man of such a character cannot show mercy to any one. He will nourish rancour and jealousy in his heart and will encourage them.

A man who becomes so aggressive with the public, can a quality like modesty prevent him from sins ? When a man falls so low, he cannot be trusted with people's valuables in his trust. How can he be made a trustee, when he is not ashamed in misappropriating the property of others or how can he be considered a watchdog of honour, when he is ever ready to make an assault on any body's honour, or how can his promises be relied upon when he does not care to keep his promises ? No responsibility can be entrusted to him, as the fear of negligence and defection will always be there. Nor can he be given a high office, because there is no guarantee against deception and trickery.

When a man loses his modesty and is deprived of trust and honesty, then he is like a mad dog and runs after his desires and in his way tramples upon the righteous and pure feelings. Then he misappropriates the wealth of the poor and the beggars, and no softness is felt by him in his heart for those unfortunates ; he observes the weak and the meek, but no waves of kindness is generated in his heart. And if at all some delicate feeling is engendered in his heart, he blindfolds himself. Then he seeks knowledge about those things, which go on throwing him in further darkness and misguidance. When a man falls down so low, then be sure that he has become free of the restrictions of the religion and he has thrown away the yoke of Islam from his neck.

There are different occasions when modesty is desirable. In conversation decency demands that man should avoid obscene talk, back-biting and fault-finding of others, and he should avoid touching upon the personal matters of the people. It is extremely disrespectful that a man should irrelevantly blurt out obscene and lewd words.

Allah's Messenger (S.A.W.) has said :

> *"Modesty is faith, and the faithful will go to Paradise, and obscene talk is tyranny and the place of a tyrant is Hell." (Ahmad)*

It is also included in modesty that Muslims should talk in a balanced way in their gatherings. Some people have the habit of making lengthy speeches in big meetings; they fret and fume and their saliva drips from their mouths, but they are not ashamed. Islam has disliked this bad habit.

The Prophet (S.A.W.) has said:

> *He who has learnt the art of conversation for the purpose of turning the hearts of the people, then on the Day of Judgment Allah will not accept his eloquence." (Abu Daud)*

In another tradition he has said:

> *Allah does not like those eloquent men who move their tongues as cows chew the cud. (Tirmidhi)*

The reason for Allah's dislike and hatred of these people is on account of the fact that their talk is full of exaggeration and falsehoods, their affairs are never devoid of hypocrisy and exhibitionism, their gatherings are a prey of various moral diseases. If these people adopt modesty, then they can get rid of all these diseases completely. For this reason in some Hadith it is mentioned that weakness and helplessness is better than eloquence. Here helplessness is of the tongue and not of the heart.

Modesty also demands that a man should feel ashamed if he is adversely criticised any where ; he should be desirous of being introduced as a person who shuns sins and keeps away from evil.

It is forbidden (Haram) to speak ill of those absent persons whose defects are hidden, but those who display their own faults and themselves show their own evils, then other people cannot spread it so speedily as they themselves spread it far and wide. Therefore, the Prophet (S.A.W.) has said that one, who has committed sin, walks hiding from the people.

When the companions of the Prophet (S.A.W.) saw him with one of his wives in a corner of the mosque, he stopped them and told them that he was not with any strange woman.

There is a man who wants, more than anything else, name and fame, and there is another man who turns away the eyes of others from his fame. Their difference is quite distinct.

The meaning of a Muslim's hiding from the people is not that he should indulge in the evil of hiding his evil and displaying his good points, but it means that he should not go on advertising his defects and evils and that he should feel ashamed of committing any sin openly.

A man who feels ashamed to disclose his defects has some element of good in him, and the man who feels proud to show his good points has some element of wickedness in him. As a man feels ashamed in the presence of others, he should have the similar feeling of being ashamed even from himself. If he dislikes that others should find any defect in him, then he should also feel hateful towards having any defect in himself. There is a well-known saying : "Whoever has done a thing secretly which he would have been ashamed to do openly, he has no respect for himself in his own eyes." Therefore it is essential for every Muslim that he should be free from all sins, open or secret, whether they may be known to him only or disclosed to all the people.

A well-known saying is: "Adopt a thing which both your ears may like to hear, and keep away from the thing which your ears may not like to hear."

Foundation of Virtue

> *Modesty is the foundation of virtue. This is the only criterion of decency in all acts. Allah's Messenger (S.A.W.) has said : "The thing, which has obscenity in it, will be spoilt by it, and the thing in which there will be modesty, it will adorn it." (Tirmidhi)*

If a man puts on the raiment or modesty, he becomes the symbol of welfare and goodness. Hadrat Aishah (R.A.A.) narrates that the Prophet (S.A.W.) has said:

> *"If modesty were to appear in the form of a man, then it would have appeared in the form of the best and virtuous man, and if obscenity takes the form of man, it would be of the worst man." (Tibrani)*
>
> *Modesty also demands that man should pay the rights of the right claimants and should give them their proper place. He should treat every man of talent in a respectable*

> *way. The relationship of the slave with his master and of the student with his teacher is that of respect and honour. It is not proper that they should raise their voices in their presence, or should walk ahead of them. In a Hadith it is written : "Treat them well from whom you learn."* *(Tibrani)*
>
> *"O Allah! Do not show me the time when the learned men of the religion are shunned and men of tolerance and forbearance are not treated with modesty."*
> *(Ahmad)*

Abdullah bin Yasar (R.A.A.) says:

> *"I have been hearing a Hadith for a long time: 'When you go to a nation, and from their faces you realise that there is none among them who is afraid of Allah, then know that the matter is extremely delicate'."* *(Ahmad)*

Modesty is not cowardice. A modest and respectable person would rather sacrifice his life than tolerate disgrace and immodesty.

Sometimes an element of fear creeps in modesty, but this fear is for safeguarding the honour lest morality and modesty may suffer in the straitened circumstances. The borders of modesty meet the limits of bravery and valour, which is praiseworthy. When the Jews avoided taking up cudgels against the invaders of the holy land :

> *Then outspoke two of those who feared (their Lord, men) to whom Allah had been gracious : Enter in upon them by the gate, for if you enter by it, surely you will be victorious.* *(Maida : 23)*

These people feared Allah. They feared disgrace and infamy. They were ashamed to take the course of running away. If there were fighting, then these people only led the people in the fight and brought victory nearer. Undoubtedly perfect modesty is given to man by nature, while there are some people in whose very nature there is shamelessness and immodesty. On the other hand there is no dearth of the people in whom the substance of modesty, sense of shame and consciousness for honour is much more. But in spite of the fact that shyness is a distinct element of modesty, it is displayed at both good and bad occasions, and sometimes a shy person commits a very serious mistake. Modesty appears within the religious limits only. A man who is cowed down by the threats of the followers of Falsehood can not be called modest or respectable. Modesty or respect will not be displayed before falsehood, and it is not required to be shown before the people who have gone astray, when helping Truth and giving assistance to the right is the need of the time. The polytheists accused Islam that its followers were abusing their gods, saying that they have no power to create anything, that they are unable to whisk away flies from their faces. They said that it is not modesty that their gods should be so insulted. This was answered by Allah thus:

> *Allah does not feel shy of using similes of the lowly things, be it a mosquito or a still lower being. Those who are believers know that it is truth from their Lord. But these who are rejectors of Faith, they say: What does Allah mean by such a simile?* *(Baqarah: 26)*

The picture drawn of the false gods is correct and Allah has no shyness in saying what is true, and a Muslim should not be afraid of proving what is truth and what is falsehood, nor should he care about it.

Modesty before your Lord : The highest peak of modesty is to be modest before the Lord Almighty, Allah, the Creator of the Universe. We eat from the provision given by Him. We breathe in His air. We grow up on His land, and we are under the shadow of His blue umbrella, the vast sky. A man does not pay his fellowman for his kindness and favour by some evil or unkind act. But it is surprising how his dealing with God is different while he is under his obligation and burden of favours from the cradle to the grave, and even after this his life is at the mercy of the Gracious Lord.

Allah has great rights on his slaves. If people appreciate this, they will rush towards righteousness and virtue without any pressure or delay, and will run away from evil and shameless acts.

Hadrat Abdullah Ibn Masood (R.A.A.) has narrated that the Messenger of Allah (S.A.W.) has said:

"Be modest before Allah as it is proper to be modest." We said : "We are modest before Allah, and for this we thank Him." The Prophet (S.A.W.) said:

> *"This is not modesty. The modesty that should be before Allah demands that you keep your head and all the parts safe from falsehood, keep your belly and your foods safe from the forbidden things, and remember the condition of death and that of the grave ; and he who wants to love the life of the Hereafter, he should give up the embellishments and grandeur of the worldly life, and should prefer Hereafter to the world. He who has done so, he has, as if, fulfilled the right of being modest before Allah."* *(Tirmidhi)*

This advice contains a majority of Islamic principles of etiquette and virtues. It is the responsibility of a Muslim that he should not let any wrong word to come out from his mouth, his eyes may not be directed towards any forbidden thing or things exciting sexual feelings, his ears should not hear wrong things ; he should not accustom his stomach to accept forbidden food, but that it should be content with permissible and clean things. Then it is also his duty that he should spend his time in seeking Allah's pleasure, and should employ all his efforts and resources and capabilities in earning sawab (reward). Carnal desires should not misguide him.

If he does all these things with the consciousness that Allah is watching him, and if he hates to be lax and defective in matters concerning Allah, then he has fulfilled the right of being modest before Allah.

In this sense modesty comprises the whole religion. When it is applicable on so many acts then it has become a part of faith.

The Messenger of Allah (S.A.W.) has said:

> *There are more than seventy aspects of faith. The highest among them is the confirmation of the words that there is no god, except Allah, and the lowest is to remove some harmful thing from the road, and modesty is an aspect of faith.* *(Bukhari)*

Man tries to display good conduct and behaviour in the presence of those whom he considers great and whom he wants to please. Before them he speaks only when necessary. Every step that he takes before them is with caution and fear. A Muslim, whose religion teaches him that he is never away from the sight of Allah, because he is in his presence day and night, feels more awe from the wrath of Allah, and he should be very cautious and careful in obeying His commands. The meaning of this Hadith is also the same: "Be modest before Allah, as you are in the presence of the powerful people of your nation."

> *On some occasions a man's feeling of hesitation and the changing colour of his face is the proof of the fact that there is a streak of virtuousness and purity in him, and "modesty is the name of perfect virtue."* *(Muslim)*

If the colour of modesty goes out from the face, then life becomes free to adopt a sinful line, and becomes the fuel of the hell. For this reason it is said: "If you have no modesty, do whatever you like."

The Kindness

Islam is a religion whose foundation has been kept on charity, generosity, and philanthropy. Narrow mindedness, greed and miserliness are evils that shake its edifice. Therefore Islam likes that its followers should be generous and charitable. It has advised them to treat others kindly, to act righteously, to help their kinsmen and to do all kinds of good and virtuous deeds. It has stressed on its followers to make righteous living a permanent policy .

> *"Those who spend (in charity) their wealth by night and by day; in secret and in public, have their reward with their Lord; there is no fear for them, nor shall they grieve."*
> *(Baqarah: 274)*

It is the responsibility of every Muslim that in meeting his needs he should act in a balanced way, so that he may not spend all his wealth on his personal needs only, but that it is his duty that he should let others also partake of the blessings which Allah has bestowed on him, and that he should allot a part of his wealth for the help and assistance of the poor and needy persons.

> *Allah's Messenger has said: "O Adam's son! Spend your wealth, it is good for you. And do not block it, it is bad for you, and the wealth according to the need cannot be reproached. Spend first for your family and dependents, and the raised hand is better than the lowered hand."*
> *(Muslim)*

Quran has very clearly hinted at this subject when it has commanded the Muslims to spend for their kinsmen and the needy persons and prevented wasteful spending. A spendthrift wastes his wealth and indulges in foolishness. He spends his excess wealth for his personal pleasures, then what can remain with him for payment of the rights of others and the necessary assistance to the needy persons?

Allah has commanded:

> *"And render to the kindred their due rights, as (also) to those in want, and to the wayfarer ; but squander not (your wealth) in the manner of a spendthrift. Verily, spendthrifts are the brothers of Satans, and the Satan is to his Lord ungrateful."* *(Bani Israil: 26, 27)*

And after this, advice is given to be mindful of the sentiments of the needy and the people in want, and their feelings should not be hurt. If there is nothing that can be given to them, they should be refused softly and in a decent way:

> *"And even if you have to turn away from them in pursuit of the Mercy of your Lord which you do expect, speak to them a word of easy kindness:"* *(Bani Israil: 28)*

Islam's call to its followers to spend in the cause of Allah and for charity is famous and well-known. Similarly its war against miserliness, greed and narrowmindedness is as clear as the day.

> *One* Hadith *has it : "A giver of charity is near to Allah, is near to humans, and is near to Paradise and away from hell. And a miser is away from Allah, is away from humans, away from the Paradise and is near to hell. An uneducated giver of charity is liked more by Allah than a miserly worshipper."* *(Tirmidhi)*

There does not exist any system in this world, and there is also no possibility of its existence, in which all the people may be indifferent to and not in need of mutual cooperation. As long as there are power and weakness, wealth and poverty side by side in the human society, it is necessary for achieving peace and satisfaction and for ensuring the success and security of the society that the strong should be kind to the weak, and that wealthy should favour the poor and needy with gifts and donations. If wealth and property are amassed as a result of the capabilities and striving of the people, then some people amass lot of riches and some people get only the bare necessities. And this cannot be objected to. The question regarding misfortune and ungratefulness arise when these people live a life away from the society, when they are concerned only with meeting their own personal needs and for providing for their own pleasures and luxuries, when Allah has caused the people to live together, and has declared this togetherness of theirs, instead of differences in their circumstances, a severe trial for them. This provides a test for their faith and an opportunity for proving their worth.

> *"We have made some of you as trials for others. Will you have patience? For Allah is One Who sees (all things)."* *(Furqan : 20)*

A community can be successful in this field of life only when the relationship among its individuals is strong and firm. No individual of the community should be so deprived that he may be facing a life of starvation and no wealthy man of the community should be so greedy that he may be spending his wealth only for his own personal pleasures and luxuries. To achieve this high objective Islam has framed very strong laws. Peoples' hearts have been prepared to indulge in righteous and virtuous deeds, and they have been tempted to cooperate with each other, help each other and act righteously. It explained to them that the benefit of spending in the cause of Allah is not only derived by the poor and needy persons but the givers of charity also achieve the invaluable riches of peace and satisfaction; their hearts are protected from the earthquakes of rancour and jealousy, and they are saved from the adverse consequences of selfishness and narrow mindedness:

> *"Behold, you are those invited to spend in the way of Allah ; but among you are some that are niggardly. But any who are niggardly are so at the expense of their own souls. But Allah is free of all wants, and it is you that are needy."* *(Muhammad : 38)*

The Tolerance

Patience (Sabr) is the exercise of restraint in trying situations. It is a virtue which enables the individual to proceed towards worthy goals, undeflected by adverse circumstances or repeated provocations. If he allows himself to become upset by opposition, taunts or other kinds of unpleasantness, he will never reach his goals. He will simply become enmeshed in irrelevancies. The only way to deal with the irksome side of daily living is to exercise patience. Patience will ensure that whenever one has some bitter experience, he will opt for the way of tolerance rather than that of reaction to provocation. It will enable one to absorb shocks and to continue, undeterred, on one's onward journey.

Patience, as well as being a practical solution to the problems faced in the outside world, is also a means of positive character building. Failure to exercise patience, gives free rein to negative thoughts and feelings, resulting in the development of a negative personality. While one who remains patient is so morally bolstered by his own positive thoughts and feelings that he develops a positive personality. Sabr is no retreat. Sabr only amounts to taking the initiative along the path of wisdom and reason as opposed to the path of the emotions. Sabr gives one the strength to restrain one's emotions in delicate situations and rather to use one's brains to find a course of action along result-oriented lines.

The present world is fashioned in such a way that everyone is necessarily confronted with unpleasant matters at one time or another. Things which are unbearable have somehow to be borne; harrowing events have to be witnessed and all kinds of pain have to be suffered. In such situations, succumbing to impatience leads to the kind of unnecessary emotional involvement which is counter-productive, while a demonstration of patience has a healing, beneficial effect, allowing one to tread the path of discreet avoidance. Success in the present world is destined only for those who adopt the path of patience in adverse circumstances.

No Reservations

During the lifetime of the Prophet of Islam many of his fellow men opposed Islam and engaged in plotting against Islam and Muslims. The Quran has mentioned this at several places. But the counter strategy advocated by the Quran was not to unearth their plots and launch movements to defeat them or even finally to wage war against them, On the contrary, the Prophet and his companions were enjoined to place their trust in God alone.

That is to say, ignoring the plots and antagonism, trusting only in God and rising above circumstances, they were to continue all activities which were of a positive nature. This was an extremely important injunction. By giving this guidance, God set them on a course of positive thinking, which left no room for negative thinking. In short, this Quranic teaching encouraged the early Muslims to live in a self-sufficient way, free of baneful influence of their opponents.

If you have this obsession that others are plotting against you, and that everyone has turned your enemy, it will result in your starting to suspect everyone, to the extent that even if a member of your own community underscores the importance of tolerance and avoidance, you will take it in a negative light and dub him an agent of the enemy. In this way, you will weaken yourselves by turning your own people away from you.

One harmful aspect of such negative obsession is that one loses all objectivity in thinking. One's entire outlook becomes partisan and prejudiced. One is unable to see reality as it is. One becomes like the man who can see only the thorns in a garden of roses or the colour blind person to whom a garden blossoming with flowers will appear in melancholy shades of grey.

Sacred Commands

Islam is the religion of peace, hence Islamic order may be defined as the divinely ordained system of life, for harmonious and peaceful coexistence, where the Unity of God is to express itself in the Unity of Man and the Sovereignty of God to manifest itself in the obedience to His Laws which avoid extremes, ensure social justice, and stand for moral excellence. Before we proceed with the concept and role of morality, in Islamic order, we deem it necessary to explain what morality is and how it is generally conceived.

Morality or ethics deals with conduct, in so far as-this is considered as right or wrong, good or bad. According to Dewey, the terms 'ethics' and 'ethical', are derived from a Greek word 'ethos' which originally meant customs, usages, especially those belonging to some group as distinguished from another, and later came to mean disposition character. They are thus like the Latin word 'moral', from mores.

It was in customs, says Dewey, that the moral or ethical made its appearance, for customs were not merely habitual ways of acting; they were ways approved by the group or society. To act contrary to the customs of the group brought severe disapproval. The customs, therefore, were strictly observed which gave birth to Customary morality. It was mainly due to their expediency that customs had the force of law and were considered as good. Being the approved standards of morality, their violation brought the censure of the whole society. But there are periods in history when a whole community or a group finds itself dissatisfied with its old customs, for they fail to adequately meet the new issues and problems of life, and this is the starting point of Reflective morality, which supplants the Customary morality.

Thoughtful Preaching Morality

Reflective morality is much advanced and progressive in that the individual is not satisfied any longer to take the group's valuation. He wants some rational method of setting up standards of values, emphasizing at the same time individual development rather than habitual response to the group needs.

Thus individuality raises its head and with it the tendencies towards self-assertion, self-interest. This being anti-social, need was felt for moral theories which emerge when men are confronted with difficult situations. Moral theory, as such, is an attempt to tackle the problem through speculation. Philosophers are the thinking minds who try to prescribe a right course of action in particular circumstances but they differ from each other according to their own lines of thought. This gives, rise to various and conflicting moral theories.

Morality is generally considered as a code or set of principles by which men live. Its theoretical study concerns itself with such questions as 'what is the good life' and 'how ought men to behave' and so on. There are many theories formulated to answer these questions but we confine our attention to the study of Classical theories of the first rank and authority.

Ethical Norms

The word 'social' in its strict sense refers to mutual relations of men in a given society. While dealing, with the social system of Islam we have, therefore, to consider the nature of society which is formed according to Divine law for the purpose of harmonious and peaceful coexistence. Islamic society, as such, is the true image of Islam which regulates the relations-between man and man on the basis of righteousness. Religion according to the Prophet is 'good human relations'.

Social system, thus, covers the whole range of mutual relations and the goodness of this largely depends upon the law which controls it. The principle of law which ensures good human relations is the saying; of the Prophet : Do not inflict injury, nor repay one injury with another'. This serves to purge the society of social evils and paves the way for peaceful coexistence. Islam is a universal religion: and whoever embraces it becomes a Muslim and integral part of its society.

In mutual compassion, love and kindness, the believers are like a body, if one of its parts feels pain the whole body responds with wakefulness and fever as said the Prophet. Such is the unity of life, while the control exercised by the law guarantees not only the uniformity of society, but also establishes good human relations. To know the moral value of Islamic social system we may consider it under two broad heads— and Politics.

Economics in Islam

Unlike other economic systems which are the products of human mind, the economic system of Islam is Divine in character and mainly based upon the Quran and the Sunnah or traditions of the Prophet. It is a system to achieve the highest standard of morality expressed under the term 'righteousness.' Islam regulates the needs of society, means of livelihood, and ways of earning and spending, in its own way. It is significant to note that Buddhism hated Wealth, while Judaism set, for wealth, a racial basis. It makes a distinction between a Jew and a non-Jew in that it allows usury with a non-Jew and forbids it to a Jew. Christianity holds that 'it is difficult for a rich man to enter the realm of Heavens and prefers the life of a cave, while Islam prohibits monasticism and lays stress on active life.

The Quran gives man full sanction to harness the forces of Nature, but makes one condition that he should not be unmindful of his brethren-in-want. The economic system of Islam demands an equitable distribution of wealth. It postulates the principle that God is the Creator of all things and wealth intrinsically belongs to Him. The talent itself which man applies to the process of production is but a gift from God. Hence God claims a share in what is produced and declares that His share must go to those in want. And, as such, it calls upon the rich to give in addition to Zakat or poor-due, whatever is surplus to the poor and the needy (2 : 219). Wealth is to serve useful purposes and not to be accumulated in a few hands (59 : 7).

Economic system of Islam has its own philosophy which is neither Capitalism, nor Communism, nor even European Socialism but a harmonious blend of the material with the spiritual. High moral standards are, therefore, prescribed in the pursuit of wealth. 'Be moderate,' said the Prophet, in this pursuit which implies that one should take what is lawful and avoid the unlawful' (Ibn Majah).

The balance maintained by Islam between Capitalism and Communism is aptly described by Prof. Gibb of the University of Oxford:

> *Within the Western world Islam still maintains the balance between exaggerated opposites. Opposed equally to the anarchy of European nationalism and the regimentation of Russian Communism, it has not yet succumbed to that obsession with the economic side of life which is characteristic of present-day Europe and present-day Russia alike. Its social ethic has been admirably summed up by Professor Massignon: Islam has the merit of standing for a very equalitarian conception of the contribution of each citizen by tithe to the resources of the community: it is hostile to unrestricted exchange, to banking capital, to state loans, to indirect taxes on objects of prime necessity, but it holds to the rights of the father and the husband, to private property and to commercial capital. Here again it occupies an intermediate position between the doctrine of bourgeois capitalism and Bolshevist Communism'*
>
> *(Gibb,* Whither Islam, *London, 1932, P-379).*

The social ethic of Islam is embodied in the Prophet's conception of mankind as a fold, every member of which is a keeper unto other and accountable for the entire fold'. Under such conception there can be neither exploitation, nor selfishness, nor greedy grasp of wealth. The economic system based on such conception is necessarily humane and good. For details we refer the reader to our work, *Economics and Islam*, Islamic Publications, Lahore (Pakistan).

Politics in Islam

While Economics deals with man's activities in pursuit of wealth, the Politics is concerned with the form, organisation, and administration of state. Since economic activities are carried oh within the framework of state we have to study the form and features of Islamic state.

Islamic state, as specified above, has to conform to the spirit of Islam which is a practical way of life, hence it does not attach much importance to the external form of government, the enforcement of Divine law being its ideal. The head of Islamic state has delegated powers and is only a Vicegerent of God and, as such, cannot be an autocrat. He himself has to obey the law of God. It is rightly remarked by Fisher that in Islam, 'Law preceded the state which only existed to enforce the law. If the state failed to enforce the law, the state's validity ceased. The Caliph or Khalifah as head of the state was charged principally with the enforcement of law (Fisher, *A History of the Middle East* p. 99).

Islam is both a religion and state. It is of interest to note that pre-Islamic religions did not think it important to study the political organisation as they were merely concerned with religious affairs. This is to the credit of Islam that it has regulated religious as well as worldly affairs. It deals not only with the relations between the Creator and the created but also with the relations between man and man. God is the Sovereign of Islamic state: 'The Command is for none but God (12 :40); 'He is best to command' (12 : 80); 'Blessed is He in Whose hands is the Sovereignty of the Heavens and the Earth and all between them' (43 ; 85). He cannot be compared to the Sovereigns of the World, nor is the Islamic state similar to democracy wherein sovereignty is vested with the people. It is a state ruled by Divine law which precedes it and to whose dictates it has ideally to conform.

The purpose of Islamic state is to endow humanity with righteous life and 'its affairs are conducted by mutual consultation' (42 : 38). But there is no single method of consultation. The number, the form of election, the duration of representation etc. are left to be adopted as it suits the given time and place, the essence of consultation being to seek the advice of such as enjoy the public confidence.

As we are chiefly concerned with morality, we point to the Quranic verses (17:23-39), which are the directives for state policy. It will be too lengthy to give here all of them. Suffice it to say that the spiritual and moral duties are, here, brought into juxtaposition. Moderation and temperance which find their expression in these directives testify to the intimate relationship which economics of Islam bears to its politics. In these verses we find principles of morality par excellence as they enjoin upon man kindness to parents, giving to the kindred and the needy their rights, keeping of covenants, giving of full measure and weight, exchange of kind words etc., prohibiting at the same time all immoral acts such as adultery, deceit, false promise etc. The state formed according to such directives cannot be designated by anyone of the terms applied to the different forms of governments known to the world. It is a state unparalleled in its norms of morality.

The moral law expounded in these verses is far in advance of the bare Decalogue (The Ten Commandments) in that it searches out what is inmost in the heart and draws pointed attention to the weak and the helpless, to the needy and the poor. It begins with the mention of the One and Only God which sweeps off other ideas of class and creed, race and nation. It aims at universal brotherhood under the Sovereignty of One God. Modern theories with regard to the forms of government and the differences of opinion therein may be traced back to Plato's absolutism and Aristotle's constitutionalism. According to Plato, absolutism or despotism is the best form of government which is rejected outright by Aristotle, a lover of law and constitutional rule. Islam has solved this problem in its form of government which is a happy synthesis of absolutism and constitutionalism as God's Sovereignty means the superiority of His Wise and Impartial laws which are to be executed by His vicegerent on earth, in consultation with such as enjoy public confidence.

We refer to the problem of collectivism and individualism which has been the issue of fundamental controversy of political thought in the history of Western civilization. Whether the individual or the community is the ultimate value, is a problem which was studied, from the point of justice, by Greek Philosophers centuries before the Christ. Legal theories assume one of three attitudes : Either they subordinate the individual to the community, or they subordinate the community to the individual, or they attempt to blend the two rival claims.

Modern totalitarianism asserts the supremacy of the community by the complete destruction of individual rights. This is achieved through the abolition of the separation of powers and judicial independence,, state supervision of all public and private activities. The Catholic theory of society makes the community supreme over the individual in a different manner, for he has to accept the place and function into which he is born. The most outstanding of all such theories-is Marxism which has completely crushed individual rights.

Hobbes stands for individualism but his doctrine leads to political absolutism. Bentham's utilitarianism, Spincer's theory of evolution all embody in different ways an individualistic philosophy but none of these theories represents perfect balance between the interests of the individual and those of society.

A synthesis "between the individual liberty and the interests of society cannot be obtained unless the life of society is based upon righteousness. It cannot be denied that society is but a collection of individuals, the problem is, therefore, to build the character of the individual in such a manner that, far from being injurious to society, he contributes his own good to its welfare. This is achieved by the process of building character through moral education and purification of soul as explained in the preceding pages. It is against such background that the individual is offered full opportunities, in Islam, to develop his personality so that he may be better qualified to serve the interests of society. In this way there can be no clash between the interests of society and those of the individual. Thus the individual is for society and society for the individual.

Perception of Morality

Mankind, according to the Prophet, are a fold, every member of which is a shepherd or keeper unto every other, and accountable for the welfare of the entire fold (Bukhari). Further, mankind are the creatures of God, and most beloved of them before Him is he who is the best to His creatures (Baihaqi). These and other sayings of the Prophet stress the point that one has to identify his interests with the interests of others. The duties to one's self and the duties to others are here placed side by side as the component parts of one's responsibility in life. Only when the individual has a developed sense of such responsibility that he is a moral being and of greater service to society. Duties are generally expressed in terms of duties to God and duties to society, but the spirit underlying duties to God is the spiritual development of one's self so as to be mindful of duties to others—a harmonious interaction between the sense of God and the sense of fellow-men resulting in righteousness. Such is the concept of morality in Islam and, therefore, Islamic law is the law of duties rather than of rights. Generally, rights have corresponding duties but in Islamic law duties are more than rights. This has its own advantages.

Right is a claim on someone and duty is a responsibility to someone. The emphasis merely on rights gives rise to the sense of one's own power and authority over others which may be injurious to peace, while emphasis on duties creates harmony in social life and is conducive to peace. A generalized sense of duty is a sense of being bound by that which is right because of its rightfulness.

Conformity to the letter of the law ' then takes the place of faithfulness to its spirit, *i.e.*, its usefulness in calling attention to the welfare of not only one's self but also of others. The sense of duty, thus, reminds us of our responsibility towards our fellow-beings. This sensitive is specially needed whenever our desire tends to blind us to everything but itself. There are occasions in life on which, under the influence of strong desire, we are apt to lose control upon ourselves and it is the sense of duty to God and to our fellow-men which keeps us away from evil-doing and directs us to the right path—the path of eternal peace and prosperity. Here we realize the importance of duty and comprehend why Islamic law is the law of duties.

Morality for Peace

The Model World according to Islam, is a world of peace. Islam in itself means a religion of peace. The Quran says: And God calls to the home of peace. This is the message of Islam to mankind. It means that a world of peace on earth so that you may be granted a world of peace in your eternal life in the Hereafter.

Now what are the basic elements of building of a culture of peace, according to Islam to be brief, these are three—compassion, forgiveness and respect for all.

Let's take compassion first. If you go through the Quran and Hadith, you will find many verses in the Quran and Hadith which lay great stress on compassion. For instance, the Prophet of Islam said: O people, be compassionate to others so that you may be granted compassion by God.

Thus, Islam makes compassion a matter of self interest for every man. As one's own future depends on one's compassionate behaviour to other fellowmen. In this way Islam motivates us to be compassionate in our dealings with each other. One who wants to receive God's grace will have to show compassion to others.

Let's take forgiveness. The Quran has to say this in this regard "when they are angered, they forgive." There are a number of verses in the Quran which promote forgiveness.

Then there is a hadith. Once a person came to the Prophet and asked him, "O Prophet, give me a mature advice by which I may be able to manage all the affairs of my life." The Prophet replied: "Don't be angry." It means that 'forgive people even at provocation.' That is, adopt forgiveness as your behaviour at all times.

Respect Others to be Respected : Now let's take the third principle—Respect for all. There is a very interesting story, recorded by al-Bukhari in this regard.

The Prophet of Islam once saw a funeral procession passing by a street in Medina. The Prophet was seated at that time. On seeing the funeral the Prophet stood up in respect. At this one of his companions said: 'O Prophet, it was the funeral of a Jew (not a Muslim), The Prophet replied: 'Was he not a human being?' What it meant was that every human being is worthy of respect. There may be differences among people regarding religion and culture, but everyone has to respect the other. For, according to Islam, all men and women are blood brothers and blood sisters. And all are creatures of one and the same God. These three principles are the basic pillars to form a peaceful society. Wherever these three values are to be found the result no doubt will be a society of peace and harmony

The above references are enough to show that Islam is a culture of peace. It is true that some Muslims are engaged in violence in the name of Islam. But you will have to differentiate between Islam and Muslims. You have to see Muslims in the light of Islam and not vice 'versa.

Perception of Peace

A believer is necessarily a lover of peace. In his mind faith and a desire for peace are so closely interlinked that, regardless of the circumstances, he will strive to the utmost for the maintenance of peace. He will bear the loss of anything else, but the loss of peace he will not endure.

The life that the true believer desires in this world can be lived only in the propitious atmosphere which flowers in conditions of peace. Conditions of unrest breed a negative atmosphere which to him is abhorrent. But if peace is to be maintained, it calls for a certain kind of sacrifice. That is, when conditions become disturbed, the believer must overlook both the misdeeds leading up to this situation and the identity of the wrongdoers. He must suffer all the harm and injustice done to him without making any attempt either to retaliate, or to bring the miscreants to book, so that a state of peace should continue to prevail. The believer has to be willing to pay this price, so that his pursuance of constructive ends should proceed unhampered.

The believer is like a flower in the garden of nature. Just as a hot wind will shrivel up a bloom and cause it to die, so will constant friction distract the believer from achieving positive goals. And just as a cool breeze will enable the flower to retain its beauty for its natural life-span, so will a peaceful atmosphere enable the believer to fulfil the obligations of divine worship in a spirit of great serenity. Peace is thus central to the life of the believer.

Islam is a religion of peace. And peace is a universal law of nature. That is because God loves the condition of peace, and disapproves of any state of unrest. God's predilection for peace is quite enough reason for the believer also to love peace. In no circumstances will the true believer ever tolerate the disruption of peace.

Human Rights: A believer has important responsibilities towards both God and man. His duty towards God means believing in Him with all His attributes, worshipping Him, regarding himself accountable to Him; and making himself ready to carry out wholeheartedly any such demands that God may make upon him.

Another responsibility of the believer is one which concerns the rights of human beings. This responsibility devolves upon him in his relations with others. Every man or woman, a relative or neighbour, a fellow townsman or compatriot or one with whom he has dealings in business - everyone has some rights over him. It is incumbent upon a believer to fulfil those rights, failing which he will not be deserving of God's succor.

What is meant by recognising the rights of human beings (Huquq ul-Ibad)? This means that whenever and wherever a believer meets another person, he should give him such treatment as is in accordance with Islamic teachings. He should refrain from such behaviour as does not come up to the standard of Islam.

Examples of proper Islamic behaviour are giving respect to other, never humiliating others while giving them help, acting for the good of others, and if unable to benefit them in any way, at least doing no one any harm, fulfilling trusts, never breaking them; never usurping the wealth and property of others; dealing justly with others regardless of the circumstances; giving the benefit of the doubt to others, not believing in allegations made against others without proper proofs; advising others in earnest.

Everyone has a duty to fulfil these responsibilities towards other human beings according to the Islamic Shariah. This is called Huququl Ibad, or human rights.

Freedom of Expression : Islam grants human beings total intellectual freedom. Rather it would be truer to say that it was Islam which for the first time in human history brought about a revolution in freedom of thought. In all the ages of history prior to Islam, the system of despotism prevailed, and man was consequently denied freedom of thought. This was a matter of the utmost gravity for it is a fact that the secret of all human progress lies hidden in such freedom. The first benefit of intellectual freedom is to enable man to achieve that high virtue which in the Quran is called "fearing the unseen." That is, without any apparent compulsion or pressure from God, man, of his own free will, acknowledges God and leads his life in this world, going in fear of Him. In the absence of an atmosphere of total freedom, no one can undergo this spiritual experience-an indescribable spiritual pleasure-which is called in the Quran, going in fear of the Lord. Without such freedom it is not possible to give credit to anyone for this highest of human virtues. Man is a thinking creature. Of necessity he forms opinions. If curbs are placed on the independent expression of his views, the content of his thought may remain unchanged, but his ideas will never find expression in his speech and writings. Curbs of this nature, imposed by a community or a state, will ultimately produce a society of hypocrites. No sincere person can ever flourish in such a repressive atmosphere. It is only freedom of thought and expression which can save man from hypocrisy.

Moreover, intellectual freedom is directly related to creativity. A society with freedom of thought will produce creative human beings; a society which places curbs on freedom of expression will necessarily witness intellectual stagnation; it will stop producing creative minds, and its development will come to a standstill.

In matters of criticism or expression of differences, the right approach is for people to end unnecessary, sensitivity to it instead of attempting to put an end to criticism and differences. This is the demand of Islam as well as of nature.

According to the hadith it is a virtue on the part of believers: to accept the truth without any reservation when it is presented to them. That is to say, a believer is one who has the ability in the perfect sense of the word to accept the truth. Whenever truth is brought before him, whenever his faults are pointed out to him, no complex comes in the way of his accepting of the truth.

This quality is present to the maximum degree in one who is ready and waiting to accept the truth when it is brought before him. Eager for his own improvement, he accepts the truth with pleasure. This keenness for self-reform through acceptance of the truth is perfectly expressed in the words of 'Umar ibn al-Khattab: "May God bless the man who sends me gifts of my own shortcomings."

It is a fact that acknowledgment of truth is worship, nay, it is the greatest form of worship. It is an act for which man has to make the greatest sacrifice. What makes it such a great sacrifice is that it involves the setting aside of one's prestige.

It amounts to the sacrifice of one's ego. But that is the occasion when man assures his entry into heaven.

When does one find the opportunity for this great form of worship and this great good fortune? This opportunity comes one's way only when there is full freedom of expression. When one can criticise another with impunity. When such an atmosphere prevails in a society which permits the speaker to air his views freely and the listener may freely appreciate what is being said. Just as a mosque is the right place for the performance of prayer in congregation, similarly freedom of expression is the right atmosphere in which to foster the great virtues of expressing the truth and acceptance of the truth.

Human Equality: According to Islamic tenets, all human beings are equal. In prayer, all members of the congregation stand in the same rows together, and on the Hajj pilgrimage, all the believers belonging to different countries don identical white seamless robes for the performance of the obligatory rites. On the occasion of the Final Pilgrimage, it is noteworthy that the Prophet of Islam declared that no Arab was superior to a non-Arab and that no white was superior to a black. All were equally servants of God. In Islamic society, everyone is accorded the same status, there being, ideally, no higher or lower social strata.

How then can we rationalise what are apparently very great differences in human beings in terms of colour and race, etc., considering that the concept of human equality ranks so high in the value system of Islam? We find the answer in the Quran, which makes it clear that such outward differences are meant to serve as means of identification and were never intended as indicators of superiority (or inferiority). People in different parts of the world may have a diversity of skin colourings and other distinctive racial characteristics, but that is only so that they may be easily distinguished from each other. By Islamic standards, this is designed to facilitate social and national interaction.

The sole basis of superiority in Islam is *taqwa* - the earnestness with which one leads a God-fearing life; as such, it bears no relation to colour or race. Physical attributes certainly have their effect on the social interaction of this world, but in the Hereafter, no value is attached to them. There, the only things which count are inner qualities, for upon them depends the essential excellence of man's distinctive character. That is why, according to a hadith, God sees the heart and not the body. He reserves a place in Paradise only for those found deserving in terms of their inner worth.

According to Islam, all greatness belongs to God. God as the Supreme Being is ineffably superior to all men. While there is this infinitely great difference between God and man, there is no difference whatsoever between man and man.

Human Brotherhood: According to Islam, all human beings have been created by one and the same God, and for this reason belong to one great brotherhood. So far as their earthly origin is concerned, they are all descendants of the first pair of human beings ever created by

God -Adam and Eve. In their subsequent spread over different parts of the world, variations in geographical conditions produced a diversity of skin colourings, languages and other racial characteristics.

The teaching of Islam in this regard is that despite differences of colour, language, etc., people should harbour no ill-will towards those who are apparently unlike themselves, for differentiating between one man and another is not approved by God. They should rather promote fellow feeling towards others, even if at first glance they appear like total strangers to them. Bearing in mind that they are all traceable back to Adam and Eve, they should be each other's well-wishers and willingly come to one another's assistance, like members of the same large family. Ideally, the relation between one man and another ought not to be one of strangeness but one of familiarity; not of distance but of nearness; not of hatred but of love.

When all human beings are descendants of the same progenitors, that means that all are equal: no one is superior or inferior. The distinction between great and small is not between one human being and another, but between God and man. And before God, certainly, all human beings are equal; all are equally His creatures and His servants. For God does not discriminate between one or the other of His creations.

Non-violence : Islam is a religion which teaches non-violence. According to the Quran, God does not love *fasad*, (violence). What is meant here by *fasad* is clearly expressed in verse 205 of the second surah. Basically fasad is that action which results in disruption of the social system, causing huge losses in terms of lives and property.

Conversely, we can say with certainty that God loves non-violence. He abhors violent activity being indulged in human society, as a result of which people have to pay the price with their possessions and lives. This is supported by other statements in the Quran. For instance, we are told in the Quran that peace is one of God's names (59:23). Those who seek to please God are assured by verse 5 of the sixteenth surah chat they will be guided by Him to "the paths of peace." Paradise, which is the final destination of the society of God's choice, is referred to in the Quran as "the home of peace"' (89:30), etc.

> *The entire spirit of the Quran is in consonance with this concept. For instance, the Quran attaches great importance to patience. In fact, patience is set above all other Islamic virtues with the exceptional promise of reward beyond measure. (39:10)*
>
> *Patience implies a peaceful response or reaction, whereas impatience implies a violent response. The word* sabr

> *exactly expresses the notion of non-violence as it is understood in modern times. That patient action is non-violent action has been clearly expressed in the Quran. According to one tradition, the Prophet of Islam observed: God grants to* rifq *(gentleness) what he does not grant to* unf (violence). *(Sunan, Abu Daud, 4 /255)*

The word *rifq* has been used in this hadith as an antithesis to *unf*. These terms convey exactly what is meant by violence and non-violence in present times. This hadith clearly indicates the superiority of the non-violent method.

God grants on non-violence what He does not grant to violence is no simple matter. It has very wide and deep implications. It embodies an eternal law of nature. By the very law of nature all bad things are associated with violence, while all good things are associated with non-violence.

Violent activities breed hatred in society, while non-violent activities elicit love. Violence is the way of destruction while non-violence is the way of construction. In an atmosphere of violence, it is enmity which flourishes, while in an atmosphere of non-violence, it is friendship which flourishes. The method of violence gives way to negative values while the method of non-violence is marked by positive values. The method of violence embroils people in problems, while the method of non-violence leads people to the exploiting of opportunities. In short, violence is death, non-violence is life.

Both the Quran and the hadith have attached great importance to jihad. What is jihad? Jihad means struggle, to struggle one's utmost. It must be appreciated at the outset that this word is used for non-violent struggle as opposed to violent struggle. One clear proof of this is the verse of the Quran (25:52) which says: Perform jihad with this (i.e. the word of the Quran) most strenuously.

The Quran is not a sword or a gun. It is a book of ideology. In such a case performing jihad with the Quran would mean an ideological struggle to conquer peoples' hearts and minds through Islam's superior philosophy.

In the light of this verse of the Quran, jihad in actual fact is another name for peaceful activism or non-violent activism. Where qital is violent activism, jihad is non-violent activism.

Non-violence therefore should never be confused with inaction or passivity. Non-violence is action in the full sense of the word. Rather it is more forceful an action than that of violence. It is a fad that non-violent activism is more powerful and effective than violent activism. Non-violent activism is not limited in its sphere. It is a course of action which may be followed in all matters.

Whenever individuals, groups or communities are faced with a problem, one way to solve it is by resorting to violence. The better way is to attempt to solve the problem by peaceful means, avoiding violence and confrontation. Peaceful means may take various forms. In fact, it is the nature of the problem which will determine which of these peaceful methods is applicable to the given situation.

Peaceful Beginning : When the Quran began to be revealed, the first verse of the revelation conveyed the injunction: "Read!" (Iqra) (96:1). By perusing this verse we learn about the initiation of Islamic action. It begins from the point where there is hope of continuing the movement along peaceful lines, and not from that point where there are chances of its being marred by violence.

When the command of 'Iqra' was revealed, there were many options available in Mecca as starting points for a movement. For instance, one possible starting point was to launch a movement to purify the Kaaba of the 360 idols installed in it. But, by pursuing such a course, in such a case the Islamic movement would certainly have had to face a violent reaction from the Quraish. An alternative starting point could have been an attempt to secure a seat in the Dar-ul-Nadwa (Mecca's parliament). At that time almost the whole of Arabia was under the direct or indirect influence of the Roman and Sasanid empires. If the freeing of Arabia from this influence had been made the starting point, this would also have been met with an immediate violent reaction on the part of the Quraish.

Leaving aside these options, the path followed was that of reading the Quran, an activity that could be with certainty continued along peaceful lines: no violent reaction would ensue from engaging in such an activity.

> *The Prophet of Islam followed this principle throughout his life. His policy was that of adopting non-violent methods in preference to violent methods. It is this policy which was referred to by Aishah, the Prophet's wife, in these words: Whenever the Prophet had to opt for one of two ways, he almost always opted for the easier one.*
>
> *(Fath ul Bari 6/654)*

What are the advantages of non-violent activism over violent activism? They are briefly stated as under:

1. According to the Quran there are two faculties in every human being which are mutually antipathetic. One is the ego, and the other is the conscience called respectively *nafs ammara* and *nafs lawwama*. (The Quran, 12:53; 75:26) What the violent method invariably does is to awaken the ego which necessarily results in a breakdown of social equilibrium. On the other hand, non-violent activism awakens the conscience. From this results an awakening in people of introspection and self-appraisal. And according to the Quran, the miraculous outcome of this is that "he who is your enemy will become your dearest friend." (41:34)
2. A great advantage of the non-violent method is that, by following it, no part of one's time is wasted. The opportunities available in any given situation may then be exploited to the fullest extent-as happened after the no-war pact of Hudaibiya. This peace treaty enabled the energies of the believers to be utilised in peaceful constructive activities instead of being dissipated in a futile armed encounter. One great harm done by violent activism is the breaking of social traditions in the launching of militant movements. Conversely, the great benefit that accrues from non-violent activism is that it can be initiated and prolonged with no damage to tradition.

Generally speaking, attempts to improve or replace existing systems by violent activism are counter-productive. One *coup detat* is often the signal for a series of coups and counter-coups, none of which benefit the common man. The truly desirable revolution is that which permits gradual and beneficial changes. And this can be achieved only on the basis of non-violence.

Good Life : Since the objective good is known to God alone, the good life is that which is lived in accordance with the law of God and men ought to behave in the manner which pleases God and what pleases God most are the righteous deeds. We are given a beautiful description of righteousness:

> *"It is not righteousness that ye turn your faces towards East or West ; but it is righteousness— to believe in God and the last Day, and the Angels and the Book, and the Messengers; to spend of your substance, out of love for Him, for your kin, for orphans, for the needy, for the wayfarer, for those who ask, and for the ransom of slaves; to be steadfast in prayer, and practise regular charity; to fulfil contracts which ye have made; and to be firm and patient, in pain (or suffering) and adversity, and*

throughout all periods of panic, such are the people of truth, the righteous'. *(2 : 177).*

The emphasis laid upon this verse is so great that most of the Quran seems to be nothing else than the exposition of its implications. Among the duties; enumerated in this verse, the first and foremost is to believe in the Unity of God. This is the basic concept into which the Quran desires to initiate human mind. The late Rev. C. F. Andrews has said :

> *"One of the greatest blessings which Islam has brought to East and West alike has been the emphasis which at a critical period in human history it placed upon the Divine Unity. For during those Dark Ages both in East and West, from 600 to 1000 A.D. this doctrine was in danger of being overlaid and obscured in Hinduism and Christianity itself, owing to the immense accretions of subsidiary worships of countless demi-gods and heroes. Islam has been, both to Europe and India, in their dark hour of aberration from the sovereign truth of God's Unity, an invaluable corrective and deterrent. Indeed, without the final emphasis on this truth, which Islam gave from its central position,—facing India and facing Europe—it is doubtful whether this idea of God as one could have obtained that established place in human thought which is uncontested in the intellectual world today"*
>
> (The Genuine Islam, *Singapore, Vol. 1, No. 8, 1936).*

Unity of God is to express itself in the Unity of man. The enforcement of the sense of Unity and brotherhood has been the chief aim of Islam. Every one who embraces Islam, enters into its fold and is treated as a brother, since believers are but one brotherhood (49 : 10). Suffice it to quote from the Prophet who says :

> *"A Muslim is a brother of another Muslim, he neither wrongs him, nor leaves him helpless, nor humiliates him"* *(Muslim).*
>
> *"It is forbidden for a Muslim to take the life, honour and property of another Muslim"* *(Muslim and Bukhari).*
>
> *"In mutual compassion, love" and kindness, you will find the faithful like a body, if one of its parts feels pain, the whole body responds with wakefulness and fever"* *(Muslim and Bukhari).*

Believe and work righteously are the injunctions to be strictly observed. These are the words that reverberate and echo in the Quran. The Quran expects man who believes in God to express that belief in an earnest endeavour to promote the unity of man, it is by action that he has to prove his belief in God, even as the Prophet said:

> *"God doth not accept faith if it is not expressed in action, and doth not accept action if it does not conform to faith"*
> *(Bukhari).*

Next to belief in God is the importance attached to the deeds of charity. So mindful is the Quran of the economically depressed classes of society that it calls upon every earning member to assign, in his earnings a share to the needy and the poor: "And in their wealth is a share of the needy and deprived" (51: 19). The supreme note in regard to social security is struck in the verse (3 : 92). It runs:

> *"Ye shall never attain righteouness unless ye give (the needy and poor) of that which ye love (particularly your wealth); and whatever ye give of a truth God knoweth it well."*

Charity is not to give something worthless but it is to give what we love and value greatly. Faith is not merely a matter of words, we must be prepared to show it in deeds of charity to our fellow-men. Practical deeds of charity are of value when they proceed from love, and from no other motive. In this respect our duties take various forms in the gradation as arranged in the above cited verse (2 : 177). The importance attached to these duties is manifest from the fact that their mention precedes that of the duties to God such as Salat (Prayers) which is one of the five pillars of Islam. These are the pillars devised to purify the soul of man and build his character in such a manner that he takes pleasure in self-sacrifice—the essence of righteousness. The above verse is remarkable in that it renders the individual conscious of his duties on which depends the welfare of society and also teaches him to be firm and patient in pain (or sufferings) and adversity and throughout all periods of panic. The virtues of firmness and patience help man preserve his dignity and enable him to bear with fortitude all that falls to his lot of the vicissitudes of life. The Arabic word 'Sabar', which occurs in this verse, is translated as patience but it implies many shades of meaning which is impossible to comprehend in one English word. In addition to its meaning of not being hasty, the word 'Sabar' connotes perseverance, constancy, steadfastness, firmness of purpose, self-restraint, endurance of sorrow, pain, and other evils. But it is never used in the sense of despair and disappointment for Islam is not passivity but active striving with the hope for the better. 'Sabar', thus, means patient perseverance and firmness of purpose which bear good fruits. In proof of the importance of this word it is enough to say that it has appeared in the Quran on more than ninety occasions and the Caliph Umar is reported to have stated that he had found the best way of life in patience, for patience is the key to success.

Here, it may be said that there is no peculiarity about Islam, for all the revealed religions profess the same truth. But their teachings are not in the original form. Further, they cannot claim to be the religions of universal character. Islam is the only religion, universal and for all time, for the Prophet Muhammad was sent as a Universal Messenger to mankind (34 : 28), and the Quran is the Book preserved in the original purity. Being universal in character Islam is neither Judaism which has the concept of a particular covenant or a specially chosen people, nor is it Christianity whose mission, as Jesus made it clear, was confined to recovering the 'lost sheep of Israel'. Further, the Christian view of the 'Kingdom of God in heaven and Kingdom of Caesar on earth' has no place in Islam.

Says Kerr : 'In professing to provide man with a political and legal system as well as a spiritual faith, Islam denies, at the outset, the conception familiar to Christendom of a separation between temporal and spiritual matters' (*Islamic Reform*, p. 3).

Observes Hitti : 'Moses was a prophet, so were Ibrahim, Nuh, Christ and others, each with a dispensation appropriate for a certain time or place. But Muhammad's dispensation, sums up as well as supersedes all earlier ones. It is final. After it there is none' (*The Near East in History*, p. 197).

Being the last of the Prophets, the message delivered by Muhammad is final and for all time and the law contained in the Quran is perfect and comprehensive. Good life is, therefore, to live in conformity with such a law.

Foreign Policy

With regard to foreign policy, Muslim international law and its precepts are based upon universal truths. Such precepts apply to the whole humanity regardless of religion and race. Islam is a religion of peace and believes in peaceful co-existence, hence treaties, pacts and covenants are respected and obligations arising out of them faithfully fulfilled:

'O ye who believe keep your covenants' (5: 1).

'Verily of the covenants enquiry, shall be made'(17: 34).

Islam tolerates on its territory, a multiplicity of laws, with autonomous judiciary for each community. A stranger, therefore, belongs to the jurisdiction of his own confessional tribunal. Further, he is allowed to practise customs that are forbidden in Islam. The consumption of alcoholic drinks, for instance, is forbidden to a Muslim, yet a non-Muslim enjoys the liberty not only of its consumption but also of its manufacture and sale. Such is the toleration of Islam which seeks to establish a world order based on the principle of belief in One God.

Status of non-Muslims : The security of life and property, and freedom of religion are ensured to non-Muslim minorities who are styled 'Dhimmi', the protected of God and the Prophet. 'Beware'! proclaimed the Prophet,' I shall myself be complainant, on the Day of Resurrection, against him who wrongs a 'Dhimmi' or lays on him a responsibility greater than he can bear or deprives him of anything that belongs to him.' (Al-Mawardi, Al-*Ahkam* al-*Sultaniyah*, p. 137). So mindful was the Prophet of their safety and welfare that a few moments before he expired, the thought of the 'Dhimmi' came to him and he said: 'Any Muslim who kills a Dhimmi has not the slightest chance of catching even the faintest smell of heaven. Protect them; they are my Dhimmis'. (Bukhari). The Caliph Umar also exclaimed in the same manner, as he lay assassinated :

> *"To him who will be the Caliph after me, I commend my wish and testament The 'Dhimmis' are protected of God and the Prophet. Respect the covenant entered into with them, and when ' necessary fight for their interests and do not place on them burden or responsibility which they can not bear'* *(Bukhari).*

In sum, non-Muslims, in the Islamic state, constitute a protected minority and it becomes the duty of the state to protect their person, property and honour. They are not to be defamed and the jurists are agreed on this point that he who violates a non-Muslim woman is to be punished as if he violated a Muslim woman.

The War : In sanctioning war, Islam has defined its aims and purposes. They are to suppress tyranny, and to guarantee freedom of belief to all: 'Permission is given (to fight) those who have taken up arms against you wrongfully. And verily, God is Most Powerful to give succour;—to those who have been expelled from you their homes for no other reason than this that they say, 'Our Lord is God'. Had not God repelled some men by others, cloisters and churches and synagogues and mosques, wherein the name of God is ever mentioned, would assuredly have been pulled down' (22: 29, 40).

These verses relate to the first occasion on which fighting, in self-defence, was allowed to those who were expelled from their homes for no other reason than their worship of One God. Thus war was forced upon the Prophet and he had to fight not only in self-defence but also to protect the places of worship of all others.

Still there are certain critics who contend that Islam was spread by the sword which is not tenable. In addition to the above verses we cite the following to prove that Islam was never aggressive but always inclined to peace:

> *'O ye who believe! take to the path of peace and do not follow in the footsteps of Satan; for he indeed is your avowed enemy' (2 : 208); And if they lean to peace, lean thou also to it, and repose thy trust in God (8 : 61); God doth not forbid you to be kind and fair to those who have not made war upon you because of your faith, or have not driven you forth from your homes, for God indeed loveth those who act with fairness (60 : 8).*

In the conduct of war, the Prophet and the Orthodox Caliphs never lost sight of humanitarian considerations enjoined by the Quran. Here we refer to Sir Thomas Arnold who in "The Preaching of Islam has given an account of the conditions drawn up when Jerusalem submitted to the Caliph Umar:

> *'I,' says the Caliph Umar, 'grant them (the inhabitants of Jerusalem) security of lives, their children, their churches, their crosses, and all that appertains to them in their integrity, and their lands, and to all, of their religion' (Arnold, The Preaching of Islam, p. 51).*

In continuation Arnold Adds : In company with the Patriarch, Umar visited the holy places, and it is said while they were in the Church of the Resurrection, as it was the appointed hour of prayer, the Patriarch bade the Caliph offer his prayers there, but he thoughtfully refused, saying that if he were to do so, his followers might afterwards claim it as a place of Muslim worship (the Preaching of Mam, p. 51). The self-restraint of the conquerors and the humanity which they displayed in their campaigns says Arnold, 'must have excited profound respect and secured a welcome for an invading army that was guided by such principles of justice and moderation.'

In view of the above facts it is unfair to say that Islam was spread by the sword. It is, indeed, the moral excellence of Islamic principles, as is evident from the following verses, which caused the spread of Islam.

'Invite (all) to the Way of thy Lord with wisdom and beautiful preaching and discuss things with them in an agreeable style. Thy Lord knoweth best who path strayed from His path, and knoweth best who is guided aright' (16 : 125); 'And (bear in mind) good and evil cannot be treated alike. Return good for evil and mark (how good is the result that follows); he who was inimical towards thee shall behave as if he were a warm friend.

Besides, there are rules and etiquette of war. Islamic law does not allow surprise attack nor does it sanction the breach of pacts and treaties. Foreign subjects or *mustamin* are entitled to rights flowing from such pacts as they cannot be violated by reason of war with their country. Even among the enemies of Islam, actively fighting against Islam, there may be individuals who ask for asylum. Full asylum will be guaranteed to them and they will be escorted to a place of safety (9 : 6).

There are also rules which forbid the killing of the aged, the young, women and others as is evident from the principles of justice and moderation laid down by the Caliph Abu Bakr for the guidance of the first expedition into Syria:

> *'Be just; break not your plighted faith; mutilate none, slay neither children, old men, nor women; injure not the date palm nor burn it with fire, nor cut down any fruit bearing tree; slay neither flocks nor birds nor camels, except for food; perchance ye may come across men who have retired into monasteries, leave them and their works in peace (Arnold,* The Preaching of Islam, *pp. 49, 50).*

The Slavery

Slavery, in Islam, is only in name, for the Prophet took away the whole spirit of this institution as is evident from the fair treatment meted out to the slaves and equal opportunity offered to them so much so that they became kings, commanders, scholars and jurists of the high rank. Here we refer to the sermon delivered by the Prophet on the occasion of Farewell Pilgrimage or

> *'And your slaves! see that ye feed them with such food as ye eat yourselves, and clothe them: with the stuff ye wear and if they commit a fault which ye are not inclined to forgive, then part them, for they are the servants of the Lord, and are not to be harshly treated*
>
> *(Ibn Hisham,* Sirat al-Nabawia, *vol. 2, p. 603).*

> *The Quran itself lays great emphasis on freeing the slaves: What is spiritual ascent asks the Quran and itself gives the answer, 'it is freeing the slave (90 :13). This is supported by the saying of the Prophet: Nothing pleases God better than to free a slave.*
>
> *(Bukhari).*

Slaves were never treated as a commodity. In striking contrast to Rome where the slaves had no social status, Islam restored to them human dignity and proclaimed: 'He who kills his slaves, we shall kill him, and who mutilates his nose, we shall cut his nose, and who gelds our slave, we shall get him gelded in return (Bukhari). The Quranic verse (4 : 36) enjoins the believers to be good to the slaves and according to verse (4 : 25) believers are permitted to marry believing bondswomen with the leave of their masters.

The Holy Prophet himself set an example of voluntary emancipation as he freed all his slaves and even brought marriage between an emancipated slave and a free Quraish woman, a relative of his own. Besides, there are other ways prescribed by the Quran which bring to the slaves their freedom. Slaves are to be set free as atonements for sins and to expiate oaths, and for slaying a believer:

> *And to who has slain a believer by mistake, he should free a believing slave, and pay an indemnity to his family, unless they forego by way of charity' (4 : 92).*

Mukataba is also a means of freeing slaves. It is the writing of freedom by the master to a slave on his asking for it in return for a certain amount of money agreed upon by both of them. The master, in such a case, has no option of refusing or delaying the freedom of the slave. He must set him free on recovery of the amount agreed upon or else the slave would bring a suit against his master for his freedom. These are the several ways which ensure the freedom of slaves.

As to the prisoners of war, they were either set free as a favour or released on payment of ransom: 'And thereafter set them free as either a favour or in return for a ransom when the war is over' (47 : 4). The verse does not mention the enslaving of prisoners, it prescribes ransoming or setting them free as a favour. Islam does not insist on taking prisoners of war as slaves.

So far as women are concerned, they are respected even in their captivity and never treated as a common property. They belong to their masters alone and have the right of freedom through 'mukataba. Further, a slave girl is considered to be free as soon as she gives birth to a child by her master and the child is also deemed free. Islam never violates the honour of women and treats them respectfully.

Principles of Faith

Islamic law is the Command of God revealed to the Prophet Muhammad. It precedes the state and is not preceded by it; it controls the society and is not controlled by it; state and society both have ideally to conform to its dictates. Observes Jackson:

> *"Islamic law finds its chief source in the will of Allah revealed to the Prophet Muhammad. It contemplates one community of the faithful, though they may be of various tribes and in widely separated locations. Religion, not nationalism or geography, is the proper cohesive force. The state itself is subordinate to the Quran, which leaves little room for additional legislation, none for criticism or dissent. This world is viewed as but the vestibule to another and a better one for the faithful, and the Quran lays down rules of behaviour toward others and towards society to assure a safe transition. It is not possible to separate political or juristic theories from the teachings of the Prophet, which establish rules of conduct concerning religious, domestic, social and political life.*
>
> *This results in a law of duties rather than of rights, of moral obligations bindings on the individual, from which no earthly authority can relieve him, and which, he disobeys at peril of his future life"(Jackson, Foreword to* Law in the Middle East, *pp. vi, vii).*

The doctrine of the Umma or one Community of the Faithful lies at the root of Islamic political concept. The Umma consists of the totality (jamaa) of individuals bound to one another by ties, not of kinship or race, but of religion, in that all its members profess their belief in the One God, and in all their relations to Him, all are equal, without distinction of rank, class or race. Differences of function are recognised, but 'the noblest among you is the most god-fearing' (49:13). See Gibb, 'Constitutional Organisation' in *Law in the Middle East*, p. 3. According to Plato, law belongs to the class of convention; it rises through use and wont, while Islamic law is based upon Divine Revelations. Being Divine in origin, Islamic law is distinct from human law which is the product of reason and outcome of customary rules which can never, with perfectness, produce uniformity of conduct within the field of action to which they apply as do the Divine laws with their specified norms of good and bad, virtue and vice.

Divine laws are the standards of right conduct and provide guidance not only in establishing a well ordered society, but also in distinguishing between 'good' and 'evil'. As a well-knit system of obligations, they safeguard the rights of all and as a product of Divine Wisdom which alone knows what the objective good is, they ensure the welfare of the entire humanity. The peculiarity of divine law is that it is eternal and immutable. The basis of life, as conceived by Islam, is spiritual. A society based on such a conception must have eternal and immutable laws, but since it does not lose sight of the material world which is subject to change, the laws contain broad principles that admit of interpretation so as to accommodate the change in life and to provide for the growing needs of society. Over and above is the Rule of Necessity and Need to provide facilities to those who are confronted with hardships.

> *Divine laws, thus, take in their sweep not only this world, but the world to come : 'Ye prefer the life of this world although the Hereafter is better and more lasting' (87 : 17). Islamic life, as such, is the harmonious blend of the material with the spiritual. Bare spirituality is never preached in Islam as it says 'yes' to life and to the worldly things. God has made all things in nature available for man so that he may harness them to suit his purpose: 'Whatever is in the heavens and whatever is in the earth are made of service unto him' (45 : 13).*

Divine law is unique in that it has its own permanent standards of justice. Hence justice according to Divine law is much higher than all other systems of justice, be they Greek, Roman or any other human law, for it searches the innermost motives. Justice, as conceived by Islam, is not only to give each his due, but also to return good for ill. What Islam suggests is the objective approach to the problem of justice, to put ourselves in the place of another, to see things from the standpoint of an impartial observer. Here are some of the Quranic verses to give an idea of impartiality :

> *'And when ye judge between people, judge with fairness' (4:58). 'O ye who believe! stand fast to justice, and for the sake of God always be truthful in giving evidence, though it be against your own selves or (your) parents or kinsfolk, whether the party be rich or poor: God safeguards the interests of both (parties). Therefore follow not your own inclinations lest you should swerve from justice. If you prevaricate or decline (to speak the truth),*

> *then verily God is aware of what you do' (4:135). 'O ye who believe! For the sake of God, stand up to uphold justice and let not ill-will towards any people impel you to deviate from justice. Act justly. This indeed is akin to piety. Be mindful of God; for assuredly, He knoweth all that ye do' (5 :9).*

Justice in Islam is conceived as a sacred trust, a duty imposed upon man to be discharged in all sincerity. 'To render justice', says Sarakhsi, 'constitutes one of the most noble acts of devotion' (*Mabsut*, vol. 16, p. 67). According to Kasani, 'it is one of the best acts of devotion and one of the most important duties after belief in God' (*Badai al-Sanai*, vol. 7, p. 4). Says the Caliph Abu Baker :

> *'By God, to me the powerful among you will be weak, and the weak among you powerful until I have taken for them their right' (Abu Ubayd,* Kitab al-Amwal, *p. 8).*

The Caliph Umar is reported to have said :

> *'No one will be allowed by me to treat others unjustly or to encroach upon their rights. Should anyone do so I will punish him severely so that he returns to others their rights' (Abu Yusuf,* Kitab-al-Kharaj *p. 167).*

The above sayings are in obedience to the Command of God which lays a preponderant stress on moral values :

> *'Verily, God enjoineth fairness of dealings and kindly behaviour (with others), and the giving to kindred (out of what you have); and forbiddeth lewdness and wrong-doing and oppression' (16 : 90). 'And do not touch the property of the orphan except to replace it with something better until he comes of age; give measured weight with, (full) justice;—no burden do We place on any soul but that which it can bear;—whenever ye speak, speak justly, even if a nearer relative is concerned; and fulfil the covenant of God: Thus doth He command you, that ye may remember' (6 : 152). Such is the morality and law of Islam. For details we refer the reader to our work Philosophy of Islamic Law I and the* Orientalists, *Islamic Publications, Lahore (Pakistan).*

Predestination : This has been the most disputed problem in the past and continues to be so in the present. For, if everything is determined or predestined by God, why should man be held responsible for his acts? This issue has given birth to two parties of opposite-views—Jabriyya or Fatalists and Qadriyya who are opposed to Fatalists.

To Fatalists, God must be tyrant and unjust if He punishes man for acts which, are not under his^ power and control. As opposed to this view, the Qadriyya hold that God is Just and is bound to be so. He would not punish man for such acts as are not in his power. Man, they say, has complete power over his actions: he has free-will and also choice and, as such, responsible for his acts.

Before we enter into further details, let us try to know, in the light of Quranic verses, the scheme of God and how it is carried out. It cannot be denied that God has power over all things (67 : 1), He created all things and ordered them in due proportions (2 : 52). He also created Death and Life, that He may try which of His creatures (men) is best in deed (67 : 2). Creation, therefore, is not without a purpose. God has created things with a measure (54 : 49) and also created their opposites, for things are known through their opposites.

Night has been created to "know the importance of Day and vice versa. Thus, world has been made a glittering show with all sorts of things to test the quality of man: 'That which is on earth, We have made but a glittering show for the earth, in order that We test them—as to which of them is of best conduct' (18 : 7). Evil and Good are both created by God as a trial, and test for us: 'And We test you by evil and by good by way of trial, to Us must ye return' (21 : 35).

As to the Will of God, 'He doeth what He will' (2 : 253). This is further supported by the Quranic verses: 'Thy Lord is doer of what He will' (11 : 107). 'His verily is all Creation and Commandment (7 : 54).

It may be noted that there are two aspects of His Commandment—Commandment relating to Creation (*amr takwini*) and Commandment relating to Right Conduct (*amr tashrii*). Creation includes both what He likes and what He dislikes, for example, He created the Devil and wickedness, while Righteousness is His love and approval. Man has to choose for himself, what is liked by God, with the help of the Rules of Right Conduct. Wickedness and sin do not fall under His liking and approval: 'He loveth not mischief (2 : 205). Ha liketh not ingratitude from His servants' (39 : 7).

And when ingratitude and wickedness transgress their limits punishment becomes inevitable. Even then God's Mercy gives every chance to the wicked to mend themselves and to repent. They are given a definite warning and if they still persist in their wickedness, the charge is proved against them and it is at this stage-that God's Commandment takes effect: 'When We decide to destroy a township, We send Commandment to its folk who live at ease, and afterwards they commit abomination therein, and so the Word (or doom) hath, effect for it, and We destroy it utterly' (17: 16); and it was never God's (part) that He should send a folk astray after He had guided them until He had made clear unto them what they should avoid' (9 : 115).

God's will is expressive of His unlimited power which renders everything possible for Him. 'He cannot be questioned for His acts but men will be questioned for theirs (21: 23). He may forgive whom He pleaseth and punish whom He pleaseth but, at the same time, He is Oft-Forgiving, Most Merciful (3 :129). This shows the tremendous Power which He commands and can use it at His Will and Pleasure but His Mercy gives chances to men so that they may correct themselves. If they fail to do so, it becomes just and fair for God to set seal on their hearts and on their hearing (2 : 7), and give rope to such as do not receive guidance and try them in their contumacy and then mete out a severe punishment for them. All this shows that God is not tyrant.

The Quranic verses which deal with God's severe penalty indicate His Power and Possibility to do any thing but the use of such power is not without justice-Although God can deal with His creatures in whatever manner He Hikes and is not bound by any law) to be just, yet 'not one will He treat with injustice' (18 : 46); 'nor shall He suffer to perish the reward of any who do a (single) righteous deed' (18 : 30). 'He never harms those who serve Him' (3 : 182); 'nor is He unjust' (41: 46).

From the foregoing it is proved that God is just and deals justly and as such, His determining of good and evil cannot be without justice. Further what is predetermined is not known to us, so why dispute it and call its fairness in question and why not believe in His Justice and Mercifulness. The best course is, therefore, to have implicit trust in the justness of God and ascribe every good to Him and evil to ourselves: 'Whatever good (O man!) happens to thee, is from God; but whatever evil happens to thee is from thyself (4 : 97). We have no reason to doubt God's fairness Who takes into consideration even an atom's weight of good and evil and passes His judgement in accordance therewith: 'And who so doeth good an atom's weight will see it then, and who so doeth the atom's weight of evil will see it then' (99: 7,8).

We cannot evaluate our acts. May be, we pride ourselves on our works and take them to be the righteous ones but in the judgement of God they are quite reverse. We may be under the impression that our efforts will be rewarded, while we are among 'those whose efforts have been wasted in this life, but they thought they were acquiring good by their works' (18 : 104). We cannot judge our acts, God alone is the best judge. Coming to the question of the Fatalists we feel that they are unnecessarily obsessed with the idea of determination. They must always expect good from God, for He does not intend anything evil for His creatures. Even' in the severe punishment which He has meted out there is our welfare. To meet the strict claims of justice equality is prescribed in cases of murder (2: 179). Life is taken for a life and in this law of equality, says the Quran, is the saving of life. And, indeed, it saves lives, being a lesson for all. Though the life of the murderer is lost but it brings peace to the society. Likewise hands of the thief are cut off (5 : 41) and in this lies the safety of property and protection of innocent people from crime. All the acts of God are, therefore, a Mercy to mankind and in their own interest.

We do not know what is really good for us and what is evil, 'Perchance ye dislike a thing which is good for you and that ye like a thing which is bad for you but God knoweth and ye know not' (2 : 216). So instead of questioning the predestination, of which we know nothing it is profitable to beseech God for His guidance and entreat Him to give what is good for us. The Prophet has rightly prescribed *istikhara* (asking good of God) in place of discussion on this topic. God in all His bountiful Mercy may grant us, what we ask for. 'Call Me', says He, 'I will answer your prayer.' (40: 60). Further, He has the power to efface the evil: God doth efface what He will and establishes what He will and with Him is the source of ordinance' (13 : 39).

Here the question may arise that God's knowledge of things would be defective if such changes take place. To this we answer that He is All-Powerful and can withhold Decree of Command which brings destiny into existence.

And it is for this reason that the Prophet laid stress on prayers. Pray often and in real earnest,' said he, 'for prayers can avert that which is inevitable (destiny).' We have to act upon it, for it is possible that God might have intended for us a better destiny on account of our entreaty and earnest prayer. Thus, His knowledge of things cannot be defective.

The followers of the Prophet asked him once as to what actually predestination meant and whether they should cease to work, for what is predestined is bound to happen. The Prophet in answer, exhorted them to work and to do righteous deeds and cited the Quranic verse:

> *'As for him who giveth (in charity) and is dutiful (toward God) and believeth in goodness: surely We will make smooth for him the Path of Bliss. But he who is greedy miser and deemeth himself self-sufficient and disbelieveth in goodness; surely We will make smooth for him the Path of Misery.* *(92 : 5-10).*

This is the best solution offered by the Prophet. Obsessed with the idea of determinism we should not cease to work, nor be indifferent to the world. The Path of Bliss will be made smooth for us if we have faith in God and do righteous deeds. For details, we refer the reader to our work Islam, its Theology and the Greek Philosophy, Islamic Publications, Ltd. Lahore (Pakistan).

Analysis and Assessment : On analysis we find that ethics is not a finished and complete subject. Socrates has rightly remarked: 'No system of ethics could be constructed until full attention had been devoted to the special features of moral experience and to the vagueness and contradictions of ordinary moral opinions. This required the philosophical intellect of the first rank concentrated on the problems of conduct' (*Ency. Britannica,* vol. 10, p. 762).

He went about showing that those who claimed to teach men how to live, poets, orators, and sophists were unable to define their views by argument or even to give adequate definitions of what they were claiming to explain. They were both inconsistent and ignorant. The problem is, therefore, to find what is absolute or objective good.

Nietzsche adopts an attitude of moral relativism. To him, that only is good which leads to enhancement of the will to power, and because in different times and climes it is possible to achieve this result with the help of different moral devices, he did not see any point in prescribing a universal code of morals. He insisted on the inversion of values because he saw in the prevailing Christian values nothing but nihilism and decadence.. Morality, he says, has been only a weapon in the hands of those who had the will to gain power, hence various systems to suit the various ends. He who is strong and powerful is on the right side, and who is weak is destined to be reckoned as false.

The classical ethical theories are characterised by their efforts to answer two questions: 'What is the good life ?' and 'How ought men to behave ?' Moral theories like Hedonism, Cynicism, Stoicism, Utilitarianism and so on seem to be of highest complex nature. We find ourselves constrained to support G. E. Moore who claimed, in his *Principia Ethica,* that the classical theories were attempts to deduce moral precepts from theological, metaphysical or scientific premises and that such arguments are fallacious, since one cannot argue from premises of one logical type (i.e., descriptions) to conclusions of a different logical type (i.e., prescriptions). Moral theories which appear plausible at a first glance, such as Hedonism, are found upon careful examination to suffer from serious defects. How can the good life be identical with a life of pleasure, since there are pleasures which are bad ? For example, pleasures such as drinking alcohol, give us momentary pleasure but may result in a life of subsequent pain and travail.

The various answers which classical theories give are in the form of advice rather than an effort to define moral words like 'good', 'bad' and so on. Hedonism, for instance, may be regarded as advising men that good life consists of pleasure, and further that they ought to act so as to acquire pleasure. But the word 'good' is not defined and, indeed, 'good' like all moral words, is indefinable and that 'goodness' is an unanalysable property. Any attempted definitions of moral words will be in terms only of their descriptive meaning and no more.

> *Good and evil are thus, described in terms of pleasure and pain. So far as 'Utilitarian Ethics' is concerned it assumes that man is motivated by the desire to secure pleasurable and avoid painful experiences. The Utilitarians have their own suspicions of reason and look to human observation and experience in order to find what men actually value. Instead of judging the conduct by the feelings and motives, they would judge it by its consequences. Each individual, they held, is really seeking his happiness above everything else. If then we are to find a moral standard in what men actually value, we must find it not in the heavens alone but in human happiness.* *(Dewey,* Ethic, *p. 167).*

> *The essence of Bentham's philosophy is that nature has placed man under the empire of pleasure and pain. We owe to them all our ideas; we refer to them all our judgements, and all the determinations of our life. He who pretends to withdraw himself from this subjection knows not what he says. His only object is to seek pleasure and shun pain... .These eternal and irresistible sentiments ought to be the great study of the moralist and the legislator. The principle of utility subjects everything to these two motives'*
>
> *(Bentham, The Theory of Legislation, p. 2).*

Bentham's theory is criticized as contradictory in itself. According to its conception of desire and motive, the whole object of all actions is the obtaining of personal pleasure, while the proper standard for judging the morality of act is its contribution to the welfare of others. In Bentham's theory 'desire for private pleasure as the sole motive of action and universal benevolence as the principle of approval are at war with each other'.

'It would be only a poor sort of happiness' remarked George Eliot in her *Romola*, 'that could ever come by caring very much for our narrow pleasures'. Personal pleasure is indeed a low sort of pleasure and it is better to be a human being dissatisfied than a pig satisfied.

Further, pleasure has no sound basis, for it depends mostly upon the existing state of a person:

> *'What is agreeable at one time, disagrees at another; what pleases in health is distasteful in illness; what annoys or disgusts in a state of repletion is gratifying when one is hungry and eager. And on a higher scale, that which is pleasant to men of generous disposition arouses aversion in a mean and stingy person; what is pleasant to a child may bore an adult; the objects that gratify a scholar are repulsive to a boor' (Dewey, Ethics, p. 213).*

In fact, there can be no standard of judgement as to know what exactly constitutes pleasure and, morally speaking, pleasure as an end cannot be considered 'good', for a villain takes pleasure in his wickedness. The Utilitarian theory, that pleasure is the good and the end, is baseless and immoral. It may have been clear by now that Morality cannot be adequately defined and Ethics fails to be a science. But the subjectivists, for instance, Hedonists contend that their moral judgements are not false but true. Moral theories, in this respect, are classified into subjectivistic and objectivistic. This raises the question of defining subjectivism and objectivism.

Subjectivism : Subjectivism is the doctrine that all knowledge is subjective only and incapable of objective proof. It is commonly held that there is no reality other than the reality of things which we see, touch, hear, smell or taste. This leads to deny the existence of an order of reality which is not open to the investigation and subject to the laws of science and equally denies, with regard to human conduct, that there is anything real in the psychological realm other than the series of emotions, desires, impulses, hopes and thoughts which make up the stream of our consciousness.

Hence a thing is good not because it is characterized by goodness or is really good but because we desire it and it gives us happiness.

Suppose if someone denies this sort of conclusion as ascetics are said to have done, maintaining that we should mortify the flesh here for the happiness to be attained in the Hereafter, what will be the reply? Further, if we ask a subjectivist, 'How do you know that pleasure is a good ?' He has no reasoned answer, he just sees to be so. Finally, as we have already-explained pleasure has no definite meaning.

The argument which is advanced in support of subjectivism may be called the argument from Sentience. The subjectivists argue that no question of good or bad can arise in a world which has no sentient being —beings that are capable of feeling, for it would not make sense to say that anything good or bad could happen to inanimate objects such as a rock or stone. It is only if some sentient being is affected by these events, or could be affected by them, that it makes sense to say that they are good or bad. Goodness and badness thus seem to depend upon the feelings, attitudes and desires of sentient beings. From considerations such as these it is argued that some form of subjectivism must be true.

But if we probe deep into such argument it becomes evident that what it proves is not the good or bad as it actually is but as it is thought or felt. Moral judgements of this type cannot be called sound ethical judgements since they depend not only upon emotions,, desires, and feelings of persons making such judgements but also on their ethical, traditional, social, economic and other sentiments. It is on this account that these judgements not only differ from one another but are also conflicting so much so that even vices and crimes-are considered virtues. Says Canon Rashdall, a well-known authority on ethical philosophy:

> *'There is hardly a vice or crime (according to our own moral standard) which has not at some time or other in some circumstances been looked- upon as a moral and religious duty. Stealing was accounted virtuous for the young Spartan and among the Indian caste of Thugs. In the ancient world Piracy, i.e. robbery and murder, was a respectable profession. To the Mediaeval Christian religious persecution was the highest of duties, and so on'* *(C. E. M. Jood,* Philosophy, *P- 31).*

Under the circumstances it may be said that just as science is content with a world of matter in motion, the subjectivist ethics is content with a world of human consciousness which consists of nothing except the stream of emotions, desires, impulses, hopes and thoughts. The peculiarity of the subjectivist theories of ethics is that they do not accept the view that there is an 'object' which possesses ethical qualities of its own, with the corollary that there can be correct ethical judgement.

For a better understanding of subjectivist theories let us call a person making an ethical judgement 'the subject' and the character to which the judgement refers 'the object'. The ethical judgements are called subjectivistic as they do not refer to the object which they support but to the subject, being judgements to the effect that the subject is experiencing certain feelings. The good according to such theories is not the good in its own right but according as is experienced by the subject, i.e., the maker of ethical judgement. It, therefore, follows that if such theories are considered to be correct then 'good' has no ethical quality of its own, for, the good, in such a case, is only what is thought 'good'. Let us turn to objectivism and see whether its ethical judgements are correct.

Objectivism : Objective means actually existing, not Subjective only. Hence objectivism is the tendency to lay stress upon what is objective or external to the mind.

> *The main argument in favour of objectivism is that; it provides a theory which corresponds more closely to the views of men of common sense about moral matters than subjectivism. To mark the difference between subjectivism and objectivism we cite an example of 'two persons who have just entered a room and asked to guess its temperature; the one is supposed to have recently emerged from a refrigerator, the other from a hot-house; the former guesses 75°F., the latter 70°F. It is clear that two subjective conditions prevailing in the bodies of the two judges have determined the guesses that they make as to the temperature of the room; what they do not determine is the temperature of the room. What both judges are purporting to assess is a certain condition which prevails in the world independently of their judgements, and most of us would agree that, since the temperature of the room can be measured by a thermometer, there is a perfectly definite sense in holding that judgement according to thermometer is Objective and correct, while another judgement to the effect that it is something else is wrong and incorrect' (C. E. M. Jood,* Philosophy, *pp. 133,134).*

The difference between the case in which we judge about the temperature and the case in which we judge about ethical qualities is that in the former we can refer to an instrument, the thermometer, by reference to which we can determine what the objective temperature is and pronounce our judgement to be nearer to the truth than the other, whereas there is no equivalent instrument wherewith to measure ethical judgements. Here is the difficulty and it is perhaps for this reason that the subjectivists contend that all knowledge is subjective and incapable of objective proof. Let us turn to Kant and see if his moral theory can solve this problem.

In his analysis of human impulses and desires Kant goes all the way with subjectivists that man is merely a creature of likes and dislikes, of wants and needs, of impulses and tastes, of preferences and prejudices, but, he says, there is one characteristic unique in nature, and man being possessed of it, cannot be adequately regarded as wholly a child of nature. In addition to the impulses and desires which tell him -what he would like to do, he is, on occasion, conscious of something else, namely, what he ought to do which may be very opposite to what he would like to do. Thus, for man there is a distinction between 'want' and 'ought', between 'desire' and 'duty'; moral sense is innate in him and not derived from experience. Moral sense, says Kant, is our unescapable feeling in the face of our temptation that this or that is wrong. An act is good not because it has good results or because it is aright, but because it is done in obedience to the inner sense of duty. Morality is not properly the doctrine how we make ourselves happy but how we make ourselves worthy of happiness.

To comprehend the unique significance of 'ought' Kant insists that man must be a member of some other order of reality. Thus, he can win free from the influences of heredity, circumstances and environment which otherwise determine his psychology. To see Kant's moral philosophy in its proper setting we have to study it in its association with his metaphysical theory. Kant says that when we will to do our duty in pursuance of ought' and in the face of disinclination, we are making direct contact not with the familiar world which appears to our senses, but with the world as it is independently of ourselves—a moral world and an order of reality which contains the value of morality such as right and good. It is not with our minds and our intellects that we recognize what is right and realize what ought to be done, but by the 'practical' as opposed to the 'theoretical' reason—a faculty similar, in modern concept, to intuition. The central feet of morals appeared to him to be the voice of duty from within the soul itself. Thus the familiar world of common sense is not the only world, there is another world and order of reality which is spiritual and which contains values of morality. This implies the existence of a mind, other than our own, which not only knows but also creates values—a Law-giver who lays down the moral law or order of the universe. The argument, in this way, passes over from ethics to religion.

With God as the Law-giver the problem is solved. He alone knows the objective good and we cannot know it as we often dislike a thing which is good for us and like a thing which is bad for us: 'Perchance you dislike a thing which may be good for you ; and perchance you like a thing which may be bad for you'. To know the objective good is beyond our power and it is in His law alone that we find the required instrument and standard for correct ethical judgements. 'Good', here is not what is thought 'good' but the 'objective and absolute good'. The question, is now, 'What is the good life, in its real sense, and' how ought men to behave?'

Standard Ideas

***Plato: Evil is Due to Lack of Knowledge*:** In most of the classical theories it is assumed that if we know what the good life is we will naturally behave in such a way as to try to achieve it.

Platonism, for instance, holds that evil is due to lack of knowledge; if a man discovers what is right he will never act wickedly. But the problem is how to discover 'the right' or 'the good' and how can this be done when men hold different and conflicting opinions about the good life? In answer to this Plato says that the discovery of the nature of things is an intellectual task, hence to discover what the good life is one must be trained in various disciplines such as mathematics, philosophy and so on. It is only through such intellectual training that men would have the capacity to know the nature of the good life. Even without this sort of training it is possible for some men to lead good life but they will do so haphazardly or blindly. There may be some men who do not have intellectual power to apprehend what the 'good life' is, but they will act virtuously if they follow those who have knowledge of the good. This finds expression in Plato's famous work 'The Republic', which speaks of Philosopher King as the most efficient ruler, for he is possessed of knowledge of 'the good' and can lead men to the good life.

According to Plato, there is fundamentally one and only one good life for all men to lead because goodness is something which is not dependent upon man's inclinations desires or wishes but is absolute as it exists independently of men and remains to be discovered if men can be properly trained. Such is the absolutism in Plato's philosophy.

From the above it is evident that Plato regards morality as being a matter of knowledge but only a few are intellectually gifted to have such ability. It is not sufficient to say that those of us who have not the ability- can live good lives by being led by those who have, since to behave morally presupposes that one has responsibility for one's actions and an action is not truly moral or immoral unless it is the result of free choice of the individual performing it. Aristotle seems aware of these defects in Plato's theory, since he adopts his own doctrine of morality.

Aristotle: Doctrine of the Golden Mean : Aristotle, though a great metaphysician, but, curiously enough, in his ethical writings he adopts a scientific or empirical approach to ethical problems. Instead of trying to discover the nature of the good life for all men by reflection alone, he examined the behaviour of various people in every day life. He noticed that the various lives that men of common sense consider to be good all contain, one common characteristic, i.e. happiness. Hence he frankly admits that the aim of life is not goodness for it own sake, but happiness.

His doctrine of Golden Mean is explained as follows:

Being happy, according to Aristotle, is like being well-fed. How much food should a man eat in order to be well-fed? To Aristotle, there is no general answer to this question in the sense of specific amount. It depends on the size of the man, what sort of work he does, whether he is ill or well, and so on. The proper amount for anyone to eat can be ascertained by trial and error: if we eat a certain amount of food and still feel hungry, we should eat more ; if we eat the same amount and feel uncomfortable, then we should eat less. The correct amount is a 'mean between eating too much and too little.

But the 'mean' cannot be interpreted as being synonymous with 'average'. Suppose that one pound of food per day is too little, and that two pounds is too much. Does this suggest that the average amount (i.e., one pound and a half) is the correct amount ? Aristotle's answer is that it may or may not be—but in general, one cannot say that the correct amount is exactly one pound and a half ; all one can say is that it is an amount somewhere between one pound and two pounds; and this is what Aristotle intends by the word 'mean'. Further, it will be seen from the above that Aristotle's mean varies from man to man. The golden mean, however, is not, like the mathematical mean, an exact average of two precisely calculable extremes; it fluctuates with the collateral , circumstances of each situation and is subject to flexible reason.

The theory of Aristotle is subject to some criticism as in certain situations it is difficult to follow the mean. For example, there is no 'mean' between keeping a promise and not keeping one. The same applies to telling the truth: either one does or does not tell the truth. But we have to bear in mind that the question of mean arises only when there is the possibility of going to extremes.

Hedonism : To Plato, the good life is in no way connected with pleasure, but Aristotle moderated this doctrine in holding that 'pleasure must be in some way an ingredient of happiness'. Epicurus disagreed with both of them and held a view which is called 'Hedonism', the doctrine that pleasure is the sole good. To him, morality is identical with expedience. The ethical philosophy of Epicurus consists mainly of advice for living moderately but pleasantly. While discovering pleasure to be good he also realized that if a person pursues pleasure too arduously, pain will follow. For example, if a man drinks too much, it will result in headache. Since some pleasures are obviously followed by pain, Epicurus distinguished between those pleasures which are followed by pain and those which are not and regarded only the latter as good. He called the former 'dynamic' pleasures and the latter as 'passive' pleasures. Sexual love, for example, is bad because it is accompanied by fatigue, remorse and depression. He advocated avoidance of such pleasures as are bad, for he believed that it is better to avoid pain than to seek pleasure if it will produce pain.

Hedonism, though theoretically attractive, may be seen to violate our ordinary feelings about what constitutes behaviour. The objection is not that it seeks superficial and narrow pleasures but, more fundamentally, that pleasure is not the sole object which men should strive for.

Cynicism : It is the philosophy of the Cynics, founded by Antisthenes, a pupil of Socrates, who condemned ease, -wealth, and enjoyment of life. The most famous was Diogenes who carried principles to an extreme. This is the philosophy which holds that if salvation is to be found it is to be found in a rejection of society and in a return to simple life—to a life of asceticism.

The word 'Cynic' comes from the Greek word 'Kunos', which means 'dog-like'. Diogenes, for example, is supposed to have lived in a large tub, and rejected all refinements—of dress, food, personal cleanliness. The Cynics believed that the world was fundamentally evil; in order to live properly a man must withdraw from participation in it. Cynicism is not only anti-social, but also contributed largely to undermine the social standards, contending that only individual virtue was of essential importance. As a philosophy Cynicism has had a great influence upon plain man and is considered to have been a major factor in the development of early Christian philosophy. The monk is no better than a Cynic for he casts aside the world and lives the life of a cave or monastery, while monasticism is not permissible in Islam.

Stoicism : Stoicism has been the most influential ethical doctrine of the ancient Western World before Christianity. Zeno was the founder of Stoicism and is supposed to have lectured in the third century B.C. from a porch, and stoicism gets its name from this fact, since 'stoa' is the Greek word for 'porch'. The basic tenet of stoicism for achieving personal salvation is just like that of the Cynics and can be summed up in one-sentence. Learn to be indifferent to external influences! It is a philosophy of indifference. By practising indifference one becomes independent of the world.

The Stoics believed in predestination, i.e. that all happenings in the world are fixed by God according to some preconceived plan, and that virtue consists in a will which is in agreement with the happenings of nature. Further, they considered it important to free oneself from desires and passions. Stoicism differs from Cynicism in that the Cynics felt that they were powerless to prevent the collapse of the world in which they lived and hence they renounced it, while the Stoics argued that this sort of renunciation was unnecessary, for man need not renounce the material things of the world provided that he does not become involved in them. If he remains indifferent to them and uneffected by them there is no reason why he should not continue to enjoy them. The Stoics hold that man is not free but instead is chained to his destinies in accordance with the divine-plan. But this view is inconsistent with their view that, a man can alter his character and can change his frame of mind in such a manner that he will become-indifferent to things that he formerly prized. If man is free and has power to alter his character and to-change his frame of mind, then the thesis that all events are predetermined by some master plan must be false. The problem of Freedom of the Will is the most baffling one. It has not only appeared in Stoic-philosophy but also occurs in religious philosophy as-well as in modern psychology. Islam is the religion, which has found a clue to its solution as will be explained later.

Spinoza: The Ethics : Spinoza is reckoned as one of the towering figures in the history of Ethics. He was a rigid determinist as he says, 'All things come to pass, come to pass according to the eternal order and fixed laws of Nature'. Thus he was in the metaphysical tradition of the Stoics-In holding that nothing is good or bad in itself, but is only so in relation to someone, Spinoza is a relativist. From this point of view of Spinoza riches, fame and sensual pleasure are all not inherently worthwhile. They are not worth acquiring for their own sake but only as means to making human life more happy. When these things affect men in desirable ways, they are good, but when they affect them in undesirable ways, they are bad.

According to him good life consists in the recognition of the truth that all events are determined and a man will be happy when he comes to understand that there are limits to human power and that everything which happens must happen necessarily. This sort of attitude, says he, if developed, will liberate men from fear, anxiety and unhappiness. These arise only when a man becomes slave to his emotions. Spinoza's masterpiece is The Ethics which is considered to be his great work by many philosophers but he did not effectively resolve the conflict that exists between determinism and freedom. He believed that all events in nature are determined which means that man is essentially powerless. The question is: 'how can he change his attitude and frame of mind towards life and be free from anxieties when he is powerless ?'

Bentham and Stuart Mill—Utilitarianism : One of the earliest exponents of this moral theory was Francis Hutcheson but the most famous exponents of it are Jermy Bentham and John Stuart Mill who attempted to lay down a principle for determining the rightness or wrongness of an act and called this maxim the Principle of Utility. According to this principle an action is right in so far it tends to produce the greatest happiness for the greatest number and happiness is taken to mean pleasure. The fundamental point is that it is consequences of a given action which determine its rightness or wrongness, not the motive from which it is done. The object is to separate the rightness or wrongness of an action from the goodness or badness of the person who performs the action.

There are certain objections raised against Utilitarianism and Nietzsche describes Mill as a 'block head' for his assumption that in computing the amount of happiness or unhappiness, which an action creates, each man will count equally for one unit of happiness. Nietzsche believed that some people were inherently more important than others and their happiness or unhappiness counted for more than the happiness or unhappiness of the average man. Carlyle, on the other hand, condemned Utilitarianism as 'a universal syllabus of sentimental twaddle'. Further, there are some philosophers who rejected Utilitarianism on the ground that consideration in assessing the moral worth of our action must be given to the motive from which it is done.

Kantian Moral Philosophy : According to Kant ethics is the most important subject in philosophy. He believes in the moral basis of religion. He even used ethical arguments to establish the existence of God. Since men who are not virtuous are happier in this world there must be another world for virtuous men to be rewarded and this leads him to the conclusion that there is God and an eternal life.

'What is the nature of morality' is the main question which Kant's moral theory was formulated to answer. Kant believed that the key to answer this question lay in distinguishing between acts done from 'inclination' and acts done from a 'sense duty-or obligation'. An obligations that which a map ought to do despite his inclination to do otherwise. Some philosophers have held that in matters of morality one should act upon his inclinations but Kant rejects such an account of morality. For him, a man is acting morally only when he suppresses his inclinations and obeys the command of duty. Further, he makes a distinction between actions which are 'in accord with duty' and those done 'from duty'. The former are not moral acts but the latter are. Most parents, for instance, are inclined to take care of their children because they are fond of them but this does not amount to moral act as it is in accordance with duty and not from duty. A man who understands the nature of his duty and acts upon it is moral and not otherwise. According to him the concept of goad and evil must not be determined before the law. But only after it and by means of it'. Thus he subordinates good to moral law. Briefly, a moral action is that which is done from 'a respect for duty and a moral person is he who acts 'from duty', not from inclination or even in accord with duty. Kant differs sharply from the Utilitarians in that he stresses the point that the essence of morality is to be found in the motive from which an act is done. A man who keeps promises by accident is not a moral man. Every action, says he, must be judged in the light of how it would appear if it were to be a universal code of behaviour. All that is required is to know our duty in a particular case and ask ourselves if the motive of that act can be made universal without falling into self-contradiction. For example, says he, 'May I when in distress, make a promise with intention not to keep it?'

Evidently, this principle, if made universal, simply contradicts itself, for with such a promise there would be no such thing as a promise. No one would like to be content with a false or deceitful promise. The principle of right action, in this light, may be summed up as: 'Act in a way that you would like to be paid back in your own coin' or 'Act as if the maxim of thy action were to become by thy will a universal law of nature'. This is according to Kant, the unconditional command of our conscience—a categorical imperative. Another categorical imperative formulated by Kant is: 'So act as to treat humanity, whether in thine own person or in that of -another, in every case as an end, never as a means only.' Another way of putting such maxim is 'Do unto others as you would have them do unto you.' We should treat others as ends in themselves because that is how we regard ourselves. To treat another man only as a means to achieve our end is to disregard his humanity, hence immoral. It is said that Kant's theory is inconsistent in that he has not held to his original claim that he is concerned solely with motive and not consequences. The objection is on the basis that Kant introduces consequences of the act in tacitly showing that the effect of not behaving in accordance with the categorical imperative would be to make human life impossible.

The Sympathy

Kindness is a basic quality of the human nature, which softens the heart when informed about the sufferings of the fellow creatures and makes one restless for providing relief to them. This quality makes a man feel sorry for the mistakes of others and causes him to guide them properly. This is a natural quality, because if this feeling of kindness dies, and it is not at all moved on occasions of happiness and sorrow, then a man falls to the level of animals, and all his virtues are vanished. This feeling is created by love and sympathy. Some times some vague feelings are created in animals too, on account of which they show some kindness to their offsprings, and for this reason hard-heartedness or cruelty is a trend which is lower and meaner than the tendency found in the animals. Nay, a cruel person is like the inanimate objects that have no feelings and no consciousness, and they are not moved by anything. Kindness, in its highest and vast sense, is the attribute of the Almighty, God. His kindness is for all the existing things and covers the entire universe, wherever the ray of His knowledge (which encloses the entire universe) falls. The angels, in his praise, pray to him:

> *Therefore, grant salvation to those who have repented and have followed Your path, and save them from the punishment of hell.* *(Momin:7)*

It is narrated by Hadrat Umar bin Khattab (R.A.A.) that in the presence of the Prophet (S.A.W.) a female-slave was brought along with other prisoners. This woman was running here and there and trying to expel milk from her breasts. If she saw any child, she embraced it and suckled it. The Prophet (S.A.W.) saw this condition of the woman and said:

> *"What do you think, can this woman throw her child into the fire?" They replied: "No, by God, this woman cannot throw her child into the fire." The Prophet (S.A.W.) then said: "Allah is more kind to His slaves than this woman is kind to her child."* *(Bukhari)*

Most names of Allah carry the meaning of Kindness, Graciousness, Favour, Forgiveness and the like. A *Hadith Qudsi* states:

> *"My kindness surpasses My anger."* *(Muslim)*

That is, to forgive humans for their lapses and errors is liked by Him more than to punish them, and therefore, He is more kind than the other people.

> *O Prophet! Say : 'My Lord, pardon, and be kind, and You are the Most Kind of all the kind people'.*
> *(Muminoon : 118)*

Today on this earth the blooming flowers of mutual love, good conduct, graciousness, and virtue that we see, are the reflections of the Divine Graciousness, only a small part of it He has placed in the hearts of His creatures. The most soft-hearted man among men is he who has received the greater portion of this kindness, and who has more sympathy with the life of the weak persons.

The cruel, the hard-hearted tyrants and the conceited persons of the nation will find their abode in the lowest part of the hell.

> *The man who is cruel and hard-hearted will be the farthest away from Allah.* *(Tirmidhi)*

Allah's Messenger (S.A.W.) considered the dryness of the eyes and hardness of the heart as signs of ill-luck.

When Allah wanted to be gracious in view of the bad conditions on the earth and to send down a person who would remove the sorrow of the people of the world, who would tend to their wounds, who would sympathise with them on their lapses, who would inconvenience himself for their guidance, who would cause the strong to give the rights of the weak, who would fight for their rights and for their protection, who would convert the rebellious and tyrant men into kind-hearted human beings, He sent down, for all these purposes, Muhammad (S.A.W.)

He placed treasures of knowledge and forbearance in his heart. He instilled in his character the light of virtue and righteousness. He made softness and kindness his second nature. He embellished his character with the qualities of charity and generosity. All these excellent qualities made Muhammad (S.A.W.) the most soft-hearted, kind, broad-minded and generous of all the men in the world:

> *It was by the mercy of Allah that you were lenient with them (O Muhammad), for if you had been stern and fierce of heart they would have dispersed from round about you.*
> *(Al-i-Imran : 159)*

This quality was also seen in action it the Battle of Uhud when the polytheists were poised to kill him. He was thrown into a pit so that he may die there. He saw his companions dying around him. His remaining companions looked at him and found that there were scratches on his cheeks and some of his teeth were broken. On this crucial occasion, they pleaded with him to subject them to a curse. He prayed: "O Allah! Give guidance to my community, they know not what they are doing." Pious men act in this manner only. The motivations of cruelty and tyranny do not excite their hearts. In the face of wrath and rage, tyranny and revenge, they always show mercy, forgiveness and kindness. Cruelty is a very wicked thing for an individual to have. In the history of nations it has caused great upheavals. We should not be surprised to learn that Islam has warned us against it, and has declared it as a rebellion against God and deviation from the right path.

> *Has not the time arrived for the believers that their hearts in all humility should engage in remembrance of Allah and of the Truth which has been revealed to them and that they should not become like those to whom was given Revelation aforetime, but long ages passed over them and their hearts grew hard ? For many among them are rebellious transgressors.* *(Hadid : 16)*

Islam has commanded Muslims to be kind to all creatures and all humans, and has considered it a proof of perfect faith. A Muslim meets all Muslims. For them he has a feeling of love, sympathy and kindness in his heart. For them he extends his hand of cooperation and tries, as far as it is in his power, to remove their troubles and difficulties.

Allah's Messenger (S.A.W.) has said:

> *"You cannot be a Momin until you are not kind among yourselves." The companions said that they were all kind. He said: "Kindness is not this that you sympathise with your companion, but kindness is this that you should think all men deserving of it."* *(Tibrani)*

When a man meets his friends, sympathy is naturally created. When a man looks at his children, feelings of love and kindness are generated. This is a common thing. Bat for a Muslim it is certain that the sphere of his kindness is widest. He treats all humans with kindness and love and meets them with a smiling face.

There are many traditions in which this general kindness has been recommended for Muslims. The Prophet (S.A.W.) has said:

> *He who does not show mercy to the people, Allah also does not show mercy to him.* *(Bukhari)*

In another tradition it is said : "He who does not forgive others, Allah also does not forgive him."

Yet another *Hadith* says:

> *"How lucky is that man who adopts humbleness without having scarcity, who considers himself inferior without having to beg for anything, who spends his own earned money in the right causes without disobeying Allah, who is kind to the inferior and mean persons, and remains in the company of the learned men and the intellectuals." (Tibrani)*

Allah has stated that the characteristic of the Muslim Society is that it is humble towards its own people and stern towards the others.

> *Humble towards believers, stern towards disbelievers. (Maidah : 54)*

At another place it is said:

> *Hard against the disbelievers, kind among themselves. (Fath : 29)*

Humble towards their Own People and Stern towards Others : Here a question can be raised: What is the relevance of discussing hardness and sternness when the talk is about Rahmat and kindness? The fact is that Islam talks of general kindness and does not keep out any person, animal or bird from it, and the authorities quoted above, all support the exhortation for the general kindness. But some men and animals are such as are a cause of danger and a source of terror for others. In their cases the demand of the public benefit is that their evil should be cut short and their menace should be put a stop to. Sometimes sternness with a person proves to be beneficial to him and serves as a whip against his going astray.

Islam is entirely a religion of peace. It commands its followers to be gracious and kind to all mankind. Allah addresses His Messenger (S.A.W.) and says:

> *"We sent you not save as a Mercy for the peoples." (Ambiya : 107)*

All the Quranic Surahs are commenced with this verse:

> *In the name of Allah, Most Gracious, Most Merciful.*

Chapter 5

Islamic Jurisprudence

Traditional Islamic Jurisprudence

In Islamic jurisprudence, slavery was an exceptional condition, with the general rule being a presumption of freedom (*al-'asl huwa 'l-hurriya* — "*The basic principle is liberty*") for a person if his or her origins were unknown, though enslavement was sanctioned by God as punishment for unbelief. Lawful enslavement was restricted to two instances: capture in war (on the condition that the prisoner is not a Muslim), or birth in slavery. Islamic law did not recognize the classes of slave from pre-Islamic Arabia including those sold or given into slavery by themselves and others, and those indebted into slavery. Though a free Muslim could not be enslaved, conversion to Islam by a non-Muslim slave did not require that he or she then should be liberated. Slave status was not affected by conversion to Islam.

Treatment

In the instance of illness it would be required for the slave to be looked after. Manumission is considered a meritorious act. Based on the Quranic verse, the Islamic law permits a slave to ransom himself upon consent of his master through a contract known as *mukataba*. Azizah Y. al-Hibri, a professor of Law specializing in Islamic jurisprudence, states that both the Quran and Hadith are repeatedly exhorting Muslims to treat the slaves well and that Muhammad showed this both in action and in words.

Levy concurs, adding that "cruelty to them was forbidden." Al-Hibri quotes the famous last speech of Muhammad and other hadiths emphasizing that all believers, whether free or enslaved, are siblings.

Lewis explains, "the humanitarian tendency of the Quran and the early caliphs in the Islamic empire, was to some extent counteracted by other influences," notably the practice of various conquered people and countries Muslims encountered, especially in provinces previously under Roman law (even the Christianized form of slavery was still harsh in its treatment of slaves). In spite of this, Lewis also states, "Islamic practice still represented a vast improvement on that inherited from antiquity, from Rome, and from Byzantium." Murray Gordon writes: "It was not surprising that Muhammad, who accepted the existing socio-political order, looked upon slavery as part of the natural order of things. His approach to what was already an age-old institution was reformist and not revolutionary. The Prophet had not in mind to bring about the abolition of slavery. Rather, his purpose was to improve the conditions of slaves by correcting abuses and appealing to the conscience of his followers to treat them humanely." The adoption of slaves as members of the family was common, according to Levy. If a slave was born and brought up in the master's household he was never sold, except in exceptional circumstances.

Legal Status

Within Islamic jurisprudence, slaves were excluded from religious office and from any office involving jurisdiction over others. Freed slaves are able to occupy any office within the Islamic government, and instances of this in history include the Mamluk who ruled Egypt for almost 260 years and the eunuchs who have held military and administrative positions of note. With the permission of their owners they are able to marry. Annemarie Schimmel, a contemporary scholar on Islamic civilization, asserts that because the status of slaves under Islam could only be obtained through either being a prisoner of war (this was soon restricted only to infidels captured in a holy war) or born from slave parents, slavery would be theoretically abolished with the expansion of Islam. Fazlur Rahman agrees, stating that the Quranic acceptance of the institution of slavery on the legal plane was the only practical option available at the time of Muhammad since "slavery was ingrained in the structure of society, and its overnight wholesale liquidation would have created problems which it would have been absolutely impossible to solve, and only a dreamer could have issued such a visionary statement." Islam's reforms stipulating the conditions of enslavement seriously limited the supply of new slaves. Murray Gordon does not: "Muhammad took pains in urging the faithful to free their slaves as a way of expiating their sins. Some Muslim scholars have taken this mean that his true motive was to bring about a gradual elimination of slavery. Far more persuasive is the argument that by lending the moral authority of Islam to slavery, Muhammad assured its legitimacy. Thus, in lightening the fetter, he riveted it ever more firmly in place." In the early days of Islam, a plentiful supply of new slaves were brought due to rapid conquest and expansion. But as the frontiers were gradually stabilized, this supply dwindled to a mere trickle. The prisoners of later wars between Muslims and Christians were commonly ransomed or exchanged.

According to Lewis, this reduction resulted in Arabs who wanted slaves having to look elsewhere to avoid the restrictions in the Quran, meaning an increase of importing of slaves from non-Muslim lands, primarily from Africa. These slaves suffered a high death toll. Patrick Manning states that Islamic legislations against the abuse of the slaves convincingly limited the extent of enslavement in Arabian peninsula and to a lesser degree for the whole area of the whole Umayyad Caliphate where slavery had existed since the most ancient times. He however notes that with the passage of time and the extension of Islam, Islam by recognizing and codifying the slavery seems to have done more to protect and expand slavery than the reverse.

In theory free-born Muslims could not be enslaved, and the only way that a non-Muslim could be enslaved was being captured in the course of holy war. (In early Islam, neither a Muslim nor a Christian or Jew could be enslaved.) Slavery was also perceived as a means of converting non-Muslims to Islam: A task of the masters was religious instruction. Conversion and assimilation into the society of the master didn't automatically lead to emancipation, though there was normally some guarantee of better treatment and was deemed a prerequisite for emancipation. The majority of Sunni authorities approved the manumission of all the "People of the Book". According to some jurists-especially among the Shia-only Muslim slaves should be liberated. In practice, traditional propagators of Islam in Africa often revealed a cautious attitude towards proselytizing because of its effect in reducing the potential reservoir of slaves.

Rights and Restrictions

"Morally as well as physically the slave is regarded in law as an inferior being," Levy writes. Under Islamic law, a slave possesses a composite quality of being both a person and a possession. The slave is entitled to receive sustenance from the master, which includes shelter, food, clothing, and medical attention. It is a requirement for this sustenance to be of the same standard generally found in the locality and it is also recommended for the slave to have the same standard of food and clothing as the master. If the master refuses to provide the required sustenance, the slave may complain to a judge, who may then penalize the master through sale of her or his goods as necessary for the slave's keep. If the master does not have sufficient wealth to facilitate this, she or he must either sell, hire out, or manumit the slave as ordered. Slaves also have the right to a period of rest during the hottest parts of the day during the summer. Evidence from slaves is rarely viable in a court of law. As slaves are regarded as inferior in Islamic law, death at the hands of a free man does not require that the latter be killed in retaliation.

The killer must pay the slave's master compensation equivalent to the slave's value, as opposed to blood-money. At the same time, slaves themselves possess a lessened responsibility for their actions, and receive half the penalty required upon a free man. For example: where a free man would be subject to a hundred lashes due to pre-marital relations, a slave would be subject to only fifty. Slaves are allowed to marry only with the owner's consent. Jurists differ over how many wives a slave may possess, with the Hanafi and Shafii schools allowing them two, and the Maliki school allowing four. Slaves are not permitted to possess or inherit property, or conduct independent business, and may conduct financial dealings only as a representative of the master. Offices of authority are generally not permitted for slaves, though a slave may act as a the leader (Imam) in the congregational prayers, and he may also act as a subordinate officer in the governmental department of revenue. Masters may sell, bequeath, give away, pledge, hire out or compel them to earn money. By the view of some madh'hab (but not others), a master may compel his/her slave(s) to marriage and determine the identity of their marriage partner(s).

The mahr that is given for marriage to a female slave is taken by her owner, whereas all other women possess it absolutely for themselves.

Concubinage

Slave women were required mainly as concubines and menials. A Muslim slaveholder was entitled by law to the sexual enjoyment of his slave women. While free women might own male slaves, they had no such right. The purchase of female slaves for sex was lawful from the perspective of Islamic law, and this was the most common motive for the purchase of slaves throughout Islamic history. The property of a slave was owned by his or her master unless a contract of freedom of the slave had been entered into, which allowed the slave to earn money to purchase his or her freedom and similarly to pay bride wealth. The marriage of slaves required the consent of the owner. Under the Hanafi and Shafii schools of jurisprudence male slaves could marry two wives, but the Maliki permitted them to marry four wives like the free men. According to the Islamic law, a male slave could marry a free woman but this was discouraged in practice. Islam permits sexual relations between a male master and his female slave outside of marriage. This is referred to in the Quran as *ma malakat aymanukum* or "what your right hands possess". There are some restrictions on the master; he may not co-habit with a female slave belonging to his wife, neither can he have relations with a female slave if she is co-owned, or already married.

In ancient Arabian custom, the child of a freeman by his slave was also a slave unless he was recognized and liberated by his father. In theory, the recognition by a master of his offspring by a slave woman was optional in Islamic society, and in the early period was often withheld. By the high Middle Ages it became normal and was unremarkable in a society where the sovereigns themselves were almost invariably the children of slave concubines. The mother receives the title of "umm walad" (*lit.* mother of a child), which is an improvement in her status as she can no longer be sold. Among Sunnis, she is automatically freed upon her master's death, however for Shia, she is only freed if her child is still alive; her value is then deducted from this child's share of the inheritance. Lovejoy writes that as an *umm walad*, they attained "an intermediate position between slave and free" pending their freedom, although they would sometimes be nominally freed as soon as they gave birth.

There is no limit on the number of concubines a master may possess. However, the general marital laws are to be observed, such as not having sexual relations with the sister of a female slave. In Islam, "men are enjoined to marry free women in the first instance, but if they cannot afford the bridewealth for free women, they are told to marry slave women rather than engage in wrongful acts." One rationale given for recognition of concubinage in Islam is that "it satisfied the sexual desire of the female slaves and thereby prevented the spread of immorality in the Muslim community." Most schools restrict concubinage to a monogamous relationship between the slave woman and her master, According to Sikainga, "in reality, however, female slaves in many Muslim societies were prey for members of their owners' household, their neighbors, and their guests." Under the legal doctrine of *kafa'a* (lit."efficiency"), the purpose of which was to ensure that a man should be at least the social equal of the woman he marries, a freedman is not as good as the son of a freedman, and he in turn not as good as the grandson of a freedman. This principle is pursued up to three generations, after which all Muslims are deemed equally free. Lewis asserts that since kafaa "does not forbid unequal marriages", it is in no sense a "Muslim equivalent of Nuremberg Laws of Nazi Germany or the apartheid laws of South Africa. His purpose, he states, is not to try to set up a moral competition-to compare castration and apartheid as offences against humanity."

Manumission

The Quran and Hadith, the primary Islamic texts, make it a praiseworthy act for masters to set their slaves free. There are numerous ways in which a slave may become free. One way is through expiation for certain sins committed by the master, such as involuntary manslaughter or perjury. Other ways include emancipation through becoming an *umm walad*, who is freed upon her master's death along with her children, or an independent act of piety by the master, as recommended by the Quran. It is also commendable to manumit a slave who demands his freedom and is considered worthy of it. Another method is the *mukataba* contract: Levy states that "the slave may redeem himself if his master agrees and contracts to let him go on payment of a stipulated sum of money, which may be paid in two or more instalments, or on the giving of stipulated services or other consideration. If the consideration is a sum of money, the master must grant the slave the right to earn and to own property." If the master makes a declaration of the slave's freedom, whether in jest or earnest, in the presence of the slave or another, then such a declaration becomes legally binding. Similarly, the master may promise manumission (verbally or in writing) that the slave is to be freed upon the former's death. Lastly, a slave is also freed automatically if she or he comes into the possession of a master who is directly related to her or him.

Gordon opines that the Quran in particular and Islamic jurisprudence in general have not placed a premium on manumission but held it out as one way for atonement of sin. He states that "Manumission was only one of several virtuous observances that the pious could avail themselves of and was by no means the most important," noting that other options include reaffirming faith in God and giving food to the poor. He concludes that "there was no contradiction between being a devout Muslim and a slave-owing one as well."

Modern Interpretations

The abolition movement starting in 19th century in England and later in other Western countries influenced the slavery in Muslim lands both in doctrine and in practice. One of the first religious decrees comes from the two highest dignitaries of the Hanafi and Maliki rites in the Ottoman Empire. These religious authorities declared that slavery is lawful in principle but it is regrettable in its consequences. They expressed two religious considerations in their support for abolition of slavery: "the initial enslaving of the people concerned comes under suspicion of illegality by reason of the present-day expansion of Islam in their countries; masters no longer comply with the rules of good treatment which regulate their rights and shelter them from wrong-doing."

According to Brunschvig, although the total abolition of slavery might seem a reprehensible innovation and contrary to the Quran and the practice of early Muslims, the realities of the modern world caused a "discernible evolution in the thought of many educated Muslims before the end of the 19th century." These Muslims argued that Islam on the whole has "bestowed an exceptionally favourable lot on the victims of slavery" and that the institution of slavery is linked to the particular economic and social stage in which Islam originated. According to the influential thesis of Ameer Ali, Islam only tolerated slavery through temporary necessity and that its complete abolition was not possible at the time of Muhammad.

According to Brockopp, some modern interpreters have accused the medieval interpreters of having subverted the Quran's demand for manumission contracts. They have used the dramatic change in the institution of slavery in the seventh and eighth centuries to argue that the Quran would not have condoned the slaving practices common in Islamic history. Others have argued that the original intent of the Quran, when understood properly, was to abolish slavery altogether (cf. Arafat, *Attitude*). The idea that Islam only tolerated slavery due to necessity has to some extent found its way into the circle of the Ulema. It has been unable to gain support among the Wahhabis.

History of Slavery under Muslim Rule

Reasons for Low Natural Increase in the Internal Slave Population

According to Bernard Lewis, the growth of internal slave populations through natural increase was insufficient to maintain numbers right through to modern times, which contrasts markedly with rapidly rising slave populations in the New World. He writes that a contributing factor was the liberation of slaves as an act of piety, but the primary drain was the liberation by freemen of their own offspring born by slave mothers. Other factors Lewis describes for the low natural increase of slave populations in the Islamic world include:

1. Castration: A fair proportion of male slaves were imported as eunuchs. Levy states that according to the Quran and Islamic traditions, such emasculation was objectionable. Jurists such as al-Baydawi considered castration to be mutilation, stipulating law enforcement to prevent it. However, in practice, emasculation was frequent. In nineteenth century Mecca, the majority of eunuchs were in the service of the mosques.
2. Liberation of military slaves: Military slaves that rose through the ranks were usually liberated at some stage in their careers.
3. Restrictions on procreation: Among the menial, domestic, and manual worker slaves, casual mating was not permitted and marriage was not encouraged.
4. High death toll: There was a high death toll among all classes of slaves. Slaves usually came from remote places and, lacking immunities, died in large numbers. As late as the nineteenth century, Western travellers in North Africa and Egypt noted the high death rate among imported black slaves.

Segal notes that recent slaves, weakened by their initial captivity and debilitating journey, would have been easy victim to climate changes and infection. Children were especially at risk, and the Islamic market demand for children was much greater than the American one. Many blacks, both slave and free, lived in conditions conducive to malnutrition and disease, with effects on their own life expectancy, the fertility of women, and the infant mortality rate.

Another factor was the Zanj Rebellion against the plantation economy of 9th-century southern Iraq. Due to fears of a similar uprising among slave gangs occurring elsewhere, Muslims came to realize that large concentrations of slaves were not a suitable organization of labour and that slaves were best employed in smaller concentrations. As such, large-scale employment of slaves for manual labour became the exception rather than the norm, and the medieval Islamic world did not need to import vast numbers of slaves.

Consequences of Muhammad's Prescriptions on Slavery

Early Islamic History

W. Montgomery Watt points out that Muhammad's expansion of Pax Islamica to the Arabian peninsula reduced warfare and raiding, and therefore cut off the sources of enslaving freemen. According to Patrick Manning, the Islamic legislations against the abuse of the slaves convincingly limited the extent of enslavement in Arabian peninsula and to a lesser degree for the whole area of the whole Umayyad Caliphate where slavery existed since the most ancient times.

Later Periods

Bernard Lewis writes: "In one of the sad paradoxes of human history, it was the humanitarian reforms brought by Islam that resulted in a vast development of the slave trade inside, and still more outside, the Islamic empire." He notes that the Islamic injunctions against the enslavement of Muslims led to massive importation of slaves from the outside. According to Patrick Manning, Islam by recognizing and codifying the slavery seems to have done more to protect and expand slavery than the reverse.

Arab Slave Trade

The 'Arab' slave trade is sometimes called the 'Islamic' slave trade. Bernard Lewis writes that "polytheists and idolaters were seen primarily as sources of slaves, to be imported into the Islamic world and molded in Islamic ways, and, since they possessed no religion of their own worth the mention, as natural recruits for Islam." Patrick Manning states that religion was hardly the point of this slavery. Also, this term suggests comparison between Islamic slave trade and Christian slave trade. Furthermore, usage of the terms "Islamic trade" or "Islamic world" implicitly and erroneously treats Africa as it were outside of Islam, or a negligible portion of the Islamic world. Propagators of Islam in Africa often revealed a cautious attitude towards proselytizing because of its effect in reducing the potential reservoir of slaves. The author Ronald Segal distinguishes the Islamic slave trade from that of the Atlantic or European slave trade by highlighting the aspects of its duration and nature: "It began in the middle of the seventh century and survives today in Mauritania and Sudan. With the Islamic slave trade, we're talking of 14 centuries rather than four." Further, "whereas the gender ratio of slaves in the Atlantic trade was two males to every female, in the Islamic trade, it was two females to every male."

In the 8th century Africa was dominated by Arab-Berbers in the north: Islam moved southwards along the Nile and along the desert trails. The Solomonic dynasty of Ethiopia often exported Nilotic slaves from their western borderland provinces, or from newly conquered or reconquered Muslim provinces. Native Muslim Ethiopian sultanates (rulership) exported slaves as well, such as the sometimes independent sultanate (rulership) of Adal. For a long time, until the early 18th century Crimean Khanate maintained massive slave trade with the Ottoman Empire and the Middle East. Between 1530 and 1780 there were almost certainly 1 million and quite possibly as many as 1.25 million white, European Christians enslaved by the Muslims of the Barbary Coast. On the coast of the Indian Ocean too, slave-trading posts were set up by Arabs. The archipelago of Zanzibar, along the coast of present-day Tanzania, is undoubtedly the most notorious example of these trading colonies. East Africa and the Indian Ocean continued as an important region for the Oriental slave trade up until the 19th century. Livingstone and Stanley were then the first Europeans to penetrate to the interior of the Congo basin and to discover the scale of slavery there. The Arab Tippu Tib extended his influence and made many people slaves. After Europeans had settled in the Gulf of Guinea, the trans-Saharan slave trade became less important. In Zanzibar, slavery was abolished late, in 1897, under Sultan Hamoud bin Mohammed. The rest of Africa had no direct contact with Muslim slave-traders.

Roles Filled by Slaves

A system of plantation labour, much like that which would emerge in the Americas, developed early on, but with such dire consequences that subsequent engagements were relatively rare and reduced. Moreover, the need for agricultural labour, in an Islam with large peasant populations, was nowhere near as acute as in the Americas. Slaves in Islam were mainly directed at the service sector-concubines and cooks, porters and soldiers-with slavery itself primarily a form of consumption rather than a factor of production. The most telling evidence for this is found in the gender ratio; among black slaves traded in Islam across the centuries, there were roughly two females to every male. Almost all female slaves had domestic occupations. This included the gratification of the master's sexual impulses. This was a lawful motive for their purchase, and the most common one. In recruiting barbarians from the "martial races" beyond the frontiers into their imperial armies, the Arabs were doing what the Romans and the Chinese had done centuries before them. In the scale of this recruitment, however, and the preponderant role acquired by these recruits in the imperial and eventually metropolitan forces, Muslim rulers went far beyond any precedent. It was not until the medieval Islamic state that we find military slaves in significant numbers, forming a substantial and eventually predominant component in their armies. While slaves were sometimes employed for manual labour during the Arab slave trade, this was usually the exception rather than the norm. The vast majority of labour in the medieval Islamic world consisted of free, paid labour. The only known exceptions to this general rule was in the plantation economy of 9th-century southern Iraq (which led to the Zanj Revolt), in 9th-century Ifriqiya (modern-day Tunisia), and in 11th-century Bahrain (during the Karmatian state).

Rebellion

In some cases slaves joined to rebels or even uprose against governors. The most renowned of this rebellions was Zanj Rebellion. The Zanj Revolt took place near the city of Basra, located in southern Iraq over a period of fifteen years (869-883 AD). It grew to involve over 500,000 slaves who were imported from across the Muslim empire and claimed over "tens of thousands of lives in lower Iraq". The revolt was said to have been led by Ali ibn Muhammad, who claimed to be a descendent of Caliph Ali ibn Abu Talib. Several historians, such as Al-Tabari and Al-Masudi, consider this revolt one of the "most vicious and brutal uprising" out of the many disturbances that plagued the Abbasid central government.

Capturing Political Power

Mamluks were slave soldiers who were converted to Islam and served the Muslim caliphs and the Ayyubid sultans during the Middle Ages. Over time, they became a powerful military caste numerously defeating the Crusaders and, on more than one occasion, they seized power for themselves, for example ruling Egypt in the Mamluk Sultanate from 1250-1517.

19th Century and Post 19th Century

Slavery in Muslim lands was influenced by the revolution against slavery in 19th century in England and later in other Western countries which gave rise to a strong abolitionist movement in Europe. Contrasting with ancient and colonial systems, slaves in Muslim lands had a certain legal status and had obligations to as well as rights over the slave owner. Slavery was not only recognized but was elaborately regulated by Sharia law. Although emancipation of slaves was recommended, it was not compulsory. Lewis elucidates that it was for this reason that "the position of the domestic slave in Muslim society was in most respects better than in either classical antiquity or the nineteenth-century Americas" and that the economic situation of such slaves were no worse than (and even in some cases better than) free poors.

Ironically, the enlightened incentives and opportunities for slaves to be emancipated meant there was a strong market for new slaves and thus strong incentive to enslave and sell human beings. The processes of acquisition and transportation of slaves to Muslim lands often imposed appalling loss of life and hardships. The hardships of acquisition and transportation of slaves to Muslim lands drew attention of European opponents of slavery.

The continuing pressure from European countries eventually overcame the strong resistance of religious conservatives who were holding that forbidding what God permits is just as great an offence as to permit what God forbids. Slavery, in their eyes, was "authorized and regulated by the holy law". Even masters persuaded of their own piety and benevolence sexually exploited their concubines, without a thought of whether this constituted a violation of their humanity. There were also many pious Muslims who refused to have slaves and persuaded others to do so. Eventually, the Ottoman Empire's orders against the traffic of slaves were issued and put into effect. According to Brockopp, in 19th century, "Some authorities made blanket pronouncements against slavery, arguing that it violated the quranic ideals of equality and freedom. The great slave markets of Cairo were closed down at the end of the nineteenth century and even conservative Quran interpreters continue to regard slavery as opposed to Islamic principles of justice and equality." Slavery in the forms of carpetweavers, sugarcane cutters, camel jockeys, sex slaves, and even chattel exists even today in some Muslim and non-Muslim countries (Some have questioned the use of the term slavery as an accurate description).

According to an article in *The New York Times* published on March 28, 1886, the Ottoman empire allowed a slave trade in girls to thrive during the late 1800s, while publicly denying it. The three main races of girls who were sold as sexual slaves in the Ottoman Empire were Circassian, Syrian, and Nubian girls. Circassian girls were described by the American journalist as fair and light skinned. They were frequently sent by Circassian leaders as gifts to the Ottomans. They were the most expensive, reaching up to 500 Turkish lira and the most popular with the Turks. The next most popular slaves were Syrian girls, with "dark eyes and hair", and light brown skin. Their price could reach to thirty lira. They were described by the American journalist as having "good figures when young". Throughout coastal regions in Anatolia, Syrian girls were sold. The *New York Times* journalist stated Nubian girls were the cheapest and least popular, fetching up to 20 lira.

Twentieth Century Suppression and Outlawry

Unlike Western societies which in their opposition to slavery spawned anti-slavery movements whose numbers and enthusiasm often grew out of church groups, no such grass-roots organizations ever developed in Muslim societies. In Muslim politics the state unquestioningly accepted the teachings of Islam and applied them as law. Islam, by sanctioning slavery-however mild a form it generally took-also extended legitimacy to the nefarious traffic in slaves.

Writing about 1862 the English traveller W.G. Palgrave says that in Arabia he constantly met with black slaves in large numbers. The effects of concubinage were apparent in the number of persons of mixed race and the emancipation of slaves he found to be common. Doughty, writing about 25 years later, made similar reports.

Slavery was common in the East Indies until the end of the 19th century. In Singapore in 1891 there was a regular trade in Chinese slaves by Muslim slaveowners, with girls and women used for concubinage.

At Istanbul, the sale of black and Circassian women was conducted openly until the granting of the Constitution in 1908.

It was in the early 20th century (post World War I) that slavery gradually became outlawed and suppressed in Muslim lands, largely due to pressure exerted by Western nations such as Britain and France.

In 1925 slaves were still being bought and sold at Mecca in the ordinary way of trade. The slave market there consisted of the offspring of local slaves as well as those imported from the Yemen, Africa, and Asia Minor.

By the Treaty of Jedda, May 1927 (art.7), concluded between the British Government and Ibn Saud (King of Nejd and the Hijaz) it was finally agreed to suppress the slave trade in Saudi Arabia. Then by a decree issued in 1936 the importation of slaves into Saudi Arabia was prohibited unless it could be proved that they were slaves at that date. In 1953, sheikhs from Qatar attending the coronation of Queen Elizabeth II included slaves in their retinues, and they did so again on another visit five years later. It was not until 1962 that all slavery practice or trafficking in Saudi Arabia was prohibited. By 1969 it could be observed that most Muslim states had abolished slavery although it existed in the deserts of Iraq bordering Arabia and it still flourished in Saudi Arabia, the Yemen and Oman. Slavery was not formally abolished in Yemen and Oman until the following year. The last nation to formally enact the abolition of slavery practice and slave trafficking was the Islamic Republic of Mauritania in 1981.

Gordon describes the lack of homegrown Islamic abolition movements as owing much to the fact that it was deeply anchored in Islamic law. By legitimizing slavery and-by extension-traffic in slaves, Islam elevated those practices to an unassailable moral plain. As a result, in no part of the Muslim world was an ideological challenge ever mounted against slavery. The political and social system in Muslim society would have taken a dim view of such a challenge. Some Muslim leaders, like Fatimid caliph Al-Hakim bi-Amr Allah did ban slavery, but it had little influence in the Islamic world.

Slavery in the Contemporary Muslim World

The issue of slavery in the Islamic world in modern times is controversial. Critics argue there is hard evidence of its existence and destructive effects. Others maintain slavery in central Islamic lands has been virtually extinct since mid-twentieth century, and that reports from Sudan and Somalia showing practice of slavery is in border areas as a result of continuing war and not Islamic belief.

Salafi and Traditionalist Juridical Support for Slavery

In recent years, according to some scholars, there has been a "worrying trend" of "reopening" of the issue of slavery by some conservative Salafi Islamic scholars after its "closing" earlier in the 20th century when Muslim countries banned slavery and "most Muslim scholars" found the practice "inconsistent with Quranic morality."

In 2003 a high-level Saudi jurist, Shaykh Saleh Al-Fawzan, issued a fatwa claiming "Slavery is a part of Islam. Slavery is part of Jihad, and Jihad will remain as long there is Islam." He attacked Muslim scholars who said otherwise maintaining, "They are ignorant, not scholars... They are merely writers. Whoever says such things is an infidel."

At the time of the fatwa, al-Fawzan was a member of the Senior Council of Clerics, Saudi Arabia's highest religious body, a member of the Council of Religious Edicts and Research, the Imam of Prince Mitaeb Mosque in Riyadh, and a professor at Imam Mohamed Bin Saud Islamic University, the main Wahhabi centre of learning in the country. According to multiple sources, religious calls have also been made to capture and enslave Jewish women. As American journalist John J. Miller said, "It is hard to imagine a serious person calling for America to enslave its enemies. Yet a prominent Saudi cleric, Shaikh Saad Al-Buraik, recently urged Palestinians to do exactly that with Jews: 'Their women are yours to take, legitimately. God made them yours. Why don't you enslave their women?'"

Shaykh Fadhlalla Haeri of Karbala expressed the view in 1993 that the enforcement of servitude can occur but is restricted to war captives and those born of slaves.

Dr. Abdul-Latif Mushtahari, the general supervisor and director of homiletics and guidance at the Azhar University, has said on the subject of justifications for Islamic permission of slavery:

> *"Islam does not prohibit slavery but retains it for two reasons. The first reason is war (whether it is a civil war or a foreign war in which the captive is either killed or enslaved) provided that the war is not between Muslims against each other-it is not acceptable to enslave the violators, or the offenders, if they are Muslims. Only non-Muslim captives may be enslaved or killed. The second reason is the sexual propagation of slaves which would generate more slaves for their owner."*

Islamist Opinions

Earlier in the 20th century, prior to the "reopening" of slavery by Salafi scholars like Shaykh al-Fawzan, Islamist authors declared slavery outdated without actually clearly affirming and promoting its abolition. This has caused at least one scholar (William Clarence-Smith) to bemoan the 'dogged refusal of Mawlana Mawdudi to give up on slavery' and the notable 'evasions and silences of Muhammad Qutb.' Syed Qutb, the scholar of the Islamist Muslim Brotherhood said in his *(Tafsir)* of the Quran;

> *"And concerning slavery, that was when slavery was a world-wide structure and which was conducted amongst Muslims and their enemies in the form of enslaving of prisoners of war. And it was necessary for Islam to adopt a similar line of practise until the world devised a new code of practise during war other than enslavement"*

Qutb's brother Muhammad Qutb contrasted sexual relations between Muslim slaveowners and their female slaves with (in his view), the widespread and depraved practice of casual consensual sex in contemporary Europe:

Islam made it lawful for a master to have a number of slave-women captured in wars and enjoined that he alone may have sexual relations with them... Europe abhors this law but at the same gladly allows that most odious form of animalism according to which a man may have illicit relations with any girl coming across him on his way to gratify his animal passions.

Maulana Mawdudi of Jamaat-e-Islami has said:

> *Islam has clearly and categorically forbidden the primitive practice of capturing a free man, to make him*

> *a slave or to sell him into slavery. On this point the clear and unequivocal words of [Muhammad] are as follows:*
>
> *"There are three categories of people against whom I shall myself be a plaintiff on the Day of Judgement. Of these three, one is he who enslaves a free man, then sells him and eats this money" (al-Bukhari and Ibn Majjah).*

The words of this Tradition of the Prophet are also general, they have not been qualified or made applicable to a particular nation, race, country or followers of a particular religion.....After this the only form of slavery which was left in Islamic society was the prisoners of war, who were captured on the battlefield. These prisoners of war were retained by the Muslim Government until their government agreed to receive them back in exchange for Muslim soldiers captured by them.....

Shiekh Taqiuddin al-Nabhani, a shariah judge and founder of Hizb ut-Tahrir movement, gives the following explanation:

> *When Islam came, for the situations where people were taken into slavery (e.g. debt), Islam imposed Shari'ah solutions to those situations other than slavery.... It (Islam) made the existing slave and owner form a business contract, based upon the freedom, not upon slavery... As for the situation of war,... it clarified the rule of the captive in that either they are favoured by releasing without any exchange, or they are ransomed for money or exchanged for Muslims or non-Muslim citizens of the Caliphate.*

Current Status

While slavery is illegal in Saudi Arabia despite Shaykh al-Fawzan's fatwa, the proclamation carries weight among many Salafi Muslims. According to reformist jurist and author Khaled Abou El Fadl, it "is particularly disturbing and dangerous because it effectively legitimates the trafficking in and sexual exploitation of so-called domestic workers in the Gulf region and especially Saudi Arabia." Organized criminal gangs smuggle children into Saudi Arabia where they are enslaved, sometimes mutilated, and forced to work as beggars. When caught, the children are deported as illegal aliens.

According to the U.S. State Department

Saudi Arabia is a destination for men and women from South and East Asia and East Africa trafficked for the purpose of labour exploitation, and for children from Yemen, Afghanistan, and Africa trafficking for forced begging. Hundreds of thousands of low-skilled workers from India, Indonesia, the Philippines, Sri Lanka, Bangladesh, Ethiopia, Eritrea, Somalia, and Kenya migrate voluntarily to Saudi Arabia; some fall into conditions of involuntary servitude, suffering from physical and sexual abuse, non-payment or delayed payment of wages, the withholding of travel documents, restrictions on their freedom of movement and non-consensual contract alterations. The Government of Saudi Arabia does not comply with the minimum standards for the elimination of trafficking and is not making significant efforts to do so.

Dhimmi

A dhimmi is a non-Muslim subject of a state governed in accordance with sharia law. Linguistically, the word means "one who's responsibility has been taken". This has to be understood in the context of the definition of state in Islam, which is different from the current definition of citizenship of a state. The dhimma is a theoretical contract based on a widely held Islamic doctrine granting special status to adherents of Judaism, Christianity, and certain other non-Muslim religions ("People of the Book"). Dhimma provides rights of residence in return for taxes. Dhimmi have fewer legal and social rights than Muslims, but more rights than other non-Muslims. However often these limited rights correspond to how in modern democracies, some rights may not be available to some citizens. For example the United States President must be a citizen that was born in the United States They are excused from specifically Muslim duties, and otherwise equal under the laws of property, contract and obligation.

Under sharia law, dhimmi status was originally afforded to Jews, Christians, and Sabians. The protected religions later came to include Zoroastrians, Mandaeans, Hindus and Buddhists. Eventually, the largest school of Islamic legal thought applied this term to all non-Muslims living in Islamic lands outside the sacred area surrounding Mecca, Saudi Arabia. This status therefore applied to millions of people living from Spain and Morocco on the Atlantic Ocean to Indonesia in the Pacific, and from the 7th century CE until modern times.

As an example of the distinctions between Muslims, dhimmis, and others, sharia law permits the consumption of pork and alcohol by non-Muslims living in Islamic countries, although they may not be openly displayed. These same commodities are expressly forbidden to Muslims. As another example of this, sharia law in present-day Saudi Arabia prescribes blood money to be paid for the death of a person caused by another. The amount payable for a Christian or Jew is half that for a male Muslim; but all others are valued at 1/16. However this is a minority view, and the largest school of legal thought in Islam i.e. the Hanafi school does not make any distinction between a non-Muslim dhimmi and a muslim citizen.

Treatment of Dhimmis

The question of how tolerant Islam was, and is, towards other religions requires a definition of terms. If a lack of discrimination is the criterion for tolerance, one answer will emerge. If a lack of persecution, defined as active and violent repression, is the criterion, the question gets a different answer. Discrimination against dhimmis was institutionalized in traditional Islamic societies. Persecution, on the other hand, was rare and atypical. The dhimmi communities had their own chiefs and judges, with their own family, personal and religious laws.

Many of the dhimmi restrictions seem to go back to the early days of the Arab conquest, and to have been instituted as security precautions in order to protect occupying military and administrative personnel. Most of the restrictions were social and symbolic in nature. Various restrictions, such as dress codes, building codes, and limits on openness of worship, were enforced unevenly on the dhimmi populations. A pattern of stricter, then more lax, enforcement developed over time. In times of external threat, or under a more pious ruler, the restrictions would be rigorously enforced for a while – then more lax enforcement would again return. The major financial disabilities of the dhimmi were the jizya poll tax and the fact dhimmis could not inherit from Muslims. The jurists and scholars of Islamic sharia law called for humane treatment of the dhimmis, however the commentators were more severe. Unlike the Jews and Muslims of Spain after its reconquest by Catholic Christians, the dhimmis did not have to choose between apostasy, exile and death. Islam has become the dominant religion in much of the world primarily through three avenues. First, a gradual process of religious conversion for material and spiritual reasons. Second, interfaith marriages, which require the children to be raised as Muslims. Third, and more recently, differing rates of population growth among the religious communities. There were no large scale massacres or expulsions of dhimmi populations until the dissolution of the Ottoman Empire, and the resulting emergence of modern secular Turkey, in the 20th century.

The Dhimma Contract in the Modern World

The Dhimma Contract and Shariah Law

The dhimma contract is an integral part of traditional Islamic sharia law. From the 9th century AD, the power to interpret and refine law in traditional Islamic societies was in the hands of the scholars (ulema). This separation of powers served to limit the range of actions available to the ruler, who could not easily decree or reinterpret law independently and expect the continued support of the community. Through succeeding centuries and empires, the balance between the ulema and the rulers shifted and reformed, but the balance of power was never decisively changed. At the beginning of the 19th century, the Industrial Revolution and the French Revolution introduced an era of European world hegemony that included the domination of most of the lands of Islam. At the end of the Second World War, the European powers found themselves too weakened to maintain their empires.

The wide variety of forms of government, systems of law, attitudes toward modernity and interpretations of sharia are a result of the ensuing drives for independence and modernity in the Muslim world. Muslim states, sects, schools of thought and individuals differ as to exactly what sharia law entails. In addition, Muslim states today utilize a spectrum of legal systems. Saudi Arabia and some Gulf states enforce their interpretations of classical sharia law. Most states have a mixed system implementing certain aspects of sharia while acknowledging constitutional supremacy. A few, such as Turkey, have declared themselves secular. Local and customary laws may take precedence in certain matters, as well. Islamic law is therefore polynormative, and despite several cases of regression in recent years, the trend is towards modernization and liberalization. Questions of human rights and the status of minorities cannot be generalized with regards to Islam and the Muslim world. They must instead be examined on a case-by-case basis, within specific political and cultural contexts, using perspectives drawn from the historical framework.

The End of the Dhimma Contract in Ottoman North Africa and the Middle East

The status of the dhimmi "was for long accepted with resignation by the Christians and with gratitude by the Jews" but ceased to be so after the rising power of Christendom and the radical ideas of the French revolution caused a wave of discontent among Christian dhimmis. While Muslims opposed the abolition of dhimma laws, continuing and growing pressure from the European powers combined with pressure from Muslim reformers gradually relaxed the inequalities between Muslims and non-Muslims. The collection of the jizya tax from non-Muslims was widespread throughout the history of Islam. In the mid-19th century, the Ottoman empire significantly relaxed the restrictions and taxes placed on its non-Muslim residents under

Ottomanism. These relaxations occurred gradually as part of the Tanzimat reform movement, which began in 1839 with the accession of the Ottoman Sultan Abd-ul-Mejid I. On November 3, 1839, the Hatt-i Sharif of Gulhane edict was put forth by the Sultan, in part proclaiming the principle of equality among all subjects regardless of religion. Part of the motivation for this was a desire to gain support from the British Empire, whose help was needed in a conflict with Egypt.

On February 18, 1856, the Hatt-i Humayan edict was issued, building upon the 1839 edict. It came about partly as a result of pressure from and the efforts of the ambassadors of England, France, and Austria, whose respective countries were needed as allies in the Crimean War. It again proclaimed the principle of equality between Muslims and non-Muslims, and produced many specific reforms to this end. For example, the jizya tax was abolished and non-Muslims were allowed to join the army.

Lapses in the Protection of Religious Minorities after the End of the Dhimma Contract

With the end of the dhimma contract, various approaches have been adopted to deal with the protection of minority rights in place of traditional sharia law. Some of the results, such as those experienced by Turkish Christians and Jews during the early 20th century AD, have been disastrous, although their extent is still debated.

Views of Contemporary Islamic Scholars on the Status of Dhimmis in an Islamic Society:

- Ayatollah Khomeini in his book *On Islamic Government* indicates unequivocally that non-Muslims should be required to pay the poll tax, in return for which they would profit from the protection and services of the state; they would, however, be excluded from all participation in the political process. Bernard Lewis remarks about Khomeini that one of his main grievances against the Shah was that his legislation allowed the theoretical possibility of non-Muslims exercising political or judicial authority over Muslims.
- Allameh Tabatabaei, a prominent 20th century Shia scholar, commenting on a Hadith that claims that the verse 9:29 has "abrogated" other verses asking for good behaviour toward dhimmis, states that "abrogation" could be understood either in its terminological sense or its literal sense. If "abrogation" is understood in its terminological sense, Muslims should deal with dhimmis strictly in a good and decent manner.

- Javed Ahmed Ghamidi writes in Mizan that certain directives of the Quran were specific only to the Prophet Muhammad (Pbuh) against peoples of his times, besides other directives, the campaign involved asking the polytheists of Arabia for submission to Islam as a condition for exoneration and the others for jizya and submission to the political authority of the Muslims for exemption from death punishment and for military protection as the dhimmis of the Muslims. Therefore, after the Prophet and his companions, there is no concept in Islam obliging Muslims to wage war for propagation or implementation of Islam.
- The Shia jurist Grand Ayatollah Makarem Shirazi states in *the selection of the Tafsir Nemooneh* that the main philosophy of jizya is that it is only a financial aid to those Muslims who are in the charge of safeguarding the security of the state and Dhimmis' lives and properties on their behalf

Views of Prominent Contemporary Muslims on the Status of Dhimmis in an Islamic Society:

- Legal scholar L. Ali Khan points to the Constitution of Medina as a way forward for Islamic states in his 2006 paper titled *The Medina Constitution.* He suggests this ancient document, which governed the status of religions and races in the first Islamic state, can serve as a basis for the protection of minority rights, equality, and religious freedom in the modern Islamic state.
- Dr. Zakir Naik, a prominent Islamic preacher from India, has stated that "as far as the matters of religion are concerned we know for sure that only Islam is the true religion in the eyes of God. In 3:85 it is mentioned that God will never accept any religion other than Islam. As far as the second question regarding building of churches or temples is concerned, how can we allow this when their religion is wrong? And when worship is also wrong? Thus we will surely not allow such wrong things in our (i.e. an Islamic) country."
- Tariq Ramadan, Professor of Islamic Studies at Oxford University, advocates the inclusion of academic disciplines and Islamic society, along with traditional Islamic scholars, in an effort to reform Islamic law and address modern conditions. He speaks of remaining faithful to the higher objectives of sharia law. He posits universal rights of dignity, welfare, freedom, equality and justice in a religiously and culturally pluralistic Islamic (or other) society, and proposes a dialog regarding the modern term "citizenship," although it has no clear precedent

in classical fiqh. He further includes the terms "non-citizen", "foreigner", "resident" and "immigrant" in this dialog, and challenges not only Islam, but modern civilization as a whole, to come to terms with these concepts in a meaningful way with regards to problems of racism, discrimination and oppression.

Historical Implications for Non-Muslims Living in Islamic Lands

Over the course of many centuries, most Zoroastrians and Christians in Islamic countries converted to Islam, but the Muslim conquest had a limited impact on the Jews. Zoroastrianism was the first to crumble after the Muslim conquest of Persia. Closely associated with the power structures of the Persian Empire, the Zoroastrian clergy quickly declined after they were deprived of state support.

North Africa, the Near East and the Middle East

Christianity: For Christians, the process of conversion was slower, but no less inexorable. It is possible that as late as the time of the Crusades Christians still constituted a majority of the population. The switch from a dominant to an inferior position proved too difficult for many Christians and they converted to Islam in large numbers. Christianity disappeared altogether in Central Asia and Yemen. It disappeared from the Maghreb, when it was subjected to persecution by the Almohads. Christians continued to live in Syria, Iraq, and Egypt, but their numbers were reduced to a tiny minority. The relative resiliency of Christians in those countries stemmed from their subordinated position in the Byzantine Empire, which made them more amenable to accepting Muslim supremacy; many of them felt better off under early Muslim rule than under the Byzantines.

In 1095 AD, Pope Urban II urged European Christians to come to the aid of their Christian brethren in Palestine. The subsequent Crusades brought Latin Christians into contact with Eastern sects of Christianity which held beliefs more different from their own than they had previously been aware. The Eastern Christians were also in a more comfortable position under the rule of the Muslim Fatimid dynasty than had been supposed by the Europeans. Consequently, the Eastern Christians provided little support to the Crusaders. When the Arab East came under Ottoman rule in the 16th century AD, Christian populations and fortunes rebounded significantly. The Ottomans had long experience dealing with Christian and Jewish minorities, and were more tolerant towards religious minorities than the former Muslim rulers, the Mamluks of Egypt. By the 19th century AD, European pressure had removed all dhimma restrictions on Ottoman religious minorities. The ensuing modernizations and improvements in economic positions of the Arab Christians would eventually lead to a reduction in their relative numbers through a lowered birth rate among their population. The increase in wealth and freedom enjoyed by the former dhimmis would in turn lead to friction with the Muslim community.

Judaism

Jews were the least affected by dhimma. Accustomed to survival in adverse circumstances after many centuries of Roman and Byzantine persecutions, Jews saw the Islamic conquests as just another change of rulers, this time for the better. Voluntary conversion among the Jews was rare, and they managed to preserve their religion all over the Muslim lands. According to the scholar Mordechai Zaken, tribal chieftains (also known as aghas) in tribal Muslim societies such as the Kurdish society in Kurdistan would tax their Jewish subjects. The Jews were in fact civilians protected by their chieftains in and around their communities; in return they paid part of their harvest as dues, and contributed their skills and services to their patron chieftain.

South Asia

By the 10th century, the Turks of Central Asia had brought Islam to the mountains north of the Indic plains. It was not long before they swept south across the Punjab. The Indus basin held a substantial Buddhist population in addition to the ruling Hindu castes, and most converted to Islam over the next two centuries. At the end of the 12th century, the Muslims advanced quickly into the Ganges plain. In one decade, a Muslim army led by Turkic slaves consolidated resistance around Lahore and brought northern India, as far as west Bengal, under Muslim rule. From these Turkic slaves would come sultans, including the founder of the sultanate of Delhi. Muslims and dhimmis alike participated in urbanization and urban prosperity.

By the 15th century, Islamic and Hindu civilization had evolved in a complementary manner, with the Muslims taking the role of a ruling caste in Hindu society. Nevertheless, the Muslims retained their Islamic identities, and were in some ways regarded by Hindus in much the same light as their own lowest castes. By this time, most of the Indian subcontinent was under the influence of Islamic rulers, although resistance in the south continued. Bengal had a high rate of conversions to Islam, as Hinduism had not firmly established itself in this region. Across India, certain castes and trades converted to Islam en masse to attain equality and higher status. Areas where Buddhism was strong became strongly Muslim. There was a notable atrocity perpetrated upon

Buddhist monks in a monastery in Bengal. Forced conversions were not the source of conversions among the Buddhists, although the Muslims did not hold them in high regard. The main source of conversions was among Buddhist peasants coming to the cities. In the 16th century AD, India came under the influence of the Mughals (Mongols). Babar, a petty ruler of the Mongol Timuri empire, established a foothold in the North which paved the way for further expansion by his successors. Until it was eclipsed by European hegemony in the 18th century, the Timuri Moghul emperors oversaw a period of coexistence and tolerance between Hindus and Muslims. The emperor Akbar has been described as a universalist. He sought to establish tolerance and equality between all communities and religions, and instituted far reaching social and religious reforms. Not all the Mughal emperors endorsed the ideals espoused by Akbar, indeed Aurangzeb was inclined towards a more traditional, communal approach. The entire subcontinent fell under European colonial rule during the 18th century. Independence from their former European colonial rulers, and the subsequent struggles for political power, have brought ethnic and religious strife to this area of the world in modern times.

The Far East

The most populous Muslim country in the world is Indonesia, with a population of over 200 million people. The officially recognized religions in Indonesia are Islam (87% of the population), Protestant (6%), Catholic (3.5%), Hindu (1.8%) and other religious and spiritual groups (1.3%). There are 525 languages and dialects spoken. Islam came to Indonesia with traders from India and Bangladesh, among other places, in the 13th and 14th centuries. These Muslim traders cemented their positions in port cities through intermarriage with local inhabitants. Christianity came later, with Dutch control of those ports in the 18th century. Nowhere is cultural pluralism more pronounced than in Indonesia and the other countries of the Malaysian archipelago: Singapore and Malaysia. The history of Islam and Christianity in Indonesia has largely been one of peaceful coexistence.

As is the case in India, independence from their former European colonial rulers and the subsequent struggles for political power have brought ethnic and religious strife to this area.

Development of the Dhimma in the Early Islamic Period

Peace Terms

A precedent for the dhimma contract was established with the agreement between the Islamic Prophet Muhammad (Pbuh) and the

Jews of Khaybar, an oasis near Medina. Khaybar was the first territory attacked and conquered by Muslims. When the Jews of Khaybar surrendered to Muhammad after a siege, Muhammad allowed them to remain in Khaybar in return for handing over to the Muslims one half their annual produce. The Khaybar case served as a precedent for later Islamic scholars in their discussions on the issue of dhimma, even though the second caliph, Umar I, subsequently expelled the Jews from the oasis.

As the early Muslims expanded their territory through conquest, they imposed terms of surrender upon some of the defeated peoples. Courbage and Fargues write:

> Before launching an attack the ruler would offer them three choices – conversion, payment of a tribute, or to fight by the sword. If they did not choose conversion a treaty was concluded, either instead of battle or after it, which established the conditions of surrender for the Christians and Jews – the only non-Muslims allowed to retain their religion at this time. The terms of these treaties were similar and imposed on the *dhimmi*, the people 'protected' by Islam, certain obligations.

After Mecca was brought under Islamic rule, deputations from tribes across Arabia came to make terms with Muhammad and the Muslims. Some tribes converted and became Muslim, other Jewish and Christian tribes agreed to pay the poll tax in order to keep their religion and stay in their homes. Most of the Bedouin pagans were given no other choice but conversion to Islam.

One hundred years from its beginnings, the Islamic Arabian empire had expanded to include the lands of the Persians and the eastern half of Byzantine Rome. Sharia law was still in its infancy, and tribal law was more influential. The Arab conquerors included Christian as well as Muslim tribes. The Christian Arabs were regarded as fellow Arabs rather than dhimmis. The Arabs generally established garrisons outside towns in the conquered territories, and had little interaction with the local dhimmi populations for purposes other than the collection of taxes. The conquered Christian, Jewish, Mazdean and Buddhist communities were otherwise left to lead their lives as before.

Byzantine and Persian Precedents

As small minorities in the newly conquered territories of the Byzantine and Persian empires, the Muslim ruling class needed administrative personnel and expertise. In addition, the Islamic tradition carried the principles for governing these new subjects, but lacked the procedures. The existing personnel, procedures and traditions for ruling religious minorities were adapted to conform to Islamic principles, and used to govern these new dhimmi subjects.

Relevant Texts

Quranic verses as a Basis for Islamic Policies Toward Dhimmis

Lewis states;

- The phrase "...there is no compulsion in religion...", from , has usually been interpreted in the Islamic legal and theological traditions to mean followers of other religions should not be forced to adopt Islam.
- The phrase "...To you your religion, to me my religion...", from , has been used as a "proof-text for pluralism and coexistence".
- Verse has served to justify the tolerated position accorded to the followers of Christianity, Judaism, and Sabianism under Muslim rule.

Hadith

A Hadith by Muhammad, "Whoever killed a *Mu'ahid* (a person who is granted the pledge of protection by the Muslims) shall not smell the fragrance of Paradise though its fragrance can be smelt at a distance of forty years (of traveling)", is considered to be a foundation for the protection of the People of the Book in Muslim ruled countries. Majid Khadduri cites a similar Hadith in regard to the status of the dhimmis: "Whoever wrongs one with whom a compact (treaty) has been made *[i.e., a dhimmi]* and lays on him a burden beyond his strength, I will be his accuser."

Constitution of Medina

The Constitution of Medina, a formal agreement between Muhammad and all of the significant tribes and families of Medina (including Muslims, Jews and pagans), declared that non-Muslims in the *Ummah* had the following rights:

1. The security (*dhimma*) of God is equal for all groups,
2. Non-Muslim members have equal political and cultural rights as Muslims. They will have autonomy and freedom of religion.
3. Non-Muslims will take up arms against the enemy of the Ummah and share the cost of war. There is to be no treachery between the two.
4. Non-Muslims will not be obliged to take part in religious wars of the Muslims.

Pact of Umar

The Pact of Umar, believed by many Muslims to be between caliph Umar I and the conquered Christians of Jerusalem, was another source of regulations pertaining to dhimmis. The document enumerates the obligations and restrictions that the Christians proposed to the Muslim conquerors as conditions of surrender. However, Western orientalists doubt the authenticity of the Pact, arguing it is usually the victors and not the vanquished who impose rather than propose, the terms of peace, and that it is highly unlikely that the people who spoke no Arabic and knew nothing of Islam could draft such a document.

Academic historians believe the Pact of Umar in the form it is known today was a product of later jurists who attributed it to the venerated caliph Umar I in order to lend greater authority to their own opinions. The striking similarities between the Pact of Umar and the Theodesian and Justinian Codes suggest that perhaps much of the Pact of Umar was borrowed from these earlier codes by later Islamic jurists. At least some of the clauses of the pact mirror the measures first introduced by the Umayyad caliph Umar II or by the early Abbasid caliphs.

Historical Status of Dhimmis

Gradual Expulsion of Dhimmis from the Arabian Peninsula

After Mecca was brought under Islamic rule, deputations from tribes across Arabia came to make terms with Muhammad and the Muslims. Some tribes converted and became Muslims, other Jewish and Christian tribes agreed to pay the poll tax in order to keep their religion and stay in their homes. Most of the Bedouins pagans were given no other choice but conversion to Islam.

By the end of the Middle Ages, most Jews and Christians from the Arabian peninsula had been resettled in the Fertile Crescent, in spite of their protected status as dhimmis. There they were given land in compensation for their loss. Arabia was never completely cleared of all non-Muslims, but agreement was reached they should not be allowed in the vicinity of Mecca and Medina, even as visitors.

Religious Aspects

From an Islamic legal perspective, the pledge of protection granted dhimmis the freedom to practice their religion and spared them forced conversions. The dhimmis were also serving a variety of useful purposes, mostly economic, which was another point of concern to jurists. Religious minorities were free to do whatever they wished in their own homes, provided they did not engage in illicit sexual activity in ways that could threaten public morals. In some cases, religious practices that Muslims found repugnant were allowed. One example was the Zoroastrian practice of incestuous "self-marriage" where a man could marry his mother, sister or daughter. According to the famous Islamic legal scholar Ibn Qayyim (1292–1350), non-Muslims had the right to engage in such religious practices even if it offended Muslims, under the conditions that such cases not be presented to Islamic Sharia courts and that these religious minorities believed that the practice in question is permissible according to their religion. This ruling was based on the precedent that the Prophet Muhammad (Pbuh) did not forbid such self-marriages among Zoroastrians despite coming in contact with them and having knowledge of their practices.

Conversions to Islam

The spread of the Muslim faith in the first centuries of the Islamic rule was mainly by persuasion and inducement. Many Christians, Jews and Zoroastrians converted to Islam, however there were significant differences among the conversion rates and scales of these three religions. Judaism, on the whole, survived throughout the Islamic lands. Lewis explains the reason for the rapid conversion of Zoroastrians was the close association of the Zoroastrian priesthood and the structure of power in ancient Iran, and neither possessing "stimulation of powerful friends abroad by the Christians, nor the bitter skill in survival possessed by the Jews." For the Christians, the process of Arab settlement, of conversion to Islam and assimilation into the dominant culture caused their gradual conversion. For many of them, transition to a inferior status, which involved disadvantages and discrimination, was too much to endure. In some places, like the Maghreb, Central Asia, and southern Arabia, Christianity died out completely. Jews in contrast were more accustomed to such adversity. For them, the Islamic conquest was just a change of master. They had already learned how to adapt themselves and "endure under the conditions of political, social and economic disability."

Jewish Encyclopedia reports a high rate of conversion to Islam of informed Jews in the 12th century. Kohler and Gottheil in Jewish Encyclopedia agree with Grätz who thinks the reason was 'the degeneracy that had taken hold of Eastern Judaism, manifesting itself in the most superstitious practises,' and their being 'moved by the wonderful success of the Arabs in becoming a world-power.' Jewish Encyclopedia also reports outward conversions of Jews to Islam at around the year 1142 in southwestern Europe due to the rise of the Almohades.

Forced Conversions

In the first several centuries after the Islamic conquest and subsequently in the Ottoman Empire, forced conversions were rare. Forced conversions occurred mostly in the Maghreb, especially under the Almohads, a militant dynasty with messianic claims, as well as in Persia.

In the 12th century, rulers of the Almohad dynasty purged Muslims who would not submit to their particular brand of Islam, and killed or forcibly converted Jews and Christians in Al-Andalus and the Maghreb, putting an end to the existence of Christian communities in North Africa outside Egypt. In an effort to survive under Almohads, most Jews resorted to practicing Islam outwardly, while remaining faithful to Judaism; they openly reverted to Judaism after Almohad persecutions passed. Maimonides, the great Jewish author and philosopher, was among those forced to profess allegiance to Islam for a period of time. He wrote about the theological basis for the outward practice of Islam by Jews in terms of the perceived similarities between the strict monotheism of Judaism and Islam as compared to Christianity.

Although Lewis claims they were very rare overall, most forced conversions of dhimmis that did happen occurred in Persia. In 1656, Shah Abbas I expelled the Jews from Isfahan and compelled them to adopt Islam, although the order was subsequently withdrawn, possibly because of the loss of fiscal revenues. In the early 18th century, Shia'a clergy attempted to force all dhimmis to embrace Islam, but without success. In 1830, all 2,500 Jews of Shiraz were forcibly converted to Islam. In 1839, Jews were massacred in Mashhad and survivors were forcibly converted. The same fate awaited the Jews of Barforoush in 1866, even though they were allowed to revert to Judaism after an intervention from the British and French ambassadors.

Restrictions on Practice

Although dhimmis were allowed to perform their religious rituals, they were obliged to do so in a manner not conspicuous to Muslims. Display of non-Muslim religious symbols, such as crosses or icons, was prohibited on buildings and on clothing (unless mandated as part of *distinctive clothing*). Loud prayers were forbidden, as were the ringing of church bells or the trumpeting of shofars.

Dhimmis had the right to choose their own religious leaders: patriarchs for Christians, exilarchs and geonim for Jews. However, the choice of the community was sometimes subject to the approval of the Muslim authorities, who might block candidates more likely to instigate political instability.

Dhimmis were prohibited from proselytizing on pain of death. Neither were they allowed to obstruct the spread of Islam in any manner. Other restrictions included a prohibition on publishing or sale of non-Muslim religious literature and a ban on teaching the Quran.

Places of Worship

The Pact of Umar puts an obligation on dhimmis not to "restore, by night or by day, any [places of worship] that have fallen into ruin", and Ibn Kathir adhered to this view. At the same time, al-Mawardi wrote that dhimmis may "rebuild dilapidated old temples and churches". As in the case of building new houses of worship, the ability of dhimmi communities to repair churches and synagogues usually depended upon their relationship with local Muslim authorities and their ability to pay the relevant taxes.

Islamic doctrine prohibited the construction of new churches and synagogues. Abbasid caliph al-Mutawakkil ordered the destruction of all churches and synagogues built after the Islamic conquest. In the 11th century, the Fatimid caliph al-Hakim ordered the demolition of the Church of the Holy Sepulchre in Jerusalem.

When non-Muslim houses of worship were built in cities founded after the Islamic conquests, Muslim jurists usually justified such evasions of Islamic law by claiming that those churches and synagogues had existed in the pre-existing non-Muslim settlements. This reasoning was applied in Baghdad, which was built on the grounds of an eponymous Persian village, as well as in some other cities.

Blasphemy

Blasphemy by both Muslims and by dhimmis was severely punished. The definition of blasphemy included defamation of Muslim holy texts, denial of the prophethood of Muhammad, and disrespectful references to Islam. Scholars of the Hanbali and Maliki schools, as well as the Shi'ites, prescribed a death penalty for blasphemy, while Hanafis and to some extent Shafi'is advocated flogging and imprisonment in some cases, reserving the death penalty only for habitual and public offenders. Al-Mawardi treated blasphemy as a capital crime.

In general, prosecutions and condemnations for this crime were not common, but they occurred. Although some deliberately sought martyrdom, many blasphemers were insane or drunk; it was not uncommon for the blasphemy accusation to be made due to political considerations or private vengeance, and the fear of a blasphemy charge was a big factor in the fearful and subservient attitude of dhimmis under Muslim rule.

As Edward William Lane put it, describing his visit to Egypt: "[Jews] scarcely ever dare to utter a word of abuse when reviled or beaten by the meanest Arab or Turk; for many a Jew have been put to death upon a false and malicious accusation of uttering disrespectful words against the Kuran or the Prophet".

Taxation of Dhimmis

The main tax imposed upon dhimmis was the *jizya*, with the revenues going primarily to the defense and expansion of the Islamic state. Dhimmis were exempted from the *zakaat* tax, paid by Muslims and used to alleviate the suffering of the poor. Later, the *kharaj* emerged as a tax payable on land by a farmer regardless of his religion. In addition, various tolls and duties were levied upon both Muslims and non-Muslims.

The Jizya Tax

Payment of the *jizya* obligated Muslim authorities to protect dhimmis in civil and military matters. Sura 9:29 stipulates that *jizya* be exacted from non-Muslims as a condition required for Jihad to cease. Failure to pay the *jizya* could result in the pledge of protection of a dhimmi's life and property becoming void, with the dhimmi facing the alternatives of conversion, enslavement or death (or imprisonment, as advocated by Abu Yusuf, the chief *qadi* — religious judge — of Abbasid caliph Harun al-Rashid).

Taxation, from the perspective of dhimmis who came under Muslim rule, was "a concrete continuation of the taxes paid to earlier regimes" and, from the point of view of the Muslim conqueror, was a material proof of the Dhimmi's subjection to Muslim control. Lewis observes that the change from Byzantine to Arab rule was welcomed by many among the Dhimmis who found the new yoke far lighter than the old, both in taxation and in other matters, and that some even among the Christians of Syria and Egypt preferred the rule of Islam to that of Byzantines.

The importance of dhimmis as a source of revenue for the Muslim community is illuminated in a letter ascribed to Umar I and cited by Abu Yusuf: "if we take dhimmis and share them out, what will be left for the Muslims who come after us? By God, Muslims would not find a man to talk to and profit from his labors."

Most Islamic scholars agree that *jizya* must be levied only upon adult males. In an important early account, Malik's Muwatta reports that the jizya was collected from non-Muslim men only, and additional taxes were to be levied against dhimmis who travelled on business:

> *"The Sunnah is that there is no jizya due from women or children of people of the Book, and that jizya is only taken from men who have reached puberty. The people of dhimma... do not have to pay any zakat... This is because zakat is imposed on the Muslims to purify them and to be given back to their poor, whereas jizya is imposed on the people of the Book to humble them...If in any one year they frequently come and go in Muslim countries then they have to pay a tenth every time they do so, since that is outside what they have agreed upon, and not one of the conditions stipulated for them. This is what I have seen the people of knowledge of our city doing." (Al-Muwatta, 17 24.46)*

The 8th-century scholar Abu Ubayd advised that dhimmis must not be burdened above their capacity or caused to suffer. Al-Nawawi, however, dissents, demanding "the poll tax to be paid by dying people, the old, ... the blind, monks, workers, and the poor, incapable of practicing a trade." The latter view was often applied in practice, as contemporary non-Muslim sources give witness of taxation even of dead persons, widows, and orphans. Al-Nawawi demands that the unpaid amount of poll tax remain a debt to the dhimmi's account until he becomes solvent.

Although in general dhimmis had to pay higher taxes (despite not having to pay Zakat), Lewis notes there are varying opinions among scholars as to how much of an additional burden this was. According to Norman Stillman: "*Jizya* and *kharaj* were a crushing burden for the non-Muslim peasantry who eked out a bare living in a subsistence economy." Both agree that ultimately, the additional taxation on non-Muslims was a critical factor that drove many dhimmis to leave their religion and accept Islam. The early Islamic scholars took a relatively humane and practical attitude towards the collection of *jizya*, compared to the 11th century commentators writing when Islam was under threat both at home and abroad.

- In his commentary on Sura 9:29, Ibn Kathir writes that dhimmis must be: disgraced, humiliated and belittled. Therefore, Muslims are not allowed to honor the people of the *dhimma* or elevate them above Muslims, for they [dhimmis] are miserable, disgraced, and humiliated.
- The jurist Abu Yusuf, the chief judge of the Caliph Harun Al-Rashid, rules as follows regarding the manner of collecting the jizya.

No one of the people of the dhimma should be beaten in order to exact payment of the jizya, nor made to stand in the hot sun, nor should hateful things be inflicted upon their bodies, or anything of that sort. Rather they should be treated with leniency.

Legal Aspects

Use of Muslim and Dhimmi Courts

Religious pluralism existed in medieval Islamic law and ethics. The religious laws and courts of other religions, including Christianity, Judaism and Hinduism, were usually accommodated within the Islamic legal framework, as exemplified in the Caliphate, Al-Andalus, Ottoman Empire and Indian subcontinent. In medieval Islamic societies, the *qadi* (Islamic judges) usually could not interfere in the matters of non-Muslims unless the parties voluntarily chose to be judged according to Islamic law. The dhimmi communities living in Islamic states usually had their own laws independent from the Sharia law, such as the Jews who had their own *Halakha* courts.

Dhimmis were allowed to operate their own courts following their own legal systems in cases that did not involve other religious groups, capital offences, or threats to public order. However, in the Ottoman Empire of the 18th and 19th centuries, dhimmis frequently attended the Muslim courts. This was not only when their appearance was compulsory (for example in cases brought against them by Muslims) but also in order to record property and business transactions within their own communities. Cases were taken out against Muslims, against other dhimmis and even against members of the dhimmi's own family. Dhimmis often took cases relating to marriage, divorce or inheritance to the Muslim courts so these cases would be decided under sharia law. Oaths sworn by dhimmis in the Muslim courts were sometimes the same as the oaths taken by Muslims, sometimes tailored to the dhimmis' beliefs. When a case pitched a Muslim against a dhimmi, the word of a Muslim witness nearly always carried more weight than that of a dhimmi. According to Hanafi jurists, dhimmi testimony and oaths were not valid against Muslims. On the other hand, Muslims could testify against dhimmis.

Punishment for Murder of a Dhimmi

The Hanafi school, which represents the vast majority of Muslims, believes that the murder of a dhimmi must be punishable by death, citing a Hadith according to which Muhammad ordered the execution of a Muslim who killed a dhimmi. In other schools of Islamic jurisprudence the maximum punishment for the murder of a dhimmi, if perpetrated by a Muslim, was the payment of blood money; no death penalty was possible. According to the Maliki and Hanbali schools of jurisprudence, the value of a dhimmi's life was one-half the value of a Muslim's life; in the Shafii school, Jews and Christians were worth one-third of a Muslim and Zoroastrians were worth just one-fifteenth.

Leniency in Case of Murder of a Dhimmi, in the Tribal Kurdish Society

An expert of the Jewish Kurdish society, Mordechai Zaken, revealed recently the term used in the tribal Kurdish society "kafir kusht", i.e., murder of non-Muslims, infidels, or un-belivers, according to which murder of non-Muslims has been generally treated with much leniency, in comparison to murder of tribal Muslim Kurds that could have led to a major blood-feud between the tribes. Mordechai Zaken shows in his book that the tribal Kurdish society treated the murder of Jews and Christians with relative leniency. Some cases were resolved in financial compensation paid, ironically, to the patron chieftain of the Jew who was murdered (and not to the family of the victim), to compensate him for the future financial loss in terms of dues and services because of the murder of his Jewish protégé.

Inheritance

The general rule in Islamic law is that a difference in religion is an obstacle to inheritance, so dhimmis could not inherit from Muslims, nor could Muslims inherit from dhimmis. However, some Muslim jurists maintained that a Muslim could inherit from a dhimmi, while a dhimmi could not inherit from a Muslim. Shia scholars went so far as to argue that if a dhimmi died leaving even one Muslim heir, all the estate belonged to the Muslim heir at the expense of any dhimmi heirs. This provision was a subject of frequent complaints from Persian Jews.

Personal Safety

Despite a common prohibition on carrying weapons, Muslim jurists allowed dhimmis to serve as auxiliary soldiers. In the border provinces, dhimmis were sometimes recruited for military operations. In such cases, they were exempted from *jizya* for the year of service; however, they were not entitled to a share in the booty, receiving only a fixed stipend.

Being forbidden to bear arms, non-Muslims relied on the Muslim authorities for personal safety. Usually these authorities managed to protect dhimmis from violence, but such protection was likely to fail at times of public disorder. In the Maghreb during changes of reign and periods of instability, non-Muslim quarters were pillaged and their inhabitants either massacred or abducted for ransom.

Prohibition on Enslavement

Islamic law and custom prohibit the enslavement of free dhimmis within lands under Islamic rule. In some Islamic societies, non-Muslim boys were pressed into service in the slave armies of Muslim rulers. These slaves were ordinarily purchased or captured in military actions along the frontier, in accordance with sharia law, as dhimmi status was not available to non-Muslims beyond the borders of the Islamic state. The practice goes back to the Abbasids, who recruited such slave warriors, mainly from non-Muslim Turkic populations. Descendants of those slaves later formed the Mamluk dynasties.

An exception to the right of personal freedom guaranteed by the *dhimma* is seen in the Ottoman system known as devshirmeh: the enslavement of boys from the Christian population of the Ottoman Balkan provinces in order to muster Janissary troops and administrative personnel. These boys were often taken first to the households of local Muslim rulers and gentry, where they learned the Turkic language and converted to Islam. Refusal of conversion was rare, and some families were happy to have their sons receive this opportunity. Later, they would travel to Istanbul, the Ottoman capital, for training in their occupations. They were considered personal slaves of the monarch. Most were destined to serve in the infantry, but some would receive an advanced education and go on to serve in the highest military and administrative leadership positions in the empire.

Social and Psychological Aspects

Distinctive Clothing

For dhimmis to be clearly distinguishable from Muslims in public, Muslim rulers often prohibited dhimmis from wearing certain types of clothing, while forcing them to put on highly distinctive garments, usually of a bright colour. The scholars cited the Pact of Umar in which Christians supposedly took an obligation to "always dress in the same way wherever we may be, and... bind the zunar [wide belt] round our waists". Al-Nawawi required dhimmis to wear a piece of yellow cloth and a belt, as well as a metallic ring, inside public baths.

Riding

Dhimmis were forbidden to ride horses or camels; they were only allowed to ride donkeys and only on packsaddles, a prohibition that has its roots in the Pact of Umar. In the 18th century, Damanhuri, rector of Al-Azhar University, summed up the consensus of Islamic jurists: "Neither Jew nor Christian should ride a horse, with or without saddle. They may ride asses with a packsaddle." An additional requirement for dhimmis was not ride astride, but only sidesaddle, like a woman. In the Mamluk Egypt, where non-Mamluk Muslims were not allowed to ride horses and camels, dhimmis were prohibited even from riding donkeys inside cities. The same prohibition imposed on dhimmis was recorded in the 19th century in Damascus, as well as in Tunisia.

European travellers passing through the Middle East in the 18th and 19th centuries left ample evidence of the careful enforcement of prohibitions on horseback riding. Danish traveller Carsten Niebuhr wrote in 1761 that in Egypt, Jews and Christians were forced to alight while passing the houses of notable Muslims and when meeting such notables in the street. A Frenchman visiting Cairo in 1697 recorded the same situation. In Yemen and in the rural areas of Morocco, Libya, Iraq, and Persia, dhimmis had to dismount from a mule when passing a Muslim.

Dwelling Places

The dhimmis' obligation not to build houses higher than those of Muslims is one of the clauses of the Pact of Umar, supported as a desirable condition of "dhimma" by the consensus opinion of Islamic scholars. According to Bat Ye'or, the rule was not always enforced; for example, no such laws were recorded in Muslim Spain, and in Tunisia Jews owned fine houses. Sometimes, Muslim rulers issued regulations requiring dhimmis to attach distinctive signs to their houses.

In the 9th century, Abbasid caliph al-Mutawakkil ordered dhimmis to nail wooden images of devils to the doors of their homes. At about the same time in Tunisia, a *qadi* of the Aghlabid dynasty compelled dhimmis to nail onto their doors a board bearing the sign of a monkey. In Bukhara, Jews had to hang a piece of cloth out of their houses so that they could be distinguished from those of Muslims. Dhimmis were seldom prohibited from living in certain places, but there were some exceptions. In Morocco, beginning from the 15th century, and especially since the early 19th century, Jews were confined to mellahs (walled quarters similar to European ghettos). Jews were also forced to live in separate quarters in Persia. Neither Jews nor Christians were allowed to live in Hejaz after Umar I had expelled them.

Marriage between Muslims and Dhimmis

Muslim men may generally marry dhimmi women who are considered "People of the Book," however Islamic jurists reject the possibility any non-Muslim man might marry a Muslim woman. Traditionally, the prohibition of marriage between Muslim women and dhimmi men was enforced with the utmost rigor. All schools of Islamic jurisprudence, with the exception of the Hanafi, treated dhimmi men who married Muslim women as adulterers, for whom the punishment was death by stoning.

In cases where a non-Muslim wife converts to Islam, while her non-Muslim husband does not, their marriage is annulled. According to some early Muslim scholars, marriage between a dhimmi and a Muslim woman would lead to an incompatibility between the superiority of the woman, by virtue of her being a Muslim, and her unavoidable subservience to a non-Muslim husband. Some traditionalists compared marriage to enslavement; as dhimmis were prohibited from having Muslim slaves, so dhimmi men were not allowed to have Muslim wives.

Conversely, Muslim men were allowed to marry dhimmi women because the enslavement of non-Muslims by Muslims was allowed. Azizah Y. al-Hibri states that the relevant Hadith regarding marriage and slavery draw an analogy between the status of women and slaves in Muhammad's society in order to beseech the male audience to treat them kindly: "Be good to women; for they are powerless captives (awan) in your households. You took them in God's trust, and legitimated your sexual relations with the Word of God, so come to your senses people, and hear my words..."

Cultural Interactions and Cultural Differences

During the Middle Ages, local associations known as futuwwa clubs developed across the Islamic lands. There were usually several futuwwah in each town. These clubs catered to varying interests, primarily sports, and might involve distinctive manners of dress and custom. They were known for their hospitality, idealism and loyalty. They often had a militaristic aspect, purportedly for the mutual protection of the membership. These clubs commonly crossed social strata, including among their membership local notables, dhimmi and slaves – to the exclusion of those associated with the local ruler, or amir. Muslims and Jews were sometimes partners in trade, with the Muslim taking days off on Fridays and the Jew taking off on the Sabbath. Andrew Wheatcroft describes how some social customs such as different conceptions of dirt and cleanliness made it difficult for the religious communities to live close to each other, either under Muslim or under Christian rule. For Muslims and Christians alike the experience of living in close proximity to unbelievers was disquieting.

The social customs of each group invariably sought to minimize contact with the people of other faiths. Each often spoke of the other in terms of fear and sometimes disgust.

Shia Islam devotes much attention to the issues of ritual purity – tahara. Strict Shi'as consider Non-Muslims ritually unclean – najis – so that certain physical contact with them or things they touched with wet hands would require purification before undertaking religious or ritual duties. In Persia, where Shi'ism is dominant, these beliefs brought about restrictions that aimed at limiting physical contact between Muslims and dhimmis.

Chapter 6

Guidance and Teaching of Shariah

"Shariah is the guidance, the teachings, the rulings, and the way of life Allah sent through His messengers for humanity to attain success in this life and the eternal life. The final seal of this guidance is the Shariah of Islam sent to Prophet Muhammad (pbuh). The word Shariah is misunderstood by many Muslims and non-Muslims and it is often confined to criminal law. This limited understanding of Shariah takes away the beauty of Islam and its values and virtues. It is very important for us as Muslims in general, and American Muslims in particular, to understand our Shariah, learn its attributes, and know about the values it promotes and the objectives it aims to achieve.

This chapter is meant to shed some light upon the definition of Shariah and fiqh and the relationship between them. It also helps us understand some of the important attributes of Shariah and how these attributes distinguish it from any other value system. It also describes, in brief, the major objectives of Shariah rulings and their importance in Islamic fiqh, and aims to help us develop a sense of pride in being Muslims, and encourages us to embrace the values of Shariah in our lives. After going through the article, we hope to be able to use those values and objectives to better present Islam to people around us. The article also highlights the need to join hands in promoting such values and working hard to instill them in our society."

Islamic Banking

With world markets suffering extreme turbulence in the wake of the credit crunch and subsequent banking crisis, it is an opportune time to examine the merits of an alternative banking model which adopts a different attitude to risk and finance, based on the principles of Shariah-law. Islamic Banking had grown substantially in the decade or so until the start of the present global economic turmoil; arguably, the events of the past few months will provide a spur to even further growth in the sector as non-Muslim bank customers opt for the relative safety of institutions based on the principles of Islam.

The Impact of Economic and Demographic Changes

In the past decade, the world's economic centre of gravity has begun to increasingly tip in favour of developing economies such as China, India and the Gulf States, to the extent that leading multinationals such as GE and P&G expect more than half of their future growth to come from these emerging markets. Experts such as the leading fund manager, Antoine van Agtmael, have predicted that the combined Gross National Product of emerging markets will overtake that of developed economies within 30 years. Already these emergent economies hold 75% of the world's foreign exchange reserves.

At the same time, there has been a demographic change, with an increase in the population in Muslim countries at the expense of developed markets where populations are stagnating or falling. There are now approximately 1.6 bn. Muslims worldwide, comprising 24% of the total world's population.

These Muslim populations are increasingly looking for financing tools which comply with the tenets of Islamic (Shariah) law, while offering the flexibility and range of traditional banking products. Choosing Shariah-compliant products has become a means for many Muslims of asserting their Islamic identity.

Islamic Banking is not, however, necessarily confined only to Muslims. It has been recently argued that the tenets of Islamic Banking are applicable to a wider population, and that the principles offer safeguards that may counter the excesses which caused the sub-prime crisis and frauds perpetuated by rogue traders.

Islamic Tenets

Islamic Finance is governed by Shariah (Islamic law), which is sourced from the Quran and Sunnah. The key tenet of Islamic financing is the prohibition of interest, Riba, the principle being that it is unacceptable to increase the value of any commodity merely by lending it to another person. Shariah law also prohibits Masir, which is involvement in speculation and gambling transactions, Gharar, which is uncertainty about the terms of contract or subject matter (prohibiting, for example, selling something which you do not own), and investing in businesses which are considered unlawful or undesirable e.g. alcohol, drugs, gambling, arms.

The Dynamics of Islamic Finance

The recent rise of Islamic Finance has coincided with the record revenue generated from 5 years of high oil prices which has attracted funds into the Gulf States, prompting Muslim investors to pull money out of the US and developed markets and invest it within the region. At the same time, even for Muslims who are not particularly devout, using Shariah-compliant products has become a means of asserting their Islamic identity, and of enhancing their status in the local community.

Islamic Financing, however, is not confined to Islamic banks – non-Islamic banks can produce Islamic products, provided a Fatwa, a decree, is issued by a Shariah qualified scholar or board deeming that they are compliant. Western banks have thus enlisted respected Shariah scholars to review banking products, and issues Fatwas legitimising them. As a consequence, qualified Shariah scholars are in high demand, charging a substantial premium for their services.

This reliance on a few, highly-qualified Shariah scholars, is giving rise to concern at several levels. The paucity of qualified scholars means that they may divide their time among several banks, which may compromise their independence. The UK's Financial Services Authority, for example, in November 2007, highlighted possible "significant" conflicts of interest in such concentration of expertise. At the same time, the lack of scholars is slowing down development of the industry, and raises questions about the ability of Shariah supervisory boards to provide enough challenge and supervision of banking products and services.

At a wider level there are issues of consistency and transparency, as there are differing interpretations of Shariah law and whether products and services are compliant. Malaysia has attempted to resolve this issue by adopting one set of rules for all Islamic banking products and services, but their lead has not yet been followed by other Muslim markets. More broadly, two international organisations, AAOIFI (Accounting and Auditing Organisation for Islamic Financial Institutions) and IFSB (Islamic Finance Standards Board) have been created to promote and enhance the soundness and stability of the Islamic financial services industry. However, at this stage, the regulatory environment for Islamic Finance remains relatively fragmented.

The Opportunity

Islamic banking is now one of the world's fastest-growing economic activities, comprising over 300 institutions in more than 75 countries. Currently a $400 bn. market, it is expected that it will grow to $4 tn. over the next 5 years (Torsten Hinrichs, Standard & Poor's). While Islamic banking is concentrated in the Middle East and South-East Asia (with Bahrain and Malaysia representing the largest hubs), it is also starting to appear in Europe and the United States, in countries where there are large Muslim minority populations. In all dimensions of financial services, Islamic financing is now prevalent, from debt and capital markets and insurance, to asset management and structured and project financing. Since its early evolution, the complexity of products offered has increased dramatically, starting with commercial banking in the 1970 through to the present day where a full range of banking and financial products is available.

There is considerable room for growth as well, particularly in Asia, where there are very large Muslim populations and low coverage by Islamic banks. In Indonesia, with a Muslim population of 195 million, only 1.2% of total banking assets are under Islamic Finance. India, Pakistan and Bangladesh have 439 million potential customers but less than 10% of the market in each case has been tapped into by the banks offering Shariah-compliant products. Even in the Middle East and North Africa, which may be regarded as the natural home for Islamic banking, the penetration by Islamic banking is still relatively small. The potential for development of the sector, is, therefore, very large, especially given the relative population growth of the Muslim world versus the global population.

Product Development

To serve the growing market, financial institutions have developed a range of products catering for housing and consumer finance, business loans and infrastructure project funding. "Islamic equity" investment funds have been launched and both the Dow Jones and FTSE provide indices to monitor these funds. However, the major instruments utilised by Islamic banks still closely resemble conventional banking products. There is currently a relative lack of pure risk sharing instruments where gains and losses are shared equitably between investors and providers. This gap is expected to be addressed in the next generation of Shariah-compliant products.

For the past 30 years or more, financiers in the Muslim world have been trying to find ways of mixing Islamic laws with modern finance. These efforts started with the creation of so-called Islamic banks in countries such as Malaysia, Pakistan and Dubai, but have gradually expanded to include the creation of more complex and sophisticated products. These include Murabaha, where a financier buys a commodity and sells it to a purchaser at a higher price; Mudarabah which involves a bank providing funds to entrepreneurs who share the profits of any venture, without the entrepreneur being required to provide any capital; and Musharakah where a bank provides funding to entrepreneurs who contribute capital, with the profits from the venture shared.

The most common Islamic Finance products and their characteristics are outlined in Appendix A.

Islamic Banking and the Credit Crunch

The Islamic Banking model has developed on principles which, theoretically at least, are inherently less risky than the prevailing western alternatives. The current global economic crisis stemming from subprime mortgage debt write-downs is attributable to two main factors. The first was the relaxation of mortgage credit criteria in developed economies, such as the US, on the assumption that rising house prices would offer sufficient collateral against the lending risk. The second was the use of securisation to repackage these mortgage-based obligations into tradable financial products which diluted the underlying asset-backing. Once house prices began to stall, these financial securities became "toxic", dragging down in their wake the banks with the greatest exposure to them. Banking instability and failure, in turn, led to a failure in confidence and a reluctance of banks to lend to each other, causing money markets to dry-up.

An Islamic Bank, theoretically at least, is less exposed to the type of lending and financing practices which are at the root of the present crisis. Because of the principle of Riba, Islamic banks do not borrow or lend on international money markets because interest is not allowed; traditionally they have a larger proportion of their assets in reserve accounts with central banks. Islamic banking is based on the principles of risk-sharing between depositor and investor – in theory, meaning that customers practice greater oversight of an Islamic bank's lending performance than their Western banking counterparts. Shariah-law stipulates that Islamic securities should be asset-based, which means that a trader must own the asset being traded as opposed to the complex derivative products which have had such an adverse impact on Western banks. This, in turn, proscribes most forms of futures trading, as goods that the seller does not own or will not deliver cannot be the subject of an Islamic contract. Practices such as short-selling, consequently, are not a feature of Islamic Banking.

A note of caution, however, may be introduced at this point. Whilst the underlying precepts of Islamic Banking prohibit many of the practices which have imperiled Western banks, the efforts to offer an expanded range of Shariah-compliant offerings have led to the development of financial products which closely resemble more conventional financial instruments, such as Tawarruq and Sukuk, with exposure to the same type of risks, albeit not to the same degree. News may yet emerge in the coming months of an Islamic Bank suffering losses because of these new products.

The Saudi Market

The Saudi banking system is by far the largest in the Middle East, with Saudi banks accounting for nearly 50% of all private sector deposits held by GCC, and 25% of all private sector deposits in Middle Eastern banks. Traditionally, the Saudi market was dominated by local banks offering the traditional range of Consumer and Investment banking products. However, the market for Islamic finance has taken off to the extent that now 64% of Saudi banking transactions are Islamic in nature.

In a parallel development, the Saudi government was forced to open up the banking and insurance sectors to foreign investors as a condition of WTO (World Trade Organisation) membership. Traditional Islamic banks, which had historically prospered due to the highly protected local market, now find themselves having to compete with new market entrants, hybrid banks offering a mixture of Islamic and conventional products. Generally more nimble, these banks tend to offer superior marketing and customer service skills. At the same time, banks such as HSBC and NCB (National Commercial Bank) have created Islamic-branded subsidiaries and networks in response to customer needs. As a result, customers no longer have to choose between Shariah-compliant banks and western levels of service. Faced with increasingly knowledgeable and demanding customers, a generic positioning as an Islamic bank is no longer sufficient.

Islamic Banking is increasingly starting to dominate the industry. Al Rajhi Bank, headquartered in Riyadh, for example, is not only vying with NCB to be the largest bank in the Saudi Arabia and the Middle East, but is the biggest Islamic bank in the world, with 100% of its products totally Shariah-compliant. It consciously promotes itself as an Islamic bank and, for the majority of its customers, this is a strong component of their loyalty and attachment to the bank. Not to be outdone, most of the other banks in Saudi Arabia now emphasise the Islamic nature of much of their products, even when conventional services are offered alongside the Shariah-compliant ones.

From a research perspective, financial institutions need to conduct the appropriate studies to evaluate the appeal of existing and new Islamic products in comparison with conventional products, and how best to communicate the functional as well as more emotive and intangible benefits of such products. This is emerging as one of the key research topics in the Gulf region, and is likely to become even stronger in the future. For the research to be at its most effective, the researcher-consultant needs to combine in-depth knowledge of appropriate methodologies with a fundamental understanding of both the conventional banking sector and its Islamic variants.

Islam's Doctrines of Deception

To better understand Islam, one must appreciate the thoroughly legalistic nature of the religion. According to Shariah (Islamic law) every conceivable human act is categorised as being either forbidden, discouraged, permissible, recommended, or obligatory.

"Common sense" or "universal opinion" has little to do with Islam's notions of right and wrong. Only what Allah (through the Quran) and his prophet Muhammad (through the Hadith) have to say about any given issue matters; and how Islam's greatest theologians and jurists – collectively known as the ulema, literally, "they who know" – have articulated it. According to Shariah, in certain situations, deception – also known as 'taqiyya', based on Quranic terminology, – is not only permitted but sometimes obligatory. For instance, contrary to early Christian history, Muslims who must choose between either recanting Islam or being put to death are not only permitted to lie by pretending to have apostatised, but many jurists have decreed that, according to Quran 4:29, Muslims are obligated to lie in such instances.

Origins of Taqiyya

As a doctrine, taqiyya was first codified by Shia Muslims, primarily as a result of their historical experience. Long insisting that the caliphate rightly belonged to the prophet Muhammad's cousin and son-in-law, Ali (and subsequently his descendents), the Shia were a vocal and powerful branch of Islam that emerged following Muhammad's death. After the internal Islamic Fitna wars from the years 656 AD to 661 AD, however, the Shia became a minority branch, persecuted by mainstream Muslims or Sunnis – so-called because they follow the example or 'sunna' of Muhammad and his companions. Taqiyya became pivotal to Shia survival.

Interspersed among the much more numerous Sunnis, who currently make up approximately 90 per cent of the Islamic world, the Shia often performed taqiyya by pretending to be Sunnis externally, while maintaining Shia beliefs internally, as permitted by Quranic verse 16:106. Even today, especially in those Muslim states where there is little religious freedom, the Shia still practice taqiyya. In Saudi Arabia, for instance, Shias are deemed by many of the Sunni majority to be heretics, traitors and infidels and like other non-Sunni Muslims they are often persecuted. Several of Saudi Arabia's highest clerics have even issued fatwas sanctioning the killing of Shias. As a result, figures on the Arabian kingdom's Shia population vary wildly from as low as 1 per cent to nearly 20 per cent. Many Shias living there obviously choose to conceal their religious identity. As a result of some 1,400 years of Shia taqiyya, the Sunnis often accuse the Shias of being habitual liars, insisting that taqiyya is ingrained in Shia culture.

Conversely, the Sunnis have historically had little reason to dissemble or conceal any aspect of their faith, which would have been deemed dishonourable, especially when dealing with their historic competitors and enemies, the Christians. From the start, Islam burst out of Arabia subjugating much of the known world, and, throughout the Middle Ages, threatened to engulf all of Christendom. In a world where might made right, the Sunnis had nothing to apologise for, much less to hide from the 'infidel'. Paradoxically, however, today many Sunnis are finding themselves in the Shias' place: living as minorities in Western countries surrounded and governed by their traditional foes. The primary difference is that, extremist Sunnis and Shia tend to reject each other outright, as evidenced by the ongoing Sunni-Shia struggle in Iraq, whereas, in the West, where freedom of religion is guaranteed, Sunnis need only dissemble over a few aspects of their faith.

Articulation of Taqiyya

According to the authoritative Arabic text, Al-Taqiyya Fi Al-Islam: "Taqiyya [deception] is of fundamental importance in Islam. Practically every Islamic sect agrees to it and practices it. We can go so far as to say that the practice of taqiyya is mainstream in Islam, and that those few sects not practicing it diverge from the mainstream. Taqiyya is very prevalent in Islamic politics, especially in the modern era."

The primary Quranic verse sanctioning deception with respect to non-Muslims states: "Let believers not take for friends and allies infidels instead of believers. Whoever does this shall have no relationship left with Allah – unless you but guard yourselves against them, taking precautions." (Quran 3:28)

Al-Tabari's (838-923 AD) Tafsir, or Quranic exegeses, is essentially a standard reference in the entire Muslim world. Regarding 3:28, he wrote: "If you [Muslims] are under their [infidels'] authority, fearing for yourselves, behave loyally to them, with your tongue, while harbouring inner animosity for them... Allah has forbidden believers from being friendly or on intimate terms with the infidels in place of believers – except when infidels are above them [in authority]. In such a scenario, let them act friendly towards them."

Regarding 3:28, the Islamic scholar Ibn Kathir (1301-1373) wrote: "Whoever at any time or place fears their [infidels'] evil, may protect himself through outward show."

As proof of this, he quotes Muhammad's companions. Abu Darda said: "Let us smile to the face of some people while our hearts curse them." Al-Hassan said: "Doing taqiyya is acceptable till the day of judgment [in perpetuity]." Other prominent ulema, such as al- Qurtubi, al-Razi, and al-Arabi have extended taqiyya to cover deeds. Muslims can behave like infidels – from bowing down and worshipping idols and crosses to even exposing fellow Muslims' "weak spots" to the infidel enemy – anything short of actually killing a fellow Muslim.

War is Deceit

None of this should be surprising considering that Muhammad himself, whose example as the "most perfect human" is to be tenaciously followed, took an expedient view on the issue of deception. For instance, Muhammad permitted deceit in three situations: to reconcile two or more quarreling parties; husband to wife and vice-versa; and in war.

During the Battle of the Trench (627 AD), which pitted Muhammad and his followers against several non-Muslim tribes collectively known as "the Confederates", a Confederate called Naim bin Masud went to the Muslim camp and converted to Islam. When Muhammad discovered the Confederates were unaware of Masud's conversion, he counseled him to return and try somehow to get his tribesmen to abandon the siege. "For war is deceit," Muhammad assured him.

Masud returned to the Confederates without their knowledge that he had switched sides and began giving his former kin and allies bad advice. He also went to great lengths to instigate quarrels between the various tribes until, thoroughly distrusting each other, they disbanded and lifted the siege. According to this account, deceit saved Islam during its embryonic stage.

More demonstrative of the legitimacy of deception with respect to non-Muslims is the following account. A poet, Kab bin al-Ashruf, had offended Muhammad by making derogatory verse about Muslim women. Muhammad exclaimed in front of his followers: "Who will kill this man who has hurt Allah and his prophet?"

A young Muslim named Muhammad bin Maslama volunteered, but with the caveat that, in order to get close enough to Kab to assassinate him, he be allowed to lie to the poet. Muhammad agreed. Maslama travelled to Kab and began denigrating Islam and Muhammad, carrying on this way till his disaffection became convincing enough for Kab to take him into his confidences. Soon thereafter, Maslama appeared with another Muslim and, while Kab's guard was down, they assaulted and killed him. They ran to Muhammad with Kab's head, to which the latter cried: "Allahu akbar" or "God is great".

The entire sequence of Quranic revelations are a testimony to taqiyya and, since Allah is believed to be the revealer of these verses, he ultimately is seen as the perpetrator of deceit. This is not surprising since Allah himself is often described in the Quran as the "best deceiver" or "schemer." This phenomenon revolves around the fact that the Quran contains both peaceful and tolerant verses, as well as violent and intolerant ones. The ulema were uncertain which verses to codify into sharia's worldview. For instance, should they use the one that states there is no coercion in religion (2:256), or the ones that command believers to fight all non-Muslims until they either convert or at least submit to Islam (9:5, 9:29)? To solve this quandary, they developed the doctrine of abrogation – naskh, supported by Quran 2:105. This essentially states that verses "revealed" later in Muhammad's career take precedence over those revealed earlier whenever there is a discrepancy.

Why the contradiction in the first place? The standard answer has been that, because Muhammad and his community were far outnumbered by the infidels in the early years of Islam, a message of peace and co-existence was in order. However, after Muhammad migrated to Medina and grew in military strength and numbers, the militant or intolerant verses were revealed, urging Muslims to go on the offensive.

According to this standard view, circumstance dictates which verses are to be implemented. When Muslims are weak, they should preach and behave according to the Meccan verses; when strong, they should go on the offensive, according to the Medinan verses. Many Islamic books extensively deal with the doctrine of abrogation, or Al-Nasikh Wa Al-Mansukh.

War is Eternal

The fact that Islam legitimises deceit during war cannot be all that surprising; strategist Sun Tzu 722-Italian political philosopher Machiavelli (1469-1527) and English philosopher Thomas Hobbes (1588-1679) all justified deceit in war.

However, according to all four recognised schools of Sunni jurisprudence, war against the infidel goes on in perpetuity, until "all chaos ceases, and all religion belongs to Allah" (Quran 8:39). According to the definitive Encyclopaedia of Islam (Brill Online edition): "The duty of the jihad exists as long as the universal domination of Islam has not been attained. Peace with non-Muslim nations is, therefore, a provisional state of affairs only; the chance of circumstances alone can justify it temporarily. Furthermore there can be no question of genuine peace treaties with these nations; only truces, whose duration ought not, in principle, to exceed ten years, are authorised. But even such truces are precarious, inasmuch as they can, before they expire, be repudiated unilaterally should it appear more profitable for Islam to resume the conflict."

The concept of obligatory jihad is best expressed by Islam's dichotomised worldview that pits Dar al Islam (House of Islam) against Dar al Harb (House of War or non-Muslims) until the former subsumes the latter. Muslim historian and philosopher, Ibn Khaldun (1332- 1406), articulated this division by saying: "In the Muslim community, holy war [jihad] is a religious duty, because of the universalism of the Muslim mission and the obligation to convert everybody to Islam either by persuasion or by force. The other religious groups did not have a universal mission, and the holy war was not a religious duty for them, save only for purposes of defence. But Islam is under obligation to gain power over other nations."

This concept is highlighted by the fact that, based on the ten-year treaty of Hudaibiya, ratified between Muhammad and his Quraish opponents in Mecca (628), ten years is theoretically the maximum amount of time Muslims can be at peace with infidels (as indicated earlier by the Encyclopaedia of Islam). Based on Muhammad's example of breaking the treaty after two years, by citing a Quraish infraction, the sole function of the "peace-treaty" (hudna) is to buy weakened Muslims time to regroup for a renewed offensive. Muhammad is quoted in the Hadith saying: "If I take an oath and later find something else better, I do what is better and break my oath This might be what former PLO leader and Nobel Peace Prize winner Yasser Arafat meant when, after negotiating a peace treaty criticised by his opponents as conceding too much to Israel, he said in a mosque: "I see this agreement as being no more than the agreement signed between our Prophet Muhammad (Pbuh) and the Quraish in Mecca."

On several occasions Hamas has made it clear that its ultimate aspiration is to see Israel destroyed. Under what context would it want to initiate a "temporary" peace with the Jewish state? When Osama bin Laden offered the US a truce, stressing that "we [Muslims] are a people that Allah has forbidden from double-crossing and lying," what was his ultimate intention? Based on the above, these are instances of Muslim extremists feigning openness to the idea of peace simply in order to bide time.

If Islam must be in a constant state of war with the non-Muslim world – which need not be physical, as radicals among the ulema have classified several non-literal forms of jihad, such as "jihad-of-the-pen" (propaganda), and "money-jihad" (economic) – and if Muslims are permitted to lie and feign loyalty to the infidel to further their war efforts, offers of peace, tolerance or dialogue from extremist Muslim corners are called into question.

Religious Obligation?

Following the terrorist attacks on the United States of 11 September 2001, a group of prominent Muslims wrote a letter to Americans saying that Islam is a tolerant religion that seeks to coexist with others.

Bin Laden castigated them, saying: "As to the relationship between Muslims and infidels, this is summarised by the Most High's Word: 'We renounce you. Enmity and hate shall forever reign between us – till you believe in Allah alone' [Quran 60:4]. So there is an enmity, evidenced by fierce hostility from the heart. And this fierce hostility – that is battle – ceases only if the infidel submits to the authority of Islam, or if his blood is forbidden from being shed [a dhimmi – a non-Muslim subject living as a "second-class" citizen in an Islamic state in accordance to Quran 9:29], or if Muslims are at that point in time weak and incapable [a circumstance under which taqiyya applies]. But if the hate at any time extinguishes from the heart, this is great apostasy! Such, then, is the basis and foundation of the relationship between the infidel and the Muslim. Battle, animosity and hatred, directed from the Muslim to the infidel, is the foundation of our religion. And we consider this a justice and kindness to them."

This hostile world view is traceable to Islam's schools of jurisprudence. When addressing Western audiences, however, Bin

Laden's tone significantly changes. He lists any number of grievances as reasons for fighting the West – from Israeli policies towards Palestinians to the Western exploitation of women and US failure to sign the Kyoto protocol – never alluding to fighting the US simply because it is an infidel entity that must be subjugated. He often initiates his messages to the West by saying: "Reciprocal treatment is part of justice." This is a clear instance of taqiyya, as Bin Laden is not only waging a physical jihad, but one of propaganda. Convincing the West that the current conflict is entirely its fault garners him and his cause more sympathy. Conversely, he also knows that if his Western audiences were to realise that, all real or imagined political grievances aside, according to the Islamic worldview delineated earlier, which bin Laden does accept, nothing short of their submission to Islam can ever bring peace, his propaganda campaign would be compromised. As a result there is constant lying, "for war is deceit".

If Bin Laden's words and actions represent an individual case of taqiyya, they raise questions about Saudi Arabia's recent initiatives for "dialogue". Saudi Arabia closely follows Shariah. For instance, the Saudi government will not allow the construction of churches or synagogues on its land; Bibles are banned and burned. Christians engaged in any kind of missionary activity are arrested, tortured, and sometimes killed. Muslim converts to Christianity can be put to death in the kingdom.

Despite such limitations on religious freedom, the Saudis have been pushing for more dialogue between Muslims and non-Muslims. At the most recent interfaith conference in Madrid in July 2008, King Abdullah asserted: "Islam is a religion of moderation and tolerance, a message that calls for constructive dialogue among followers of all religions."

Days later, it was revealed that Saudi children's textbooks still call Christians and Jews "infidels", "hated enemies" and "pigs and swine". A multiple-choice test in a book for fourth-graders asks: "Who is a 'true' Muslim?" The correct answer is not the man who prays and fasts, but rather: "A man who worships God alone, loves the believers and hates the infidels". These infidels are the same people the Saudis want dialogue with. This raises the question of whether, when Saudis call for dialogue, they are merely following Muhammad's companion Abu Darda's advice: "Let us smile to the face of some people while our hearts curse them"?

There is also a philosophical – more particularly, epistemological – problem with taqiyya. Anyone who truly believes that no less an authority than God justifies and, through his prophet's example, sometimes even encourages deception, will not experience any ethical qualms or dilemmas about lying. This is especially true if the human mind is indeed a tabula rasa shaped by environment and education. Deception becomes second nature. Consider the case of former Al-Qaeda operative, Ali Mohammad. Despite being entrenched in the highest echelons of the terrorism network, Mohammed's confidence at dissembling enabled him to become a CIA agent and FBI informant for years. People who knew him regarded him "with fear and awe for his incredible self-confidence, his inability to be intimidated, absolute ruthless determination to destroy the enemies of Islam, and his zealous belief in the tenets of militant Islamic fundamentalism", according to Steven Emerson. Indeed, this sentiment sums it all up: for a zealous belief in Islam's tenets, which, as has been described above, legitimises deception, will certainly go a long way in creating incredible self-confidence when deceiving one's enemies.

Exposing a Doctrine

All of the above is an exposition on doctrine and its various manifestations, not an assertion on the actual practices of the average Muslim. The deciding question is how literally any given Muslim follows Shariah and its worldview.

So-called "moderate" Muslims – or, more specifically, secularised Muslims – do not closely adhere to Shariah, and therefore have little to dissemble about. On the other hand, "radical" Muslims who closely observe Shariah law, which splits the world into two perpetually warring halves, will always have a "divinely sanctioned" right to deceive, until "all chaos ceases, and all religion belongs to Allah

Evolution of the Idea of Human Rights and Duties in Islam

The contemporary notion of human rights— embodied in theory, practice and law— does not have a parallel provenance in pre-modern Islamic thought and practice.

There are no similar "moments" in Islamic history comparable to Magna Carta, the French Revolution's Declaration of the Rights of Man, or the framing of the US Constitution and Bill of Rights.

Neither does Islam have a tradition of theorising about individual rights and freedoms, in the vein of Locke, Hobbes, Montesquieu, Rousseau, Paine and JS Mill in pre-modern times.

Therefore, in as much as the modern principles of human rights can be related, in part, to an accumulation of systematic thinking on the rights of individuals, groups and communities, then Islamic thought does not exhibit the same or similar progression of the set of ideas and principles that underpin modern human rights. However, there is little doubt that Islamic thought and jurisprudence, in the pre-modern era, did deal with many aspects of the rights and duties of various categories of human beings; but in a framework that was conceptually and methodologically different from the western tradition.

"Huqooq al-Insan" in Arabic are the contemporary rendering of "human rights". However, they cannot be located as such in pre-modern Islamic literature. But *Huqooq* itself is a word derived from the root word *Haqq*— a word which can mean equally truth or right or rights over others, or share. (*Al-Haqq* or the Truth, is one of Allah's attributes).

It is in this form that the equivalent principle of human rights and duties in Islam is found in a huge array of original Islamic sources.

Such sources can include documents on the principles and maxims of government; sayings of rulers and judges; actions of the *muhtassib*, (a type of ombudsman); treatises on justice, equality, ethics, political and moral philosophy, accountability, toleration, treatment of minorities, property rights, freedom of conscience and expression, and so on.

Human Rights in the Classical Islamic Period

The Quran

For the mass of believing Muslims throughout history, the Qur'an has always been the key text upon which Islamic life and civilization has been built. Muslims have found in the Qur'an numerous verses from which an understanding of human being's position in the cosmos has been derived; as well as the enumeration and exposition of the rights and duties of human beings to their Creator, to each other and to themselves.

Such verses cover the dignity and moral perfectibility of human beings; mankind as God's vice-regents on earth; the inherent equality of human beings; elevated status of human beings in the cosmic order; as well as the obligation to consult others in governing; the toleration of non-Muslims and the rejection of compunction in matters of faith and religion.

Human beings (*insan*) and *Haqq* are mentioned over 70 and 250 times respectively.

However, the pre-modern reading and interpretation of the Qur'anic text was not done with the specific intent of developing a human rights doctrine. This only emerged in the 20th century mainly in response to the challenge of the modern human rights movement.

The Early Medinan 'Constitution'

This document reports the heads of agreement between the Prophet Muhammad (Pbuh) and his followers after the hegira to Medina and the people of Medina and the surrounding tribes— both pagan Arabs, Christian Arabs and Jews. It is narrated by Ibn Ishaq, the earliest of the Prophet Muhammad's biographers.

The document regulates the relationship between the various components of the Medinan society and confirms the principles of toleration, freedom of religion and rights granted to the tribes and to non-Muslims, in the context of building a civic order.

Instructions and Decisions of the Rightly Guided Caliphs

Instructions from the Caliphs Abu Bakr and Omar on the treatment of non combatants and non-Muslims in conquered territories; and on the dispensation of justice.

Discourses, Orders and Sermons of the 4th caliph, Imam Ali[2]

The key document here is the detailed letter written by Imam Ali to Malik al-Ashtar, the governor of Egypt, where Imam Ali sets out the rights and duties of the ruler and the ruled, and guidelines on the proper and appropriate conduct of the state towards its subjects. (This document surfaces later in the design of the Iranian constitutions of 1906 and 1979).

The discourses of Imam Ali that were collected in a compilation called *Nahj ul-Balagha* (the Peaks of Eloquence), are an important source for the evolution of Shia Muslim ethical doctrines, some of which relate to the idea of human rights and duties.

Jurisprudential Treatises and the Idea of Human Rights

These sources fall into a number of categories including: treatises on government and power, emphasising humanistic principles such as equality, access to justice, provision of personal security and public order, and enhancing social and economic welfare.

Such treatises include the writings of Al-'Amir (d. 991), al-Ghazali (d.1111), al-Tartoushi (d.1126), Abi Asiba'a (d.1269), Al-Taqtaqi (d.1309), Ibn Jama'a (d.1332), al-Zayani (d.1388). Al-Tartoushi's book, *Siraj al-Muluk* (The Lamp of Kings) in particular comes close to discussing issues of equality before the law, and the rights of subjects not to be oppressed by state power in ways that approximate contemporary human rights discourse.

Human rights were also implicit in the writings of Islamic political philosophers such as al-Farabi in his *Virtuous City;* philosophers of history such as Ibn Khaldun and moralists and ethicists such as Ibn Hazm of Andalusia and ibn Muskawayh.

The Epistle of Rights by Imam Ali Zain al-Abidin

This is a document that has been authoritatively attributed to Imam Ali Zain al-Abidin (d.714), the fourth Imam of the Shia Muslims. It sets out eight categories of rights, mainly expressed in terms of the classical understanding of rights that others have over the individual.

These include: individual rights and obligations couched in religious terms; spiritual and religious rights; the rights and obligations of the ruler and ruled; the rights of parents and children; social rights (such as the rights of neighbours); economic and financial rights; the rights of those seeking reform (a uniquely Islamic category); ethical and moral rights.

The Rights of 'Adamic Creatures' of al-Mawardi

Al-Mawardi (d.1058) is a key political philosopher in Islam and the author of the famous treatise on government *al-Ahkam al-Sultaniyya* ('The Principles of Government').

His treatise on the rights of man (Adamic Creatures) is less well known but nevertheless a significant document. It is written mainly as a manual for rulers to curb their excesses in the exercise of power and not to trample on the rights of human beings as ordained by religion.

In summary, the classical period did not treat human rights as a separate category of inquiry but included aspects of them in treatises on government, power and authority.

In general, rights arose as a correlative of duties and obligations, and this was so expressed in the jurisprudential terms of the Shariah. It is the human being as an obligor (*Mukallaf*) rather than one with inherent rights that is the foundation of Shariah rulings that have a bearing on human rights and duties.

Modernity and Human Rights

The impact of the European powers on Islamic institutions and laws was felt especially forcibly in the Ottoman Empire. The demand for a constitution to contain the powers of the Sultan/Caliph introduced the idea of citizenship in place of the *millet* system.

The *millet* system was based essentially on the recognition of each religious community in the Empire as a separate unit, directly connected to the Sultan/Caliph. Each *millet* (e.g. the Greek orthodox, the Catholics, the Jews) set most of its own laws and regulations in light of religious ordinances and customs. The Sultan/Caliph in turn had his power limited to those areas for which the Shariah had no ruling.

The constitutional movement thus undermined both the principle of Sultan/Subject and the division of autonomous communities according to religious affiliations. The Political rights were therefore recast in modern terms of constitutional arrangements, representation, elections, separation of powers, and the institutions and laws that accompanied impact of modernity in the 19th century also affected intellectuals, writers and high officials in the Muslim World in ways that further undermined the familiar concepts and categories of Islamic thought and practice. The principles of the French Revolution, profoundly significant in the early construct of human rights doctrines in the West, seeped into Muslim lands and influenced a whole range of opinion leaders.

Rifa'a Tahtawi (d.1873) wrote regarding the meaning of liberty and freedom. In Islamic thought liberty was not an inherently desirable trait but merely one that stood in contrast to a state of slavery. Syed Ahmad Khan (d.1898) introduced reason and the scientific method in his Qur'anic hermeneutics.

Muhammad Abduh (d.1905) discussed the importance of free expression and conscience as a fundamental human right. Ali Abd el-Razzik dismissed the ideal of the Caliphate as a significant and necessary institution in Islam, allowing thereby legitimacy to the notion of the nation state. Qasim Amin (d.1908) and Jamil Zahawi (d.1936) sought to elevate the status of women in Islam.

But all of these reformers met with strong resistance from traditional circles and their claims only gradually entered the public consciousness. In many cases, it was only through the efforts of autocratic regimes (such as Ataturk) that their principles (for example the emancipation of women) were accepted at the level of government.

The principles of limited and constitutional government were most profoundly expressed in the Iranian Constitutional Revolution of 1906. The author of the most famous treatise on the necessity of constitutional government in Islam was Grand Ayatollah Muhammad Hussein al-Naini (d.1936). It was his theoretical writings and pronouncements (especially *Tanbih al-Umma wa Tanzih al-Milla*) that inspired the revolutionaries of the period and reconciled the ideals of Islamic government with the demands of a constitutional order that limited the powers of the ruler.

Naini's treatise introduced important qualifications to the principles of government of Islam *viz.* The idea of deputising a person to represent one's political interests and limiting the duration of such deputation. Choosing one's representative in an assembly of such people, with delegated, limited but renewable powers becomes a critical aspect of a government in Islam. At the same time, the people are recognised as politically sovereign in the absence of a divinely guided Imam.

Naini's political and constituional ideas revolved around four basic points:

1. A description of the evils of an unrepresentative and oppressive government.
2. The promulgation of a constitution.
3. The establishment of a parliament through elections.
4. Elaboration on the ideas of freedom, equality, supervision and transparency.

Nevertheless Naini also introduced the idea of guardianship over the political process by the establishment of a council of elders that would supervise the constitution and government, and ensure that no laws are passed that contravene Islamic ordinances.

The ideals of the Iranian constitutional revolution of 1906 resurfaced in the 1979 revolution, but key aspects of Naini's vision were distorted or overlooked in the constitutional arrangements of the Islamic republic. Following the end of WW I, most Muslims resided in one form or another under colonial or imperial rule. The evolution of human rights doctrines were naturally subservient to the struggle for independence, and for expanding the scope of political freedoms where a form of parliamentary government was followed (e.g. in Egypt).

UN's Universal Declaration of Human Rights

The role of Muslim majority countries in the formulation of the UN's Universal Declaration of Human Rights (UDHR) in 1948 was minimal. That is not to say that Muslim majority did not particpate in the negotiations that resulted in the final document, but their concerns, when expressed, were not taken into account.

There were few Muslim majority countries in the UN at that point and apart from the interjections of Saudi Arabia— which abstained in the final vote— the other Muslim nations ratified the document without any reservations or comments.

Muslim countries all participated in later international conferences in 1966 which set out the civil, political, social, economic and cultural rights, and the collective International Bill of Rights have been ratified in their present form by nearly all Muslim majority countries.

The fact that a number of the provisions of these covenants contravened generally accepted Islamic norms (for example, Article 18 of the UDHR on the right to change one's religion) could be attributed to the nature of the governments (and their diplomatic representatives) of that period. Most of the newly independent Arab countries were run by secular elements who were not over concerned with the nuances of the contradictions between certain Shariah rulings and the covenants of the human rights declarations. It was only after the rise of political Islam on the world stage in the 1970's which culminated in the Islamic revolution in Iran, did a serious questioning of the conditions under which the international human rights covenants were drawn become a subject of dispute. The UDHR became depicted as an unequal imposition of a purported universal doctrine by ascendant western powers.

However, at the non-governmental level the UNDHR and the other human rights covenants spurred a critical examination of the Islamic retort to the human rights movement, and an attempt to update Islamic rulings and understandings of the concept. The literature on human rights and Islam grew exponentially in the period after 1950 with several writers attempting to evolve a specifically Islamic notion of human rights built on key Qur'anic concepts, such as human beings acting as God's' vice regents on earth and the inherent dignity of human beings endowed with a spiritual essence.

In addition, the literature on Islam and human rights began to mine the principles of the Shariah as well as new renderings of Shariah rulings to build a body of human rights that purported to be in accordance with the teachings of Islam. Parallel to this entirely new literature on human rights, Muslim countries meeting in various conclaves began to formally introduce the idea of human rights, albeit in a specific Islamic formulation.

The first such attempt to introduce specific provision for human rights in a model Islamic state was the Pan Islamic conference held in Karachi in 1950, which was attended by the leading Islamic ideologue of the times, Abul 'Ala al-Mawdudi. The Karachi conference produced a model constitution for an ideal Islamic state. The provisions of this model constitution became the building block for several similar schemes promoted by Islamist political parties, such as the Muslim Brotherhood's proposals for an Islamic constitution (1952) and that of Hizb-ul-Tahrir (also 1952). These schemes culminated in the famous Azhar University's 1978 proposal for an Islamic constitution, whose significance lies in that it was proposed by the pre-eminent Sunni Muslim religious institution. In one form or another, the idea of a specific Islamic formulation of human rights as a counterpoint to the International Bill of Rights can be traced to these proposals, all of which were triggered by the UDHR and the inadequate response of Muslim governments of the time to the (Islamically) controversial or problematic provisions of the covenants.

In the 1970's Saudi Arabia began to sponsor a series of meetings and conferences with a view to systematising an Islamic bill of human rights; as well as propagating the role of religion and religious doctrine in the formulation of international covenants of human rights. These efforts started in 1972 by the Saudi Ministry of Justice, directly and through the offices of the Saudi-financed World Islamic League. In 1980, the Islamic Council of Europe, an independent organisation that had then a link to the World Islamic League, produced the first specifically Islamic doctrine of human rights, called the Universal Islamic Declaration of Human Rights (UIDHR). This was as a result of a conference held in London and attended by over 50 representatives from various Muslim governments. The UIDHR acquired a semi-legal status in the Islamic world and was seen as a counterpoint to the UHDR.

The Declaration involved the stipulation of 23 human rights, all of which were justified explicitly by Qur'anic verses and sayings (*Hadith*) of the Prophet Muhammad (Pbuh). The rights listed did not follow the sequence of the UDHR and included rights that did not feature at all in the UDHR, couched as they were in the language of religion. The UIDHR became in time the main foundational document and support for all subsequent elaborations on human rights by Islamic organisations. The UIDHR was unveiled to the world at an elaborate conference at UNESCO attended by a number of former leaders of Muslim countries such Ben Bella of Algeria and Ould Dadah of Mauretania.

The UIDHR was soon followed by a meeting of Muslim jurists, lawyers and judges in Kuwait in December 1980 that elaborated in detail on the UIDHR's covenants. A specifically Arab version of human rights emerged out of a conference organised by the Arab League's legal department. The conference, held in Syracuse in Italy in 1986 grouped a large number of Arab legal, academic, religious and governmental figures. The conference produced a document, *The Project for The Declaration of the Rights of Human Beings and Peoples in the Arab Nation.* The document detailed the nature of civil rights.

- Recognition of legal rights.
- A right to life.

- o A right to personal security.
- o Freedom to travel, and so on.
- o The nature of social, economic and cultural rights.
- o Political rights (such as freedom of assembly, freedom to form associations.
- o A right to nationality.
- o And finally, group rights such as the right to self-determination, the right to resist the invader or foreign tutelage.

The conference also recommended the formation of a specific Arab Human Rights Committee as well as the establishment of an Arab Human Rights Court.

The conferences of the late 1970's and 1980's were partly in response to the enormous challenge thrown at the Muslim world by the promulgation of a specifically Islamic constitution in Iran. Many countries were moved to question the specifically Shia aspects of the Iranian constitution, especially to the innovative and controversial idea of the Rule of the Jurisprudent (*wilayat al-faqih*). Partly in response to the increasing diversion of various Islamically-inspired constitutions and declarations on human rights, the Iranian revolutionary government organised a Pan Islamic conference on human rights in Tehran in 1987. The final communiqué of the Tehran conference on human rights detailed ten recommendations nearly all of which related to the legitimation of the new Iranian state and the privileged role of its *ulema* leaders; and the denunciation of imperial powers and the various enemies of the Iranian state. Only one recommendation specifically related to the issue of human rights in Islam.

The Cairo Declaration on Human Rights in Islam which was issued in 1990, is the most authoritative official pronouncement on the issue. It was approved by the foreign ministers of all the member countries of the Organisation of Islamic Conference (OIC) after a decade long process of debate, review and consultation, and three summit conferences of the OIC. It was subsequently ratified by a summit of the OIC leaders.

The Cairo Declaration however did not try to reconcile or resolve the differences in emphasis and context with the International Bill of Rights, leaving many OIC countries in the uncomfortable position of endorsing two often conflicting interpretations of human rights. Neither did it result in the establishment of a permanent office or secretariat to monitor human rights in OIC countries. The Cairo Declaration was soon followed by a separate charter for the Arab world, the Arab Charter of Human Rights, which was issued by the Arab league in 1994. This charter seemed to defeat its purpose by granting governments the right to suspend the provisions of the charter "in the interest of national security, economic emergencies and threats to public order."

Partly in response to a heightened awareness internationally of human rights issues, the 1990's and 2000's saw a significant increase in the number of conferences in the Islamic world that examined the issue of human rights in Islam.

In 1996, a conference in Jeddah grouped jurisprudential leaders (*fiqh* experts) to develop the Shariah-basis of human rights legislation. This was followed in 1997 by a conference held in Amman under the auspices of the Ahl-ul-Bayt Foundation, an official Jordanian institution. The conference was aimed at reconciling differences between Islamically-based human rights conventions and prevailing international standards, with a strong emphasis on developing an interfaith basis for human rights legislation.

In 2000, Rome was the venue for a conference organised under the auspices of the World Muslim League, a Saudi-linked institution, which produced the Rome Declaration on Human Rights in Islam. This was followed by a conference in 2001 in Riyadh in which human rights were examined within the historic and legal legacy of Islam. These two conferences were the partly in response to increased agitation regarding the human rights record of Saudi Arabia.

In a related development which had a number of human rights implications, a conference was organised in 2005 in Amman to encourage inter-sectarian concord within Islam. This was partly in response to increasing Sunni-Shia violence mainly in Iraq, but also in Lebanon, Pakistan and Afghanistan. It was also intended to isolate and negate the influence of extremist Islamic political movements in appropriating for themselves the right to issue binding religious decrees. Some of the pronouncements of the extremist organisations and leaders impacted directly on human rights abuses.

The Amman Message which emerged from the conference, and which was subsequently endorsed by a number of Islamic countries, called for inter-sectarian harmony, defined the formally acknowledged Islamic groups and sects, and denounced unauthorised religious decrees that did not abide by the strict rules of orthodoxy as expounded by the officially acknowledged sects and groups. The accumulated effect of decades of engagement between Muslims and the modern human rights has been uneven. There is still no definition of an 'Islamically' acceptable standard, with a common agreed methodological and theoretical basis to which all parties would agree.

The documentary evidence clearly reflects this ambiguity and uncertainty. The Cairo Declaration for example stated categorically that the Shariah was the basis of all human rights legislation, ignoring the fact that the Shariah is understood differently by different sects. The UIDHR in contrast based human rights in Islam on the Qur'an and Prophetic sayings, a different emphasis in important ways from a strictly Shariah basis. The Arab Charter and the Syracuse Declaration relied on a different theoretical basis for human rights, and privileged *raison d'etat*over other considerations in extremis.

Critiques of the Concept of a Specifically Islamic Construct of Human Rights

The idea that there should be a specifically Islamic basis for Human Rights, that would meet the religious criteria of Islam has proved problematic. The critiques of the justification of a separate category of human rights notions in Islam cover the entire spectrum of opinion, from extremely conservative Muslims to the outer reaches of opinion regarding the compatibility of Islam with most aspects of modernity.

Traditional Muslim thought has always looked askance at categories of law and policy that are not rooted in the Islamic tradition. Thus, human rights as a separate aspect of the human condition requiring its own set of definitions of rules and processes is alien to the structure of traditional thought. The refrain of this group to any crystallization of the principles of human rights, to which Muslims ought to abide, is an affront to the Shariah and to the notion of Islam as a perfected religion. In this mode of thought, there is no need for any separate body of law and doctrine on human rights for Muslims, as their lives, if ordered according to the Shariah, is bound to lead to a felicitous outcome for humanity.

This line of reasoning has retreated in modern times, especially in official and governmental circles; as well as in the formal religious institutions of Islam. However, it has been adopted, in one variant or another, by the forces of extreme political Islam, that do not acknowledge the need for any separate body of law and policy that covers the area of human rights. A second line of reasoning among a number of conservative Muslims is that the entire human rights movement, from the UDHR through to the conventions of 1966, and the gamut of official institutions and NGO's that manage and supervise the human rights movement are linked to an ongoing western onslaught to dominate the world and are no different in form and intent from other projects of political and cultural domination. The fact that Muslim countries mostly signed on to these conventions is of no significance to these critics, as the argument is often made that these governments were subservient to western interests in any case.

A corollary to this position is that there is no need for specific concern with human rights in the methodological form of the human rights conventions; but there should, nevertheless, be a heightened awareness of the issues of abuses and oppressive laws and customs within the Muslim world, and that these should be tackled and erased in the context of Shariah law. A third line of reasoning can be broadly termed the rejection of the principles of the universality of human rights on the grounds of cultural relativism. This was best expressed by the 1984 statement by Iran's UN representative, Rajaei-Khorassani, who rejected the *universality* of the UDHR by claiming that it was an outcome of a secular understanding of the Judeo-Christian tradition, and thus could not be foisted on people whose traditions and values originate from other premises.

A fourth line of reasoning acknowledges that individuals and groups would benefit from a codification of their rights and duties; and that while the international conventions might not reflect the ideal mechanism to do so, their form and purpose should be adopted in the design of a specifically Islamic framework of human rights.

This implicitly accepts that international conventions cannot be ignored, and that they have seeped into the political discourse of Muslim countries. Muslim countries cannot stand by anymore as mute bystanders in the human rights debates of modern times and that their interests as states and governments are best served if they pro-actively engage the human rights movement by expressing an Islamic variant of the definition of human rights. It is the combination of the last two perspectives that have driven the articulation of official human rights conventions in Islamic countries.

Finally, there is a significant body of opinion amongst Muslims whose political and philosophical perspectives are rooted in Islam (rather than, say, western liberalism), that there are indeed human rights that cross cultural and religious boundaries, and these are best expressed in the form of binding international conventions that stipulate individual and group rights primarily as a break on the powers of a rampant state. This group works from the assumption that the declared human rights of international conventions must be legitimated by a re-reading of Islamic texts and doctrine to arrive at a similar understanding of human rights; in essence generating an Islamic sanction for issues where traditionally authoritative readings would indicate otherwise.

A variant of this line of thought is that of the Iranian philosopher Abdolkarim Soroush, who expressly denies that the idea of the duties-bound human being of classical Islamic thought has any relevance to the modern construct of mankind as endowed with inherent rights. Similarly, the Sudanese-born legal theorist Abdullahi An-Naim, starting from the perspective of a devout believer, has called for a re-reading of the Shariah in light of the primacy of human rights and international law. The critique of modern Islamic doctrines of human rights emanating from western sources or from secular Muslims tend to fall into the following categories:

1. The need for international standards in defining human rights cannot be undermined or abrogated by Islamic "exceptionalism".
2. The modern understanding of rights has no counterpart in a religious tradition that emphasises the nexus of duties and obligations that determine a human being's condition.
3. International conventions are better mechanisms for protecting individuals against deprivations than Shariah-based criteria that are frequently vague and uncertain.
4. The above applies in particular to provisions relating to the treatment of non-Muslims and women where classical Shariah readings seem to deny the principle of equal protection under the law. By affirming the primacy of Shariah law, the Islamic human rights schemes undermine other provisions that appear to accord with international conventions.
5. The issue of freedom of religion, in particular the ability of Muslims to change their religion, appears to be treated evasively in the Islamic human rights conventions.
6. The Islamic Human rights conventions assume that there is a singular Islamic position on the matter; while in reality Islam presents a far more nuanced and complex understanding of the issues of human rights. In essence, the modern Islamic human rights schemes are only a reflection of an ideological and theoretical position formulated by Islamic modernists and revivalists, who seek to monopolise the Islamic political space.

Finally

The evolution of the principles of human rights in Islam will always be a complex process. On the one hand are claims that Islam should not demand an exceptional status in international conventions and agreements; and that Muslim countries and their citizens are best served if they abide by the international bill of rights. These should be adhered to even if some of their provisions may be problematic from the perspective of traditionally authoritative rulings.

On the other hand are the variants of claims that Muslims cannot blithely abandon the bases of their culture and civilisation to a system where the idea and ideals of rights might stray even further from commonly agreed norms of Islam. It is incumbent upon them to produce therefore their own version of the principles of human rights and hew to them in defence of their values and faith.

Of course it is possible that in time, the two systems may co-exist but for this to have any significance in terms of the rights of individuals and peoples, the real abuses that abound in Muslim countries must be reined in. Peoples must see a real improvement in their wellbeing, their rights and freedoms as a result of nations abiding by the stipulations of an Islamic code of human rights, irrespective of its provenance. Lastly, the final word on what constitutes Islamic norms has not been given, nor will it ever be definitively determined. In this respect, certain aspects of the Islamic legacy with profoundly humanistic overtones, from which an entirely new perspective on human rights can evolve, can be rediscovered after centuries of neglect and marginalisation.

This especially relates to the area of ethics in Islam (*akhlaq*) and the field of *tassawuf* (sufism) and gnosis (*irfan*) from which important insights on the nature of human beings and their duties and rights can be derived. This will be the theme of possible subsequent lectures on the matter— whether a human rights doctrine in Islam can be partly rooted in Islam's gnostic and sufic tradition.

Muslims believe that Shariah is the law of God, but differ as to what exactly it entails. Modernists, traditionalists and fundamentalists all have different points of view of Shariah, as the followers of different schools of Islamic thought and scholarship. Different countries and cultures have different interpretations of the Shariah as well. Shariah deals with many issues addressed by the secular law, including crime, politics and economics, as well as personal issues like sexuality, hygiene, diet, prayer and fasting. Where it enjoys official status, the Shariah is implemented by Islamic judges, or Kadis.

The magnet has different responsibilities depending on the interpretation of the Shariah, while the term is commonly used to refer to the leader of communal prayer, the magnet can also be a scholar, religious leader or political leader. The reintroduction of the Shariah is a longstanding goal of the Islamist movements in Muslim countries. Some Muslim minorities in Asia (eg India) have maintained the institutional recognition of Shariah law to rule on personal business and community.

In Western countries where Muslim immigration is more recent, Muslim minorities have introduced Islamic family law, for use in their own conflicts, with varying degrees of success (for example, Muslims in Britain Court of Arbitration.) Attempts to impose Shariah law has been accompanied by controversy, violence and even war (cf. Sudan Civil War). The Shariah is the sacred law of Islam. Most Muslims believe that Shariah is derived from two main sources of Islamic law, established the divine revelations in the Quran and the example set by the Islamic Prophet Muhammad (Pbuh) in the Sunnah. Fiqh jurisprudence interprets and extends the application of Shariah to the questions that are not directly aimed at the primary sources through the inclusion of secondary sources.

These secondary sources often include the consensus of scholars of religion enshrined in the ijma, and the analogy of the Quran and Sunnah through qiyas. Shia jurists qiyas replace analogy with 'aql, reasoning. In the spirit of Islamic law, Professor Bernard G. Weiss states "archaic Arabic, 'path to the waterhole." Shariah Means within When we consider the importance of a well-trodden path to a source of water for man and beast in the arid desert environment, you can easily see why this term in the Muslim use have become a metaphor an entire way of life ordained by God.

"In Understanding Islamic Law: from classical to contemporary, Professor Irshad Abdal-Haqq states "Shariah, or more properly Al-Shariah, which literally means the path, the path to follow, or clear to follow, and has come within the meaning the route by which the believer has to go. Shariah, In the original use meant the road to wash or path that leads to water, ie, the shape of the source of life. The technical implementation of the expression as a reference to the law of Islam is directly traceable to the Quran, where the followers of Islam, believers are admonished by Allah (God) to keep clear and accurate way, the path of Shariah, then you put in the road (right) of the religion to follow you that (road) and not follow the wishes of those who do not know "According to Abdul Mannan Omar. His Dictionary of the Quran, is derived from the "root of the Quran leads Sharaa include.

Sharaa meaning "order", which appears once in the Quran; Sharau (prf. third pluralism of late..). "It was decreed (law)", Shiratun (n.) "spiritual law", used at 5:48, finally, Shariatun "system of divine law, Way of belief and practice" is used to 45:18. Definitions and descriptions of the Shariah has been defined as "Muslim or Islamic law, both civil and criminal justice, and the regulation of individual behaviour, both personal and moral. The custom body based on the law based on the Quran and religion of Islam. Because, by definition, Muslim states are theocracies, religious texts are the law, it is distinguished by the Islam and Muslims in their application, according to the Shariah or Islamic law.

"A debate on the rights of Muslims, "Alexander Hamilton Rosskeen Gibb" a long tradition of diverse, complex intellectual, rather than a "well-defined specific rules and regulations that can be easily applied to life situations "-Hunt Janin and Andre Kahlmeyer" a view shared by the community [Islamic], based on a literature that is extensive, but not necessarily consistent or approved by one agency, "Knut-S. Vikor From the ninth century, the authority to interpret and refine the law in traditional Islamic societies was in the hands of the scholars (ulama). This separation of powers serves to limit the range of actions available to the ruling, which could not easily reinterpret the law decree or independently and have the continued support of the community.

Through centuries and empires, the balance between the ulama and the rulers changed and reformed, but the balance of power has not changed permanently. In the early nineteenth century, the Industrial Revolution and the French Revolution ushered in the era of European world hegemony includes mastery of most of the lands of Islam.

At the end of the Second World War, European powers were too weak to maintain their empires. The variety of forms of government, legal systems, attitudes towards modernity and the interpretation of the Shariah are the result of the units that followed independence and modernity in the Muslim world. Traditional perspectives on the Shariah Most Muslims consider themselves as belonging car finance to either Sunni or Shiite sect of Islam. Among these sects, there are different schools of religious study and scholarship. Schools within each sect have common characteristics, although each is different in its details.

If you're planning on developing a website for your business or personal life, you no doubt have considered using to help save you both time and money. There are pros and cons in using a web template and you'll have to weigh out all of your options before making a decision. The biggest pro would be that you can save time, money, and a big headache. One of the cons would be that if you aren't familiar with HTML, you may have trouble editing or customizing your website.

Sunni addition to the "Professional Code" of the Quran and Sunnah, traditional Sunni Muslims also joined in the consensus (ijma) of the companions of Muhammad (Sahaba) and Islamic jurists (ulama) on certain issues. In situations where no specific provision exists in the sources, scholars use law qiyas - various forms of reasoning such as analogy, to derive the law of the essence of the divine principles and previous resolutions. The consensus of the community, interest groups, and other sources are used in addition to the Shariah in the primary and secondary sources allow. This description can be applied to the major schools of Sunni Islamic jurisprudence, including the Hanafi, Shafii, Maliki and Hanbali. Salafi perspective Main article: The Salafi movement sees the actions and sayings of the first three generations of Muslims for guidance, in addition to the Quran and Sunnah. Salafi Muslims take these first copy as the source of fiqh. The Salafi movement has attracted thousands of followers of Muslim cultures and schools of fiqh.

The Wahhabi Muslims who subscribe to the teachings of Muhammad Denver Dentist ibn Abd-wise al-Wahhab considered part of the Salafi movement. Main article Shiite perspective: Shiite Muslims Shiites also expand the "Code of" the fiqh, but strongly reject analogy (qiyas) as an easy way to innovations (bidah), and reject the consensus (ijma) as having no particular value in own. During the period when scholars developed two tools Sunni, Shia Imams were alive, and the Shiites see them as an extension of the Sunnah, so they see themselves as deriving their laws (fiqh) only of the Quran and the Sunnah. A recurring theme in Shia jurisprudence is the logic (Mantiq), something that most Shiites believe that mention, employment and the value of a degree higher than the majority of Sunnis learn how to become a ticket broker. They see no logic as a third source of law, but a way to see if the derivative work is compatible with the Quran and Sunnah. In Imami-Shii law, the sources of law (Usul al-fiqh) are the Quran, anecdotes of Muhammad's practices and those of The Twelve Imams, and the intellect ('aql). The practices called Shariah today, however, also have roots in comparative law and local customs (URF). Most Shiite Muslims followed Ja'fari school of thought, modern perspectives on Islamic law Muslims have responded in various ways to the forces of modernity.

Stone is one of the most sturdy, strong, and impressive materials to put in your home. Are a great way to accentuate the living area in your home and give your space a unique look. No matter what kind of material you put in your home, you should definitely consider stone.

Islamic Law is Not Acceptable in a Democratic Republic Period

it should be clear that there must be a zero tolerance policy for Islamic law in the US. Islamic worship – no problem. But the religion must change in the US context – just as there are no state churches making civil and criminal claims on individuals in the US. They had to adapt from the state church models of old Europe." Another example of efforts to usurp the Constitution are the actions of the global Organisation of Islamic Cooperation (OIC), whose main agenda is to have "hate speech" laws enforced against anyone who criticizes Islam. And, unfortunately, there are those determined to enforce Shariah on their own who attack and murder any nearby dissenters. The Quran justifies and protects these people's violence by declaring that it is blasphemous to mock or degrade any component of Islam. According to Shariah law, such activity is punishable by death."

The Case for Banning Shariah Law in America

The incompatibility of Islamic Shariah law with secular courts stems from the underpinning of Islamism — the unyielding union of the laws and punishments of the Quran and Hadiths with the country's legal and political system. Shariah law is the legislation of these religious and criminal rules, which *rejects* America's constitutional secularism and legal penalties. The Quran commands Muslims to change secular laws to conform to Shariah, eventually establishing Islamic law worldwide. Islamic courts want their fatwas to supersede the civil and criminal laws, untying Muslims from civil secular courts.

The facts reveal that in 2008, when the first Shariah court was recognized in the U.K., within one year, over 85 recognized Shariah courts were established within the U.K.'s Tribunal Court system. The problem with this rapidly spreading dogma is that several of these courts have issued some fatwas that are completely incompatible with British and European law. As Islam is a male-dominated ideology, the laws of the Quran make half of its devotees, its female population, second-class citizens. This inequality has drawn recent attention to the need for additional British legislation to rein in these courts so they abide by British law. It appears that once any legal system opens its doors to Islamic law, that door will be hard to close and eventually, the only thing missing will be a parallel Islamic government.

But even with this reality in front of Americans, there are still many who insist that our laws will prevent such circumstances from ever occurring in the U.S. And because of this nonchalant attitude, there are numbers of people, both Muslim and non-Muslim, who believe that Shariah law is not a threat to non-Muslim Americans or to the Western liberal democratic rule of law.

Shariah Law Is in the U.S.

The possibility that Muslim-only towns and urban enclaves could be created in the U.S. seems unimaginable to most Americans, but it already is a reality. Just travel 150 mile northwest of New York City to the woods of the western Catskills, and you will find Islamberg, a private Muslim community founded in 1980 by Sheikh Syed Mubarik Ali Shah Gilani. Sheikh Gilani is said to be one of the founders of Jamaat al-Fuqra, a terrorist organisation believed to be responsible for dozens of bombings and murders in the U.S. and abroad.

Islamberg is only one of twenty to thirty Muslim-only communities and training compounds that this Pakistani group supports through Muslim affiliates in America. This radical group has purchased land in isolated areas close to city networks and infrastructure. Jamaat al-Fuqra now has sites in Alabama, Georgia, Oklahoma, South Carolina, Tennessee, Virginia, Pennsylvania, California, Washington, Colorado, Michigan, and Illinois, as well as Canada, Venezuela, and Trinidad.

The Shariah debate in the U.S. is heating up as more and more Americans are reacting to lawyers requesting rulings based on Shariah law, and local judges agreeing to make them. This has happened in a New Jersey divorce case, a Maryland child custody case, and most recently in a Florida property case. These cases are now a precedent for other American-Muslim communities. In addition, according to the Centre for Security Policy study that was published in May 2011, there are actually over fifty Appellate Court cases from 23 states that all involve conflicts between Shariah law and American state law.

There are numbers of Muslim community leaders challenging the delicate line between religious freedom and the laws against state religion by petitioning in favour of living under Shariah law. The moment one court allows the establishment of an independently ruled enclave, others courts in liberal cities across the nation will petition for the same opportunity.

Another example of efforts to usurp the Constitution are the actions of the global Organisation of Islamic Cooperation (OIC), whose main agenda is to have "hate speech" laws enforced against anyone who criticizes Islam. And, unfortunately, there are those determined to enforce Shariah on their own who attack and murder any nearby dissenters. The Quran justifies and protects these people's violence by declaring that it is blasphemous to mock or degrade any component of Islam. According to Shariah law, such activity is punishable by death.

It is this ongoing effort to shut down public criticism of Islam that presents the gravest danger to America — one that the Muslim Brotherhood and its Salafist organisations regard as key to limiting individual rights over the rights of the community. The Council on American-Islamic Relations (CAIR), along with other Islamic activist groups, continues to push back, often with demonization of character and follow-up lawsuits. Recently, intimidation and character assassination have been used against U.S. politicians who question Islamism or want hearings on issues relating to radical Islamic terrorism, along with those Congressmen who introduce state legislation to ban all foreign law.

Why Muslim Cultures Lag Behind? A Muslim Perspective

Recently, in a discussion here at Jihad Watch as to why Muslim cultures noticeably lag behind much of the rest of the world, the following eight traits were summarised as characteristics of the dysfunctional societies of Islam:

1. Belief in magic
2. Belief in conspiracies
3. Lack of innovation
4. Lack of devotion to non-family/non tribal/non clan organisations
5. Lack of empowerment of women
6. Lack of personal responsibility
7. Lack of skilled labour
8. Lack of meritocracy.

Interestingly enough, an article appeared today in one of Malaysia's English daily newspapers that addresses this very topic. Entitled "The Muslim dilemma today", its author Dr. Wan Azhar Wan Ahmad, Senior Fellow/Director at the Centre for the Study of Syariah [Shariah], Law, and Politics, attempts to also summarise the reasons why Muslim nations are stagnating and falling behind. As the Doctor is the director of a major organisation in Malaysia and writing an editorial in a government-backed newspaper, it can be reasonably surmised that he is in fact writing on behalf and with the full backing of Malaysia's Muslim-controlled government.

I started reading Doctor Azhar's article eagerly, hoping that the distinguished, esteemed writer (at least to Muslims) and 'Islamic scholar' would have had the decency to be plainspoken and the courage to let loose at least a little of the truth. It's probably hardly surprising to the 'Islamophobes' reading this, but I was soon to be disappointed. Worse than that, I found the good Doctor's words plainly wrong-headed and disturbing, in yet another instance of denial and self-deception.

Regardless, the good Doctor's words are worth analysing, deconstructing and given a thorough debunking. The analysis is especially needed because Doctor Azhar, as a quasi bureaucrat, writes in encoded bureaucratic language that will baffle many outsiders who try to follow his thinking.

First, the doctor starts by saying this:

MUSLIMS, regardless of times and locations, have been facing a varied magnitude of challenges since the very inception of Islam. This will never cease to happen. But how could all these 'challenges' happen? After all, Islam is supposed to be the perfect 'deen', the perfect religion and the best way of life for everyone. That's the pitch, at any rate. So why is life so hard for Muslims? Maybe because Islam is not all that it's cracked up to be? But never mind that for the moment.

Let's examine the conditions of Muslims in this country today. They are generally in a state of crisis almost in every respect of life – religiously, socially, economically and politically.... But the above phenomenon can be discerned, among other things, from the increasing number of ignorant, secular and non-practising Muslims.

The first sentence is true enough. But while the first part is blindingly obvious, the second sentence is an oblique nod to the usual Islamic sham; namely, any difficulties for Muslims are either due to the scheming of evil outsiders (i.e. non Muslims) or due to the fact that many Muslims are insufficiently pious. This typical drivel should warn the clear-thinking that this 'doctor's' writing is not to be taken seriously. In terms of politics, Muslims basically rule the country, but have been perceived as compromising too much, even on fundamental matters, at the expense of their own interests and dignity.

The references to 'compromise' and 'dignity' are not explained, so allow me to elucidate. It means anytime when Muslims treat the followers of other belief systems in Malaysia (Christians, Buddhists, Hindus) too much like equals. Namely, if a Buddhist is ever treated as the equal of a Muslim, or anything approaching equal terms, then this is seen as a 'compromise' to Islam's/Muslims' 'dignity'. And note the author's use of passive voice — *perceived as compromising* by whom? This bureaucrat of a writer fails to specify, but I strongly suspect he is referring to the various Muslim pressure groups in Malaysia (Perkasa et al) who constantly agitate for more Islamic 'purity' and 'devoutness' for Malaysians (i.e. more Shariah).

On with the Good Doctor's Argument

Once ignorance spreads from top to bottom and defines the character of the *ummah*, the community will have no integrity and strength.... They will gradually become more fragile and vulnerable to foreign influences, especially harmful ones. It is this foregoing disintegration of internal qualities of the Muslim *ummah* that causes confusion and disunity.

Remember those scheming evil nonbelievers? According to Doctor Azhar, these 'foreign influences' are extraordinarily dangerous to Believers (Muslims), a position which adheres quite well to Muslim orthodoxy. What Azhar has primarily in mind is probably the influence of Western culture, which naturally is harmful to Muslims and their supposed 'perfect' way of life. And since everyone is failing to show up at the mosque every Friday, that's the 'disunity' he is lamenting about.

The most disturbing part of Doctor Azhar's argument is his closing, in which he states:

[Muslims should] give priority to religious consideration or interests and put aside differences in facing their common enemies.

Who are those enemies exactly, Doctor Azhar? Of course, he's keeping it vague here, but Islamic scripture makes it quite clear who he is referring to. So, if you're a non Muslim and you're reading this, you are one of those "common enemies" that he means. Doesn't this sound peace-loving, open-minded and tolerant?

So, to recap, here's Doctor Azhar's list for why the Ummah is stumbling so badly:

- Lack of Islamic piety
- Being too open to outside/'enemy' influences
- Lack of unity.

This is what we can expect from the finest minds of Planet Islam. Now, compare his list with the one at the beginning of this column. Which do you think is a better diagnosis?

Doctor Azhar, with all due respect, I suggest a different remedy for you and your co-religionists. Recognize the equality of the so-called 'infidel', embrace your 'common enemies' as 'fellow humans' instead, and acknowledge the universal brotherhood of mankind. As these are all inherently un-Islamic ideas, I am sure devout Muslims will not take heed. But there's a chance that the "ignorant, secular and non-practising Muslims" will.

Chapter 7

The Human Side of Shariah

Scholar Works with the Powerless in Navigating Islamic Law

In 2002, Amina Lawal, a young Nigerian woman, was tried for adultery under Shariah, Islam's traditional law. She was saved the following year with the help of Hauwa Ibrahim, a Harvard scholar and visiting lecturer on women's studies and Islamic law at Harvard Divinity School(HDS). Ibrahim, the first female lawyer among a population of 250,000 in northern Nigeria's predominantly Muslim Gombe region, used Shariah law to fight the Shariah system, but she also had to battle society.

You have to win these cases in the courts, said Ibrahim, but you also have to "win the hearts and minds of the villagers."

As a 2008-09 fellow at Harvard's Radcliffe Institute for Advanced Study, Ibrahim explored the theoretical foundations of Shariah penal code and examined its impact on the legal practices and the human rights of women in West Africa. Currently she is working on a book telling the story of the Shariah system through the eyes of her clients, the women, children, and men whose lives have been affected by Islamic law. She discussed her new project during a Thursday (April 7) lecture at HDS titled "Humanizing Shariah — A Memoir of the Human Face of a Legal Practice."

With her new work, Ibrahim said she hopes to convey the importance of common humanity, written in a familiar style with a language accessible to lawyers and laymen alike.

I can do that, said Ibrahim, because "I am an insider, I am a daughter of the soil." Calling her own education an accident, Ibrahim said she takes clients on for free because it "is her passion." While her husband disagrees with much of what she does, he supports her. The problem for so many of her clients, she said, is that they are poor, illiterate, and powerless.

"They don't have a voice."

With her new work, Ibrahim said, she hopes to tell their stories, and to shed light on Shariah. In working on the cases, she said she learned that Shariah is never about stoning, flogging, or amputation, but that it is actually "a path to peace."

"Are there opposing forces against this? Yes, of course ... Are there verses in the Quran contradictory? Without a doubt, just like any other religious book. But let me tell you finally I am seeking to do what is right ... through Shariah."

Unintended Consequences

A perfect storm is gathering in the Middle East. Fuelled by revolution, international interference, and the repositioning of world leaders as they try to hold on to their power in the region, the streets are now churning with what is called the 'Arab Spring'. The outcome is anything but certain. The Rolling Revolutions of 2011 have dramatically changed the playing field in countries throughout the Middle East. They have created a void in leadership as the fall of dictators opened up opportunity for Islamist organisations. Intent on taking control and redefining nations under Shariah law, organisations like the Muslim Brotherhood in Egypt and Syria, al Qaeda in Yemen and Libya, and the leaders of Iran and Turkey have been rushing to fill the vacuum.

The success of revolutions in Tunisia, Egypt, and Libya empowered a struggle that has been spreading like wildfire, sowing chaos wherever the revolutionary fever strikes. The surge of revolution has not yet subsided, and the rumours and threats of larger, impending wars that will spill across national boundaries to become regional conflagrations are real. They are the consequence of the empowerment derived from the successful revolutions that toppled governments and empowered the street. They should be taken with the utmost seriousness by Western governments, who are their ultimate target.

They represent a threat to the Western world that has not been seen since the days before World War II. Although the language of the revolutions uses words like 'freedom' and 'democracy', what is being left in their wake is anything but. Initial chaos has already given way to a new form of tyranny that will suffer neither freedom nor democracy – in Tunisia, Libya, and soon, in Egypt.

In Egypt: The young men and women who began the revolution with dreams of equality and democratic process have been out-maneuvered by the Muslim Brotherhood, Egypt's oldest and most well-organized Islamist movement. In fact, the leaders of the Brotherhood have been planning this succession for years, and were therefore able to move in swiftly when the demonstrations first erupted. In the beginning, they said that they had no interest in the political process, claiming that the Brotherhood was simply a community assistance organisation whose primary aim was to support "the people". The Brotherhood engaged in a massive organisational effort once the demonstrations started. They brought Muslims out of the mosques in the hundreds of thousands onto the streets of Egypt's cities to demonstrate for the fall of the Mubarak government. They provided food, water, and portable latrines, to keep the people in the streets once they got there.

Then something not unexpected happened. As we predicted in January, their modest assertions gave way to high political ambition. They formed a new party – the Freedom and Justice Party – and recently announced that they plan to run candidates in just under 50% of the district seats in the November election. Judging by past performance, this 'modest' aim is still likely to change, putting them in line to control the government in Egypt after the elections. Because the Brotherhood draws its support from the mosques, where it has a commanding voice, it is certain to bring out the needed votes for seats in the new parliament that will enable it to take command of the government and begin installing Shariah law, upon which their true ideology is based.

Elsewhere: The fighting still rages in Syria and Yemen, where the ferocity of the conflict is still escalating. In Libya, Gaddafi loyalists continue to stand their ground in key places like Sirte, Gaddifi's birthplace. The rebels have formed a new interim government, and their draft Constitution clearly states that "Islam is the religion of the state, and the principle source of legislation is Islamic Jurisprudence (Shariah)" A major cultural shift for this formerly secular country. Jordan's Hashemite monarchy is also on the list of ruling families to be targeted. Picking up the cue from recent events in Turkey and Egypt, a FaceBook page posted last week called for an attack on Israel's embassy in Amman. It hasn't happened yet, and King Abdullah II is not likely to take it lightly, but Jordan is ripe for the unrest among its people to erupt in one form or another, encouraged by the successes of other revolutions. Finally, Saudi Arabia's King Abdullah, another target of the Brotherhood, has been on alert against a coup for several years, cleaning up and training his military in such things as urban warfare, and waiting for the other shoe to drop. In his country, where Shariah is already law, the ground-breaking programs which King Abdullah has begun to put in place (e.g. the establishment of the first integrated, co-educational school in Saudi Arabia) make him a prime target for attack.

More Crises Brewing

In the mean time, two additional crises have been added to the mix, preparing to play out in the immediate future:

The first will take place in New York City this week. Mahmoud Abbas, President of the Palestinian Authority, has come to New York with plans to seek full membership in the United Nations. The request is unilateral and disregards all efforts to reconvene direct peace talks with Israel. Although 'Palestine' is not, in fact, an established nation, membership would provide the Palestinians with a de facto statehood, albeit one without official boundaries. It will also give the Palestinians a new bully pulpit from which to mount its ongoing and virulent campaign against Israel. America has made clear its position. Just one year ago, the President said, "the rights of the Palestinian people will be won only through peaceful means – including genuine reconciliation with a secure Israel". This means direct negotiations with Israel, something that has failed to bring about peace in the past, despite more than twenty years of trying.

But UN recognition of the Palestinian state will not ensure peace. In fact, should it happen, it may very well provoke a new war by empowering people sworn to the destruction of Israel to take matters into their own hands in an extension of the 'Arab Spring'. If it does not happen, it may still provoke war, justified by the 'frustration' of those supporting the Palestinian cause.

The Pandora's box has now been opened. The simple fact of Abbas' appeal to the UN,, whichever way it is decided, is sufficient in itself to start a chain reaction that he will not be able to control. The future impact of his determination to act unilaterally remains to be seen, but it is not likely to be a positive one.

A New Mediterranean Threat

The second crisis point is also in the Middle East, where Turkey is making major waves in a bid for power in the Arab world. Turkey's Prime Minister Recep Tayyip Erdogan has been travelling to the newly 'liberated' countries of Egypt, Tunisia, and Libya. Seeking to expand his influence in the region, he addressed audiences who shouted their approval when he told them that the creation of a Palestinian state "is not an option but a necessity." They went wild when he damned Israel for last year's attack on the blockade-busting flotilla in which nine people were killed. His hypocrisy couldn't be more blatant.

Erdogan lamented the death of nine Turks who were challenging a legitimate blockade under international law. He also talked about the 'freedom and democracy' in Turkey where he claimed that all people were treated with respect. "There are Christians, Jews and minorities [in Turkey],", he said, "but the state treats them equally." He failed to mention his country's violent war against the Kurds. According to reports, over the last twenty years Turkey has dispossessed three million Turkish Kurds and killed more than 30,000. Erdogan's open hostility to Israel and his recent saber rattling has added a new and dangerous dimension to the already crumbling stability in the region. He has recently threatened Israel with a naval confrontation by promising a naval escort for the next blockade-busting flotilla to Gaza. The consequences of such a confrontation are likely to be far beyond his ability to control, embroiling the region (and beyond) in armed conflict greater and more deadly than anything we have seen in recent years. And should Iran, with its new naval presence in Syria's port of Latakiya, also decide to get involved, the conflict will take on broad new dimensions from which the West will not be able to stay aloof.

Ironically, Erdogan (a Turk and non-Arab) seems to be competing with Ahmadinejad (an Iranian and non-Arab) to fill the leadership vacuum in the Arab world and become a pan-Arabic, pan-Islamic leader. His visits to Egypt, Tunisia, and Libya, are seen as his effort to establish himself as the new leader of the Arab world.

Meanwhile, Back in New York... While Edrogan flexes his muscles in the Middle East, the drama set to unfold in New York City will be worth your attention. Israel's Prime Minister Benjamin Netanyahu will deliver a speech at the UN on Friday. In a statement to his Cabinet on Monday, Netanyahu said, "I will meet with US President Barack Obama and other world leaders, and afterwards I will address the UN General Assembly. The UN is not a place where Israel wins praise, but I think that it is important that I go there in order to represent both the State of Israel and the truth – and the truth is that Israel wants peace and the truth is that the Palestinians are doing everything to torpedo direct peace negotiations."

Mahmoud Abbas will also speak at the UN on Friday when he applies for membership. He will no doubt talk about peace, freedom, and economic development in Palestine. He will no doubt not mention that Palestinian refugees who now live in 'Palestine' will not be given citizenship in the new state, or that no Jews will be allowed to live there (despite Palestinian demands that millions of Palestinian 'refugees' be 'repatriated' in Israel). These are both publicly stated conditions of his new state, but the world is not likely to here about them on Friday.

The discussion that follows the speeches is unlikely to bring the parties to Middle East conflict any closer together in a quest for peace. Israel will undoubtedly come under attack from other members of the General Assembly, as usual, and the Quartet – the US, the EU, Russia, and the UN – will continue to try getting the Palestinians back to the negotiating table. This will be an historic event, however it turns out. The confluence of events is looking increasingly like the perfect storm. The seeds of war are once again being sown and the laws of unintended consequences have been released in a part of the world already afflicted with a host of unresolved conflicts. Friday is likely to be a significant and irreversible tipping point in the future of the world as we know it.

Revising the Image of Shariah

Even though the implementation of *shariah* law is not publicly discussed by the activists of PKS, as a political party arisen out of a religious movement, PKS will not stray from its commitment to Islamise society and the state. The struggle of how to implement *shariah* still preoccupies its activists. One member of a PKS committee in East Java said, "Partai Keadilan has never denied the implementation of *shariah* in Indonesia because it would be foolish for an Islamic party to reject *shariah*. In political platform, however, PKS uses the term *dakwah* instead of *shariah*, using *dakwah* as a means of the purification of human beings based on their natural tendencies (*fitrah*). Becoming God's servants who also serve as good exemples and enjoin the good in order to strengthen moral foundations of the nation. Promoting freedom to all citizens to embrace and practise their religion with mutual respect PKS's position on the implementation of *shariah* can be found in a book written by a PKS activist, entitled *Yang Nyata dari PK Sejahtera*.

The book emphasises that "*shariah* is mercy for all creatures and the proper implementation of *shariah* will not bring discrimination. PKS believes that its implementation in Indonesia will provide the solution for the current multi dimensional-crisis. However, it must be done in a peaceful and constitutional way, not through violence or compulsion. Furthermore, in a different expression, which carries the same meaning, the chairman of PK in East Java has said, "We don't want to use *shariah* as a merely political commodity because it saddens us that many activists of political parties strongly demand the implementation of *shariah* in Indonesia but they themselves do not practise it.

Believing that the lack of a proper understanding of *shariah* is the chief obstacle in promoting its application, the Jemaah Tarbiyah activists who occupy the central leadership within PKS have begun to formulate their strategy for promoting its positive image. Implementing *shariah*, according to PKS, is not merely the need to impose a set of Islamic laws but rather it entails all positive aspects of human values and behaviour. For PKS, universal morality and values must take first priority in solving Indonesian political and economic crises.

In order to gain popular support, the party has worked to make *shariah* more applicable to day-to-day matters. The meaning of *shariah* has been widened in scope to include more substantive and practical issues. *Korupsi* (corruption), *Kolusi* (collusion) and *Nepotisme* (nepotism) known by the acronym "KKN" are new areas to combat, so that clean government, justice and welfare are considered to be the main ideals deriving from *shariah*. The campaign for *shariah* should be directed towards achieving prosperity, security, justice and peace in the world. In its simplest form, preserving public facilities, such transportation, parks, roads and toilets is obligatory for members of the party. In fact, PKS has tried to spiritualise all profane activities within realm of Islamic values and indeed all can be justified by religious doctrine.

In order to provide the religious grounds for these issues, the arguments are based on the Quran and Hadith and as well as on the public interest (*maslahah*). The manual and training materials of PKS state that preserving individual and public rights is important, since Allah in the Quran (XXVIII: 77) states:" ...and desire not corruption in the land. Indeed, Allah does not like corruptors. According to the activists of PKS, most people still have insufficient information about *shariah* and tend to see it from a negative point of view. They understand it merely as a legal system that prescribes the severe punishment of crimes under the *hudud* laws. Hidayat Nurwahid, former president of PKS and currently chairperson speaker of the People's Consultative Assembly (MPR) in 2004-2009 stated:

The problem is that too many people talk about *shariah* and they mean cutting off hands and wearing (head) scarves. Our main programme is how to make people better off, how to get justice. In order to make Indonesians, both Muslims and non-Muslims, comprehend the concept and essence of *shariah*, Dr. Salim Segaf al-Jufri, chairman of the *Shariah* Council of the Central Board of PKS, suggests three steps in socialising *shariah*: educating Muslims, providing good examples and creating dialogue with non-Muslims.

Educating Muslims

PKS believes that educating people to be well informed about the proper meaning of *shariah* is an important step. *Shariah* must be seen as a model that promises prosperity to all human beings. If *shariah* is described by such acts as stoning adulterers and cutting off the hands of thieves, which alarms both Muslims and non-Muslims, according to PKS, this is a wrong understanding. *Shariah* contains aspects that apply not only to the legal system but also to economic progress and social solidarity. Rofi' Munawwar, a chairman of PKS in the province of East Java (1999-2004) explained

It is true that *hudud* is part of *shariah* but a just economic distribution for all people is also Islamic. Unfortunately, the aspects of punishment within *shariah* are more dominant than efforts to encourage wealthy people to help and lift up the poor. If this other aspect of *shariah* is truly implemented and people gain prosperity, there will be no thieves and consequently the cutting off of hands will never be implemented. In this regard, PKS has succeeded in reformulating the meaning of *shariah* into more practical avenues suitable to Indonesian society. Suryadarma, a PKS member of the legislature in the province of South Sulawesi said:

I think a Muslim who understands his or her religion well will practise *shariah*. *Shariah* is very wide and not only related to the legal dimensions often exposed by the mass media in a threatening way, such as the cutting off of hands. We focus on a *shariah* that is related to the achievement of prosperity and the basic needs of the people. In addition, we need to uphold the law in order to ensure the equality of all people before it. Without considering both dimensions, prosperity and law, we think it is difficult to implement *shariah*. How do we practise a *hudud* law if the thieves are poor people? How do we observe *qisas* when we tend to agree with the abuse of politics and power? In short, when we campaign for justice and prosperity, all these are part of implementing *shariah*.

By educating people about the "essence" of *shariah*, it is hoped that they will not hesitate to put it into practice. And when Indonesian society supports the implementation of *shariah,* PKS is ready to bring the aspirations of its constituents into the legislature. PKS attitudes are always determined by the acceptance of the people.

So at this stage, making people familiar with the day-to-day aspects of *shariah* is more important than promoting its formalisation. PKS activists observe that the majority of people are ignorant of the practice of the true *shariah*. West Sumatra, for instance, is widely known as a stronghold of Muslim scholars and religious observance, but one activist from this area has acknowledged that the ordinary people are actually far from *shariah.* The campaign for formalisation in this region will not gain much popular support

PKS raises the issue of *shariah* not as a political commodity or to win votes. Our mission is to uphold *shariah* itself. In West Sumatra, this is not an issue which will win us popular political support. The impact of secularism in West Sumatra is very strong. A campaign to bring the people to live in accordance with *shariah* will face difficulties, since people feel threatened by it. The decline of the Islamic institutions in West Sumatra has made *shariah* uninteresting. We do not need to campaign for *shariah* but it does need to be socialised.

He further stated:

The important issues for West Sumatra are the economy, education and public health. What makes West Sumatra's people proud of their region in terms of economy and education? Nothing! We were strong because we had Central Sumatra, including Riau, which is well known for its petroleum. PRRI (Pemerintahan Revolusioner Republic Indonesia) was ready to confront the central government because they knew about the resources. When Central Sumatra was made a new province, we became very weak and poor. What we need is kind of a reformist Islam. Why did Partai Amanat Nasional (PAN) win success in the general elections in 1999 - because they were not too fanatic or too secular! Those who want to practise Islam rigidly and too radically will not put down roots in this society. The typology of the people is moderate, as represented by Muhammadiyah.

Being Exemplars

Besides educating Muslims about the "true meaning" of *shariah,* PKS activists try to offer themselves as living examples. Every cadre is expected to practise the teachings of *shariah* and to ensure that Indonesians, Muslims and non-Muslims, feel secure and comfortable with its concept. They firmly believe that *shariah* must avoid any possibility of causing discrimination against people, regardless of religion, gender or political aspirations and that *shariah* must be seen as an alternative solution for Indonesians. Since ideas of the implementation of *shariah* are still far from the popular mind in Indonesia, PKS activists have not voiced it during campaigns for the general elections. Even though some districts in Indonesia, such as in some areas of West Sumatra, have issued district policies (*peraturan daerah,* Perda) requiring female students and civil servants to wear head scarves, the most appropriate issue regarding *shariah* is the campaign to combat against corruption. One of the PK legislators in the Province of West Sumatra (DPRD I) emphasised:

PK cadres are persons who are in the very beginning expected to practise *shariah* in their daily activities and to demonstrate it to others around them. They must feel happy and satisfied carrying out *shariah* so that other people will be interested and follow them. *Shariah* must lead to achieve welfare and prosperity for all. For that reason PK now adds the word "*Sejahtera*"(prosperous) into its new name, Partai Keadilan Sejahtera.

PKS has also begun to promote the inclusive nature of *shariah.* As an example of its conviction of the all embracing nature of *shariah,* PKS elected a non-Muslim as branch chairman of PKS in one of the districts in Papua, while another elected Member of a regional parliament in Papua representing PKS, Natalis Kamo is a Christian.This decision to include non-Muslims within PKS was not an easy choice since it drew criticism from some members. For instance, a mailing list of PKS sympathisers, partai-keadilan-sejahtera, on March 2004 was filled with questions and criticism of the party's decision to appoint non-Muslims as members of PKS committees in the Province of Papua and for nomination as legislators as well. The main concern was that this policy did not follow the Traditions of the Prophet and the pious ancestors (*al-s}alaf al-s}alih*). One argumentation is that "appointing non-Muslims means requiring loyalty to an infidel and it is really against the teachings of the Prophet. The Quran states 'let not believers take disbelievers as allies (i.e., supporters or protectors) rather than believers. And whoever (of you) doest that has nothing (i.e. no association) with Allah, except when taking precaution against them in prudence. And Allah warns you of Himself, to Allah is the (final) destination." However, these objections did not last long, since most members of the mailing list advised those who had criticised the policy of Central Board of PKS to trust their leaders.

In order to persuade its members about the validity of its decision in this regard, the Central Board of PKS issues *bayanat* (explanations) in which it is stated that the prohibition for a Muslim against voting and electing a non-Muslim as a member of parliament is clear. However, the party considers the rights of non-Muslims within the Muslim community the same to observe their religion and to manage their affairs. This is clearly worded in the Medina Charter. The inclusion of non-Muslims within PKS committees and in the parliament reflects the policy of recognising the existence of non-Muslim communities and their representatives in Indonesia.

In the case of the amendment of the 1945 Constitution, particularly chapter 29 regarding religion, the PK, together with Partai Amanat National (PAN) did not support the Jakarta Charter. While other Islamic parties, such as PPP and PBB view the phrase of "with obligation for Muslims to carry out *shariah*" added in the 1945 Constitution to be critical for the legal acknowledgement of implementing *shariah*, for PK such recognition of the privileged status of Islam was not a priority. When the Islamic parties in the 2000 legislature raised the issue of returning to the Jakarta Charter, PK neither supported nor rejected the move.

Instead, its representatives preferred to propose what they called Piagam Medina (the Medina Charter), which gives the same freedom to all religions of Indonesia to carry out their teachings. The reason is that the party did not support any effort to impose the implementation of *shariah* because it would be undemocratic. PK preferred to see the government and the Muslim community strongly committed to the upholding of Islamic values first.

The Medina Charter was the first "constitution" regulated by the Prophet Muhammad (Pbuh) to knit all the inhabitants of his community into a single polity. However, the proposal of PK is not a new issue since Piagam Medina was widely discussed by Nurcholish Madjid in promoting pluralism within Islam. Even earlier, during the debates in the 1959 constituent assembly on the ideological direction of the state, Islamic parties had pushed for the legalization of the Jakarta Carter and they met the objections of non-Muslims and Muslims who were not members of Islamic parties.

Even though not referring to the Medina Charter as such, Djamaluddin Malik, the Third Chairman of NU's Executive Board, proposed a sentence in addition to the Jakarta Charter that "followers of other religions are under obligation to abide by the doctrines of their respective religions. In fact, the idea of proposing a new sentence by Djamaluddin Malik is similar to the idea brought by members of PKS in order to guarantee the plural religious character of Indonesian state.

PKS has shown a reluctance to promote the position of women in politics but it has started to give recognition to their role. It allows the same opportunities for women to be involved in politics and in the broader arenas of life. PKS has begun the empowerment of women by proposing them as members of the legislature. The Election Law of the 2004 elections stated that parties were required to have at least 30 per cent female legislative candidates, and PKS met this quota in 65 of 69 electoral districts. Even though only four women were actually elected as legislators because most had been put low in the candidate list, their presence is a symbol of the political will of the party in this direction. Compared to PPP, PKS is still higher in terms of female representation in the legislature. Women elected to the 2004 DPR from PKS are 4 of 45 members (8.89%) and from PPP, 3 of 58 members (5.17.Furthermore, it is interesting that in the district of Gayo Luwes in Aceh, a woman named Nurhayati is the head of the district committee of PKS. She is the only woman in the party to reach such a level of leadership. In addition, female members of the party, Nursanita Nasution and Aan Rohanah have also been appointed members of the Consultative Council, which holds the highest authority in determining the direction of the party. However, the role of women in PKS is still far from satisfactory, since most women on committees of the Central Board have been placed in a special department of women's affairs. They have not yet been accommodated in other departments on the basis of their true capacity and expertise.

Opportunities have always been open to women but they have not often been ready to take them up. For instance, the PKS Provincial Board of Central Java in 2006 is open for a woman to be elected as chairperson. Members of PKS in that area are free to choose woman as a chairperson. "There are many female cadres in PKS. So it is allowable for woman to run as a candidate for PKS chairperson. In responding to the issue of a female president, PKS has revised its objections. Yet however much PKS might prefer a man, the case of Megawati as President of Indonesia, replacing Abdurahman Wahid in 2000, was problematic. PK was actively involved in the campaign to oppose Megawati in 1999. There were two reasons to oppose Megawati's appointment. The first was ideological and political; Megawati's party and its members had an inharmonious relation with the Islamic parties. The second was a normative reason: most Islamic parties, including PK, opposed a woman president on religious grounds.

A large demonstration was held in 2000, involving thousands of PK cadres, in front of the National Parliament in Jakarta to request members of DPR/MPR not to choose Megawati. However, during the presidency of Abdurahman Wahid, cadres of PK also held simultaneous demonstrations to call for the resignation of Wahid, which indirectly gave a constitutional opportunity for Megawati to replace him. Why did PK change its stance in favour of a woman as president? They followed political expediency in the legal clause "that men and women are treated equal under the constitution. Whenever the constitution guaranteed a practice, PK preferred to follow the constitution.

By the good example of its cadres, PKS intends to lead Indonesian Muslims to willingly practise *shariah*. Even though some Islamic movements that campaign for the implementation of Islamic law argue that the Indonesian people already practise the non-legal aspects of *shariah,* PKS still considers that its introduction is urgent. It is true that some parts of *shariah* have been adopted by the state, such as the regulation of marriage and the laws of inheritance and endowment, however, for PKS, the essence of *shariah* is still wanting.

Dialogue with Non-Muslims

PKS activists believe that in order to explain the "true" meaning of *shariah,* a dialogue with non-Muslim organisations and communities needs to be established; as long as non-Muslims are honest about their religion and understand the issue of *shariah* properly they will not oppose its implementation· Through dialogue, common values among the religions in Indonesia will emerge. Salim Segaf al-Jufri, chairman of *shariah* board of PKS said

By dialogue a communication is established among different parties, including non-Muslims, if they are fair in dealing with this issue and are not overwhelmed by suspicions. I believe that even though it may raise some dispute and disagreement, we will find common agreement. For instance, whoever lives in this country must agree on the need to combat corruption and to practise justice for all, Muslims and non-Muslims alike. To protect people's rights, property and souls is the basic thing that all people must agree upon. Is not respect for others' rights in worship and the practice of their religions part of Islamic teaching (*shariah*?

Nonetheless, dialogue has not been an easy task because the elite of PKS have had little experience in initiating dialogue with non-Muslims. Their experiments within Jemaah Tarbiyah activities in the past were confined to their inner groups and rarely did they socialise beyond with the broader society. However, this last step program is still far from applicable for the rank and file of PKS. The PKS has not engaged in the interfaith dialogue that is promoted by the government and other leaders of religious organisations in Indonesia and many PKS activists still hesitate to cooperate with non-Muslims. According to al-Jufri, the socialisation of the concept of *shariah* still faces obstacles, since *shariah* itself is still seen by certain Muslims and non-Muslims as well as something that may threaten sections of society. This is because *shariah* is promoted by certain Muslim groups such as NII, MMI, FPI and many radical groups in unwise ways, tending towards force and violence. It is a real challenge for PKS to reform this image.

As many PKS activists have often said, "it is true that *hudud* is part of *shariah* but people often forget that the distribution of wealth is also a significant element of *shariah.* The problem is how to find a balance between promoting welfare and proposing *shariah,* and not to fall into the trap of formalising the sacred whilst abandoning the profane.

PKS's commitment to Islamic teachings has resulted in actions to "Islamise" non-religious issues and to use them as vehicles to promote its ideals. Other Islamic parties often tend to promote Islam from a legal point of view and "top-down" approach, but PKS starts from practical issues to lead people into the essence of *shariah.* The issue of the formalisation of *shariah* guarantees their presence in the political field, among more powerful secular parties, even though they can claim only a small number of votes. The problem is whether or not the party will retain its commitment to gradual steps towards the formalisation of *shariah* if it should gain significantly greater support than before. This question will be analysed by focussing on the issue of the implementation of *shariah* and various opinions on it among PKS activists.

Sources of Authority in Islam

Each religious tradition has its own authentic sources of authority, which are referred to for authentication of religious practices and traditions. Islam too has its own sources of authority both oral as well as written. These sources were the mainspring of Islamic law. In fact law in the form of Shariah is most central to Islam. Shariah law holds the centre stage in Islamic tradition except some Islamic sects and Sufi traditions. Shariah law being so fundamental to Islam the sources which the Shariah law is based on, assumes even greater importance.

What are these sources of authority in Islam? Needless to say some of these sources are common to all sects of Islam and some vary from sect to sect. The one which is common to all the sect of course is Holy Quran which is most authentic source for all sects of Islam. There is no sect which can ignore, let alone reject Quran as the source of authority. Even Batini sects like Qaramita and Isma'ilis and Duruzis, contrary to popular belief, consider the Quran as the most authentic source of authority. However, it does not mean that the Quran is understood in the same way by all these sects.

There are serious differences in interpretations of various verses of the Quran. The Quranic verses, according to the Quranic verse 3:7 are divided into two categories i.e. those belonging to 1) mutashabihat (allegorical) and those belonging to 2) muhkamat (decisive). Also, according to the Quran those who use allegoric verses create disorder and confusion. Thus Muslims should follow the verses which belong to the category of muhkamat i.e. decisive and clear. Despite this many Islamic sects are based on verses which belong to the other category i.e. mutashabihat i.e. allegorical verse.

This same verse above also lays down that ta'wil (original or hidden meaning) is known to Allah and those firmly rooted in knowledge (al-Rasikhun fi' al-'ilm) believe in them and say it is all from our Lord. But the Shiah sects believe that ta'wil is also known to al-rasikhun fi' al'ilm i.e. those firmly rooted in knowledge and they are nothing but imams from the progeny of 'Ali, son-in-law of the Holy Prophet (PBUH) and his daughter Fatima. Many batini sects like the Qaramita, the Ismailis and Duruzis give central position to ta'wil as far as their beliefs are concerned. They believe that it is absolutely necessary to know ta'wil of the Quranic verses. It is central to their religion. More of it later.

Islam was divided into several sects within a few decades of the death of the Holy Prophet (PBUH). There is a Hadith (Prophet's saying) that my ummah (community) will be divided into seventy- two sects. Now seventy-two should not be taken literally. What he says is that my ummah will be divided into numerous sects. In the well known work of Baghdadi Al-farq bayn al-Firaq we find that there were more than hundred sects in the first century of Islam itself. The Kharijites (Khawarij), a small extremist sect itself had subdivided into more than a dozen sects.

The Shias themselves were subdivided into numerous sects - the Zaidis, the Ithna 'Asharis, the Alavids, the Qaramitas, the Isma'ilis, the Duruzis and so on. The Alavids were themselves subdivided into various sub-sects. The Isma'ilis split into two major sub-sects the Nizaris and Must'alians. All these Shia sects, as pointed out before, believed into hidden or original meaning of the Quranic verses but no two Shiah sects agreed on common original meaning. All these sects had their own version of the meanings of the Quranic verse. The Sunni Muslims, of course maintained that the real meaning (ta'wil) is known only to Allah and those firmly rooted in knowledge only believe in ta'wil but have no knowledge of ta'wil themselves.

Thus though the Quran is most authentic source of authority yet it is interpreted so differently by different sects that one wonders whether the Quran could unify all believers in matters of beliefs. Also, like no two Shiah sects agree on the real meaning of the verses of the Holy Quran, no two Sunni sects agree on meaning of all verses of the Quran. It should be borne in mind that Sunnis and Shias are actually umbrella terms. There are several schools of thought or sects under these two umbrellas.

Among the Sunnis the Asha'irah and the Mu'tazilah differ radically from each other in understanding the Quranic verses. The Mu'tazilah believe who are popularly known as the party of al-'Adl wa al-Tawhid (i.e. party of justice and unity of Godhood) consider 'aql (i.e. reason) as very central to their beliefs. According to them 'aql enables us to understand the Quran and not naql (i.e. oral or written traditions). They differ from Asha'ira who believe in naql as the main source of understanding the Quran. Thus among the Sunnis while the Mu'tazilah (who no more exist as a sect now) stress 'aql the Asha'irah stress naql The Asha'irah take the Quran literally the Mu'tazilah do not.

Besides these two sects the Sunnis are divided into four major Madhahib (schools of law - Hanafi, Shafii, Hanbali and Maliki. All these four schools of Shariah differ in understanding some crucial Quranic verses, apart from authority of some ahadith. For Sunni Islam the second most important source of authority is Prophet's sunnah. Sunnah means sayings and doings of the Prophet. Both what the Prophet said and did was reported by chain of reporters or narrators. These reports were collected together in six authentic collections known as Sihah Sitta i.e. six authentic collections of Prophet's sayings and doing.

The different schools of law lay stress on different ahadith for deriving the laws of Shariah and formulating 'aqidah (plural 'aqa'id) i.e. dogmas. Though all books of ahadith i.e. Sihah Sittah are acceptable to Sunnis each school of Shariah (madhhab) has its own preferences for the books of ahadith. Thus Malikis would prefer Imam Malik's Muwatta' as the most authentic source after the Holy Quran. Hanafis, on the other hand, would prefer Sahih Bukhari and Sahih Muslim. Among the Sunnis again there are two other sources of authority i.e. ijma' and qiyas (i.e. consensus and analogical reasoning). Where the Quran does not contain the required answer, the Ulama' would look into ahadith and if ahadith are also silent on some problem, they will resort to qiyas and then try to develop a consensus (ijma').

Thus among the Sunnis these are four recognised sources of authority i.e. the Quran, Hadith, qiyas (analogical reasoning) and consensus (iijma'). However, here too this neat division is more theoretical. The four schools of law in Sunni Islam plays more vital role for the adherents of those respective schools than these four sources. In fact these four sources were of real importance to those who were formulating laws than the lay adherents.

The lay adherents will simply go to the Ulama of their respective schools and ask fatwa (i.e. authentic opinion of the 'alim of his/her school. Among the Sunnis ahl al-hadith or those who adhere to the schools of Hadith do not accept the two other sources of law i.e. qiyas and ijma' i.e. analogy and consensus. For them only two sources are sufficient i.e. the Quran and Hadith. It is for this reason that Ahl al-Hadith do not accept validity of triple divorce in one sitting because the validity of triple divorce is not authenticated by Hadith. It is based more on two other sources i.e. qiyas and ijma'.

For Shiah Muslims too qiyas and ijma' are not acceptable. Though Hadith is acceptable as source of law but they do not accept ahadith as compiled in The Sihah Sitta i.e. the Six authentic collections recognised by the Sunnis. The Shiahs have their own collections of ahadith like the Kulaynis and others. Again what is recognised as authentic collections of ahadith by Ithna Ashari Shiahs is not recognised by the non-Ithna 'Asharis i.e. Zaidis, Isma'ilis, 'Alavids and others. The most authentic source of ahadith or Prophet's sunnah for these Shiah sub-sects is their respective Imams. For Zaidis it is Zaidi Imams, for Ithna 'Asharis it is twelve Imams or for Isma'ilis, it is their Imams.

Some Imams are of course common for Shiah sects i.e. common up to Imam Zain al-'Abidin as far as the Zaidis are concerned; up to Imam Ja'far al-Sadiq as far as Ithna 'Asharis are concerned and up to Imam Hakim as far as Druzis are concerned and up to Imam Mustasir bi' Allah as far as Nizaris are concerned. For the Isma'ilis in general the most authentic source of law is Da'aim al-Islam. All Isma'ili Shiahs up to Musta'lians accept it as the most authentic source of Islamic law. Needless to say the Shiahs too do not accept qiyas and ijma' as valid sources of law.

For the Shiahs the valid sources of law are Quran and the Prophetic sunna as reported by the Imams. In Sunni Islam there is no concept of Imamah, it is Khilafah. But there were only four rightly guided Caliphs who too are authentic sources of Islamic law. After the four Caliphs it is authentic 'Ulama' who are looked up to as sources of authentic religious opinion. Among the Travellers the twelve Imams and among Nizaris the existing Imam (known as Hazir Imam) and among the Musta'lians the twenty one imams and after them their deputies known as Du'at al-Mutlaq.

As far as the Nizaris or popularly known as the Agakhanis are concerned they believe that one of their Imams i.e. Hasan 'Ala dhikrihi al-salam suspended application of Islamic Shariah and now the Hazir Imam is the sole source of law which is more traditional than Islamic. Perhaps this is the only Islamic sect which believes that application of Islamic Shariah has been suspended. All other sects of Islam believe in continuing validity of Islamic Shariah.

Among twelver Shiahs belief is that the 12th Imam has gone into seclusion and that he will reappear one day. But during his concealment the authority to interpret the law and to find Islamic solution to problems arising rests with what is called mujtahids. A mujtahid is a properly qualified Shai'ah 'alim (learned man). Whenever any problem arises the Shiahs consult their mujtahid. He is considered most authentic source of authority for the twelver Shias.

As for the Must'alian Isma'ilis the most authentic source of authority is Da'i al-Mutlaq. But, it is important to note that a da'i al-mutlaq is not the final authority. In all Shiah traditions whether twelver or Isma'ili, Imam is considered as infallible and hence he is supposed to be the final authority in all religious matters after the Prophet. But except Zaidis and Nizaris imam in all other Shiah traditions is in seclusion. While in twelver Shiah tradition it is 12th Imam who went into concealment and will himself reappear one day to set all wrongs right, in the Musta'lian Shiah tradition it is 21st Imam who went into seclusion and the institution of Imamat continues in his progeny and when conditions are congenial the Imam from his progeny will come out of concealment one day and will provide guidance to entire humanity.

Thus in the Must'alian tradition the da'i al-mutlaq is not the final authority but deputises for the Imam in concealment and hence the da'i is not infallible. Thus the da'I is not vested with the final authority to solve the problems arising. The Final authority will be the books like D'a'im al-Islam as far as matter pertaining to jurisprudence are concerned and books of ta'wil written by earlier da'is in consultation with Imam. In those days the da'is were in contact with the Fatimi Imams. However, now the da'is have no contacts with Imams in concealment.

Now we come to the Sunni Islam. In Sunni Islam too there is no unified religious authority. Sunnis are divided not only along the lines of schools of law (madhahib) but also along sectarian lines. As referred to above there are several sects among the Sunni Muslims. And each sect, apart from each school of law (madhhab) has its own authority. It has to be noted that, contrary to popular belief, there is no concept of church in Islam and certainly not in the Sunni Islam.

In fact there is no concept of church in Islam as such. Some sects like the Isma'ilis did develop such concept but for reasons of its own. This is not the place to throw light on it here. The Isma'ili movement being underground movement for long it developed hierarchy of authority of its own which acquired church like structure. Thus both the Nizaris and Musta'lians retained this church like structure of religious authority.

In Islam there is no concept of priesthood, let alone that of church. Each and every Muslim is responsible for all religious rites in the light of the Quran and sunnah. Quran and sunnah are the only authority. In the light of these any Muslim can perform all religious functions. However, in Sunni Islam too the institution of 'ulama developed and they acquired the authority and became pivotal in developing the law. The 'Ulama acquired a unique status of their own among the Muslims. It is these 'ulama who issue fatwas (religious edicts) on different issues.

Since new issues arose from time to time an institution called ijtihad (which means exerting oneself utmost) came into being. In fact it is the holy Prophet himself who is reported to have encouraged ijtihad. When he appointed one of his companions Ma'adh bin Jabal to the Yemen as governor the Prophet encouraged him to resort to ijtihad if he did not find answer to his problems in the Quran and sunnah. He could exert himself utmost to find solution to his problems. Thus ijtihad is a very important institution new legislation within framework of Islam.

Technically even qiyas and ijma' we have talked about above is part of the process of ijtihad. The early period of Islamic legislation clearly shows that many problems could not find direct answers in the Quran and sunnah and it was through the process of ijtihad that legislation became possible. The first two centuries of Islam witnessed the full fledged functioning of the institution of ijtihad. The Maliki and Hanbali schools of law were evolved within the confines of Mecca and Medina and hence are much closer to the Prophetic sunnah. Sunnah was naturally influenced by the local customs, traditions, institutions and what is known as the Arab 'adat. Thus these two schools are much closer to the Meccan and Madinese society. However, the two other schools i.e. the Shafii and Hanafi originated in other parts of Islamic world i.e. in Egypt and Bhaghdad and hence had to encounter many new problems which were not part of the Prophetic sunnah.

Thus Imam Abu Hanifa and Imam Shafii had to frequently resort to qiyas and ijma' to evolve new legislation. Thus the history of Islamic legislation is full of instances of ijtihad. Once the corpus of Islamic legislation came into existence the effort was to protect that corpus within the framework of those schools. The 'ulama belonging to these respective schools almost closed the gates of ijtihad i.e. the process of legislation thinking that all time comprehensive corpus of legislation has been evolved.

And during the medieval ages since socio-economic developments on one hand, and, technological developments, on the other, remained almost stagnant hardly any new problems arose. Thus they were quite content with the laws evolved by the founders of their schools. There is no doubt that the four Imams were not only great scholars of Quran and sunnah but had great insights into human affairs and legislative needs of Muslims. They did, what they could, to fulfil the legal needs of the people of their times and in the light of the problems they were confronted with. Thus the four Imams became the great source of authority in Sunni Islam.

The modern and post-modern period have witnessed breath- taking changes in social, economic and technological fields and new problems have arisen along with new consciousness among different sections of people. And, in the light of these developments new answers are needed to some of the old problems too. The concepts of criminal law have undergone drastic changes. The question of women and their rights have acquired new dimensions and new questions are arising by the day in view of swift technological developments. These questions can no more be answered in old ways nor the laws evolved centuries ago can withstand new social and moral pressures.

Thus ijtihad has acquired new urgency. The holy Prophet himself permitted ijtihad in order to confront new situations in Yemen. Thus ijtihad is, in a way, a part of the Prophet's sunnah and it was for this reason that all great imams of the time resorted to it for developing the whole corpus of Islamic legislation. Without ijtihad by these learned Imams this corpus of law would not have come into existence at all. In their own way they were facing new social pressures and they exerted themselves to find answers to those questions. The institution of ijma' was highly useful for that purpose as they could evolve the consensus among the 'ulama and through them of the community.

There is, as pointed out, an urgent need for ijtihad. It cannot be avoided for long on the grounds that there is no one qualified to do ijtihad. There may not be any single authority to do so but the new problems being faced are common to Muslims of all sects and schools and hence the prominent 'ulama of all sects and schools of law along with modern social and natural scientists must come together to evolve new corpus of Islamic legislations in these new areas. It is not being proposed that every thing has to change. Certainly not. The various Sunni and Shiah sects and schools can certainly retain much that is valuable in their existing traditions but certainly to re-examine that part which has bearing on new problems and subject to new pressures.

It is also not proper as some orthodox Muslims do that the only law giver is Allah and that no human being can legislate. This is not correct. In fact much that we have in Shariah is, as explained above, as a result of human endeavour to understand and seek guidance from the Quran and Prophetic sunnah and to use human faculty of reason gifted by Allah to solve problems arising from time to time. Thus ijtihad has been an integral part of Islamic legislation in early period of Islam. Today many new problems have arisen and new human endeavour is needed to frame legislation in the light of the Quran and Sunnah. What was in the context of these times can be rethought in the light of modern and post-modern developments.

It is also not proper to maintain that it is Allah who is sovereign and people have no rights to act. Who can question the doctrine that Allah is sovereign. But people have sovereignty as Allah's khalifah on earth. Allah has designated them to be his 'sovereign deputies' on earth and have also been equipped with the faculty of reason to solve their own problems. In any Islamic countries the source of authority could be parliament for legislation. It comes quite close to the medieval doctrine of ijma`. The parliament can, if necessary, consult the `ulama in the matter.

Iran has come out with the new doctrine of Wilayat-i-Faqih who has the status of guardian of Islamic law and no legislation by the Parliament can become law without his approval. It can be called as council of the guardian. But such council can obstruct legislation if it is vested with final authority. It should have consultative status only. Iran is facing the problem of dual authority because of this doctrine of Wilayat-I-Faqih. Dual authority can cause serious problems. Thus the 'ulama should have consultative rather than approving authority.

In view of fast developments all sects of Islam will have to rethink issues in matters of jurisprudence. New laws in keeping with the value system of Islam are highly necessary. One way is to constitute the joint council of the representatives of all sects of Islam to evolve new body of laws and this will certainly be very helpful for the Muslim ummah as a whole despite sectarian differences. The differences can be ironed out in the joint council. But such a body can help only if there are 'ulama and experts with liberal and progressive disposition. It has been experienced that the 'ulama have compulsions of their own, and often, politics of their own. They oppose new legislation, even if it is perfectly in keeping with Islamic values and traditions to retain their own authority. Thus opposition from the 'ulama is not always 'Islamic'; it is often due to other considerations also. Thus seen from whichever angle it is difficult, if not impossible, to push new legislation and to work out new consensus. It has become all the more difficult in view of the rise of conservative Islam. The irony of the situation is that the rise of conservative Islam is also more political than religious. This situation will continue to create strong impediments in the way of development of new sources of authority in Islam.

Shariah Law Creates Economic Meltdowns

Shariah law has a nasty habit of melting down the economy of any nation in which it has been implemented. Attacking the economies of western societies is a tenet of radical Islam. And, as we shall see in this article, the progressive/socialist movement in western societies has formed a dangerous partnership with radical Islam – forming a socialistic Jihad to be wielded against democracies throughout the world. David Jonnson, author of Islamic Economics and the Final Jihad has this to say as an introduction to Islamic economics:

My goal today is to put you into the mind of an Islamist to think like an Islamist. It is only possible to understand the events occurring by understanding their thinking and what it would mean to live under Shariah law. There is a well-worn Cliché "It's the economy stupid" that appears around election times. So it is with Islamic Economics and the Clash of Ideologies we are witnessing today. It should be realized that the goal of the Islamists, following in the footsteps of Muhammad, is not so much to conquer the land but to Islmanize the populations. In so doing they seek to have the lands come under Shariah law and that the lands become dar al-Islam, the land of Islam and that all non-Muslims accept the status of Dhimmis subservient to Muslim rule.

The Plan involves the incremental acceptance of basic tenants of Shariah law as applied to all aspects of life—the Islamic "Way of Life". This implies the desire to incrementally change the laws and ultimately the Constitution of the U.S.

This requires the population to accept the new laws as equally valid and acceptable. Initially this will result in parallel legal systems and progressing from there with laws that may be applied locally and ultimately nationally. Jihad can be with the pen and the tongue, just as it can be the sword and the spear as Dr. Yusuf al-Qaradawi the spiritual leader of the Muslim Brotherhood has said. Knowledge combined with economic control can be wielded with the precision of a sharp sword to effect any desired social/political change necessary for the fulfilment of Islam's goal. – David J. Jonsson.

Jonsson goes on to explain just how the Islams intend to create Shariah law within the United States and other western countries: Jihad is considered a required religious duty for Muslims. Jihad is Islam's normal path to expansion. Islamic Economics is the stealth sword of Islam. It is more powerful than the Weapons of Mass

Destruction and terrorism. It is immune to negotiation. The stealth sword is being applied for the Islamization of the West and the whole world. The goal is to create the "Islamic kingdom of God on earth." The implementation of Shariah law would have a dramatic affect on your life and that of the entire Western Civilization. Understand the nature of the evil and do not be blindsided.

Islamic economics has an impact on your life, whether you are a banker, investing in the stock market, selling a home, buying a car, purchasing food, buying a suit or a dress, or just trying to make sense of the current events. Islamic economics and Islamic banking are primary Islamist strategies to condition the West to accept Shariah law as a basis for all life in all nations. The Islamic movement is an idea movement; at the present time the leader(s) has not been identified. Many, if not most, of the participants in Islamic Financing may not even be aware that they may be supporting the Islamist agenda.

Our goal is to understand, the genesis of Islamic Economics, what it is, how it is taking place, and how it would affect our lives. And what is the means by which Shariah law gains a foothold into western societies. Through the machinations of liberal Democrats and RINOs, of course. As Sir Winston Churchill once famously said, "An appeaser is one who feeds a crocodile, hoping it will eat him last." And if there is one thing that the progressives specialize in it is appeasement. The progressive policy of appeasement is allowing Shariah law to slither its way into the United States financial system.

The twentieth century has witnessed the emergence of an economic doctrine that calls itself Islamic economics. The doctrine is significant because it advances the sprawling and headline-grabbing movement known as political Islam, Islamic fundamentalism, or simply Islamism. The movement is having a profound impact. The Islamic windows of major banks that incorporate the principles of Islamic economics represent the fastest growing sector. The banks, based on the principles of Islamic economics, raise billions of dollars in the form of Islamic bonds (sukuk) annually.

Banking laws in Islamic and Western countries are changing to accommodate Islamic economic rules. The Dow Jones Islamic Stock Index and in April 2006, Dow Jones and Citigroup announced the launch of the first Islamic Bond Index. The Dow Jones Citigroup Sukuk Index, is the first index that seeks to measure the performance of global bonds complying with Islamic (Shariah compliant) investment guidelines. – David Jonsson The Muslin Brotherhood (al-lkhwan al-Muslimun) is the main motivator behind setting up experiments in Islamic financing on a global scale. The theory and the practical requirements needed to set up an Islamic banking system come from the ranks of the Ilkwan.

"Allah is our objective. The Prophet is our leader. Quran is our law. Jihad is our way. Dying in the way of Allah is our highest hope." —*Muslim Brotherhood*

Today's progressive/leftist movement within the United States is increasingly being integrated into Shariah law. Jonsson explains this concept: The people in the West who are trying to construct a new socialism, a de-Marxified alternative to the politics of pure individualism, share the views of Islamist economists. These Westerners also accept the market as the essential driving-force of any economy, but they too wish to set it within a man-made moral framework that will ensure support for the weak through the compassion and self-discipline of the strong. What communism tried and failed to achieve through the state, one Islamic economist has written, "is to be established through the agency of man himself." It would be a good slogan for the possible new socialism of the twenty-first century. As we will see, these principles are being promoted broadly in the West. This merging of ideologies is a powerful force in today's political environment. This merging is taking the form of a Marxist/Leftist – Islamist Alliance.

Thus you see Barack Obama sympathizing with the Islamist Movement. Many people have wondered if Obama is a Muslim. It is certainly a worthy topic of discussion. But more importantly is the fact that Obama is implementing policies that are favourable to this new socialist/Islamist alliance. Professor Yusaf al-Qarasawi, in his book, The Lawful and the Prohibited in Islam, clarifies the melding of socialism and Shariah law in the realms of commerce and finance:

Islamic law on commerce is known as fiqh al-mu'amalat. Much of the laws, rules and interpretations of Shariah takes into consideration issues of social justice, equitability, and fairness, as well as practicality of financial transactions. In general, the Shariah legal maxim in relation to commercial transactions and contracts states: "They are permissible unless there is a clear prohibition." In a nutshell, prohibited elements of a commercial transaction must first be removed for it to be Shariah-compliant.

The major prohibited elements under Shariah are riba (interest), gharar (uncertainty), maisir (gambling), non-halal (prohibited) food and drinks and immoral activities.

The principles laid out by al-Qaradawi are having profound influence on all daily and commercial activities, not only in the finance sector, but also in the energy, transportation (ports and terminals), construction, and food and drink sector. The goal is to bring all commercial activity into Shariah compliance.

Mawlana Mawdudi, was a Sunni Pakistani journalist, theologian, Muslim revivalist leader and political philosopher, and a major 20th century Islamist thinker. He was also a prominent political figure in his home country (Pakistan) and was the first recipient of King Faisal International Award for his services to Islam in 1979. He was also the founder of Jamaat-e-Islami, the Islamic revivalist party.

Mawdudi had a goal of establishing a separate Muslim society. He was against integration or assimilation in to Western Culture. Examples of his philosophy have resulted in the Muslim dominated ghettos such as Clichy-sous-Bois and Bagneux outside Paris and Leicester in the U.K. This concept of a separate Muslim society is now starting to pervade major money centre banks with the concept that Muslim funds may not be comingled with those of non-Muslims.

Mawdudi saw Muslims not as people who followed the religion of Islam, but as everything: "Everything in the universe is 'Muslim' for it obeys God by submission to His laws." The only exception to this universe of Muslims were human beings who failed to follow Islam. In regard to the non-Muslim:

"His very tongue which, on account of his ignorance advocates the denial of God or professes multiple deities, is in its very nature 'Muslim' ... The man who denies God is called Kafir (concealer) because he conceals by his disbelief what is inherent in his nature and embalmed in his own soul.

His whole body functions in obedience to that instinct... Reality becomes estranged from him and he gropes in the dark".

Mawdudi believed that Islam was a "religion" in a broader sense of the term. He stated: "Islam is not a 'religion' in the sense this term is commonly understood. It is a system encompassing all fields of living. Islam means politics, economics, legislation, science, humanism, health, psychology and sociology. It is a system which makes no discrimination on the basis of race, colour, language or other external categories. Its appeal is to all mankind. It wants to reach the heart of every human being."

Maududi believed that without Shariah law Muslim society could not be Islamic:

That if an Islamic society consciously resolves not to accept the Shariah, and decides to enact its own constitution and laws or borrow them from any other source in disregard of the Shariah, such a society breaks its contract with God and forfeits its right to be called 'Islamic.'" Based on Maududi's doctrine that Islam is all-encompassing, the Muslims seek to extend Islam beyond the historical homeland of Islam unto the entire world. And they use Jihad to accomplish this end.

Islam wishes to destroy all states and governments anywhere on the face of the earth which are opposed to the ideology and programme of Islam regardless of the country or the Nation which rules it. The purpose of Islam is to set up a state on the basis of its own ideology and programme, regardless of which nation assumes the role of the standard-bearer of Islam or the rule of which nation is undermined in the process of the establishment of an ideological Islamic State.

Islam requires the earth—not just a portion, but the whole planet because the entire mankind should benefit from the ideology and welfare programme [of Islam] ... Towards this end, Islam wishes to press into service all forces which can bring about a revolution and a composite term for the use of all these forces is 'Jihad'. The objective of the Islamic ' Jihad' is to eliminate the rule of an un-Islamic system and establish in its stead an Islamic system of state rule. – Mawlana Mawdudi

The teachings of Mawdudi on no integration and/or assimilation into Western culture has far-reaching impact today on many of the issues being addressed in Europe. When immigrants came to America in its formative years, their goal was integration into a unified culture; this is what made America the strong nation it is. In Canada, the Muslim population has sought and has already achieved the separation by the creation of separate civil courts for Muslims. The goal of Islamists is the incremental Islamization of all countries and peoples.

Ummah is an Arabic word that means "community" or "nation." In the context of Islam, the word ummah is used in foreign languages as well as in Arabic to mean the "nation of the believers" (ummatul-muminin), and thus the whole Muslim world. The phrase al-ummatun wahid in the Quran (the "One Community") refers to the entire Muslim world unified. Some modern Islamists use the term Islamic Ummah or Muslim Ummah to refer to all the people in the lands and countries where predominantly Muslims reside, and which were once under the control of the Islamic caliphate.

Jonsson has this to say about Mawdudi: Whatever one thinks of his agenda, he was onto something real: with technological progress, economics was indeed becoming increasingly important to daily life everywhere. In a technologically primitive and static world, where family background determines one's career, where one plants and sells crops in the ways of one's grandparents, where one has little to spend on non-subsistence goods, and where markets offer little variety, economics may be vital to physical survival, but economic decision-making does not absorb much attention.

By contrast, in a technologically advanced world, where job choices must be made, where women pursue and interrupt careers outside the home, where investment choices require monitoring, and where markets offer abundant choice, economic decision-making absorbs considerable time. It follows that if economic choice is considered a secular activity, economic advances will make Muslim existence look increasingly secular. But if economic activity is considered a religious activity, then economic development need not reduce Islam's perceived role in the lives of Muslims.

The declared purpose of Islamic economics is to establish a new world economic order that conforms to Islamic scripture–the Quran–and Muslim tradition. (1) Its core positions took shape in the 1940s, and three decades later, efforts to implement them were under way in dozens of countries. (2) In Pakistan, Malaysia, and elsewhere, governments are now running centralized Islamic redistribution systems known as Zakat.

More than sixty countries have Islamic banks that claim to offer an interest-free alternative to conventional banking. Invoking religious principles, several countries, among them Pakistan and Iran, have gone so far as to outlaw every form of interest; they are forcing all banks, including foreign subsidiaries, to adopt, at least formally, ostensibly Islamic methods of deposit taking and loan making. Attempts are also under way to disseminate religious norms of price setting, bargaining, and wage determination. And for every such initiative, others are on the drawing board.

As seen from an Islamist perspective, Islamic finance provides financial services in accordance with Islamic law or Shariah. Islamists emphasize that Islamic financial services represent the ethical, social, and religious dimension of financial transactions to enhance equity and fairness for the general good of society.

These services are not limited to commercial banking and extend into capital markets, insurance and other channels of non-bank financial intermediation. Adoption of the principles of Islamic Finance by the western institutions is a critical step in the Islamization of the West and the acceptance of Shariah law. It is one step forward in making dar al-harb into dar a-Islam and non-Muslims becoming al-Dhimmis and subservient to Islamic rule.

Just as the proponents of "organic" foods and the Green lobby have promoted their ideologies with catch phrases, the Islamists have promoted the their ideology of "Islamic-Safe" and "socially responsible investment" as preferred words for Islamist investing and finance, signifying that the investment products are in compliance with Shariah Law. We have all heard the term "social justice" bandied about by Obama and his ilk.

But now we gain the understanding that this term actually has its roots in Shariah Law. The concept of Social Justice is part of Shariah Law. It does not mean what conservative American citizens take it to mean. Rather, it means law that conforms to the Islamic way of life. "Social Justice" therefore, is an Islamic term and Obama is using it in order to "condition" us to its use.

Obama is not using this term by accident. Obama is merely part of a larger conspiracy to subject the United States to the rule of the socialist/Islamist conspiracy. Economic jihad is a long-term incremental program being waged to Islamize the world. The Medina Charter of 622, the conquests of Muhammad and the early caliphs gave birth for all time (within the Muslim world) of an institution that places the native populations into a permanently handicapped status. The imposition of Shariah law in Iraq and Afghanistan and changing and/or implementing Shariah-compliant laws in the West all contribute to accomplishing the goal of Islamization, as called for by Muhammad. – David Jonsson

Mawdudi also largely expanded upon his view of the Islamic State and Shariah in his book Islamic Way of Life.

As David Kennedy Houck wrote in the Middle East Quarterly for Spring 2006, The Islamist Challenge to the U.S. Constitution, "First in Europe and now in the United States, Muslim groups have petitioned to establish enclaves in which they can uphold and enforce greater compliance to Islamic law. While the U.S. Constitution enshrines the right to religious freedom and the prohibition against a state religion, when it comes to the rights of religious enclaves to impose communal rules, the dividing line is more nebulous. Can U.S. enclaves, homeowner associations, and other groups enforce Islamic law?"

The goals of Islamists in establishing an economic system based on Islamic law (the Shariah) are:

- To establish credibility for Islam as a "way of life" equal to all other economic and religious doctrines

- To establish an economic system that allows control of the financial, natural resources and intellectual properties by a totalitarian, non-elected hierarchy justified on the basis of religious law–the Quran
- To bring together the global economic resources of Islamic Ummah to influence the world opinion and provide the funding for proselytizing (Da'wa) of non-believers
- To establish an economic system not based on scientific principles but on religious beliefs.

Economics under Shariah law will result in the redistribution of wealth, the confiscation of private property, the establishment of a mega-Islamic bank with global reach and financing backed by the Islamic Development Bank (IDB), control of the exportable oil and natural gas worldwide, control of major transportation systems including the Suez Canal and ports, create a new currency based on the gold dinar, establishment of an interlinked merchandise trading system and a trading block with Free Trade Agreements with other blocks. And mandating the contribution of title (Zakat) and directing the funds for economic gain, political action and the proselytizing of non-Muslims.

If this is the kind of world we wish to live under then we can continue to elect socialists, Marxists, progressives, liberals, and environmentalist whackos who worship trees and assorted flies. Their appeasement of the Islamist radicals ensures our eventual demise. On the other hand we can wake up to the threat that radical Islam presents to us and we can fight for our freedoms. The choice is ours – but not for long. If we do not take action quickly we face the reality that we might be too late to the fight to win it. The time for appeasement is over. The time for action is at hand America.

Bibliography

Abou El Fadl, Khaled. *Rebellion and Violence in Islamic Law*. Cambridge, UK: Cambridge University Press, 2002.

Abu-Rabi, Ibrahim M : *Intellectual Origins of Islamic Resurgence in the Modern Arab World,* Albany: State University of New York Press, 1996.

Al-Azmeh, Aziz: *Islamic Law: Social and Historical Contexts*. London: Routledge, 1988.

Ali, Shaheen Sardar : *Gender and Human Rights in Islam and International Law,* The Hague/London/Boston: Kluwer Law International, 2002.

Anderson, J.N.D. *Law Reform in the Muslim World*. London: Athlone Press, 1976.

Asad, Muhammad *: The Message of the Qurán*, Published by Dar Al-Andalus, Gibralter.

Bakhtiar, Laleh: *Encyclopedia of Islamic Law: A Compendium of the Major Schools*. Chicago, IL: Kazi Publ., 1996.

Bassiouni, M. Cherif: *The Islamic Criminal Justice System*, Oceana, 1982

Brown, N.: *The Rule of Law in the Arab World: Courts in Egypt and the Gulf*, Cambridge 1997

Cotran, Eugene and Mai Yamani: *The Rule of Law in the Middle East and Islamic World: Human Rights and the Judicial Process*. London: I.B. Tauris, 2000.

Coulson, J. Noel : *A History of Islamic Law*. Edinburgh: Edinburgh University Press, 1964.

Daniel Pipes : *In the Path of God: Islam and Political Power,* New York: Basic Books Inc., 1983.

Eisenman, Robert H. *Islamic Law in Palestine and Israel: A History of the Survival of Tanzimat and Shari'a in the British Mandate and the Jewish State*. Leiden: E.J. Brill, 1978.

Ferrari, Silvio and Anthony Bradney: *Islam and European Legal Systems*. Aldershot: Ashgate, 2000.

Fluehr-Lobban, Carolyn. *Islamic Law and Society in the Sudan*. London: Frank Cass & Co., 1987.

Glasse, Cyril : *The Concise Encyclopedia of Islam,* San Francisco: Harper & Row, 1989.

Hallaq, Wael B. *A History of Islamic Legal Theories: an introduction to Sunnî usûl al-fiqh.* Cambridge, UK: Cambridge University Press, 1997.

Johansen, Baber : *Contingency in a Sacred Law: Legal and Ethical Norms in the Muslim Fiqh.* Boston: Brill, 1999.

Kusha, Hamid Rez. *The Sacred Law of Islam: A Case Study of Women's Treatment in the Islamic Republic of Iran's Criminal Justice System.* Aldershot: Ashgate, 2003.

Lindholm, Tore and Kari Vogt, eds. *Islamic Law Reform and Human Rights: Challenges and Rejoinders.* Copenhagen: Nordic Human Rights Publications, 1993.

Makdisi, George. *Religion, Law and Learning in Classical Islam.* Aldershot: Ashgate/Variorum, 1991.

Motzki, Harald. *The Origins of Islamic Jurisprudence: Meccan Fiqh before the Classical Schools.* Leiden: E.J. Brill, 2001.

Peters, Rudolph. *Islamic Criminal Law: Theory and Practice from the Sixteenth to the Twentieth Century.* Cambridge, UK: Cambridge University Press, forthcoming.

Qutubuddin Aziz : *The Prophet and the Islamic State,* Islamic Media, Karachi, 1900.

Rahman I. : *Shariah: the Islamic Law.* Kuala Lumpur: A. S. Noordeen, 2002.

Rosen, Lawrence. *The Anthropology of Justice: Law as Culture in Islamic Society.* Cambridge, UK: Cambridge University Press, 1989.

Schacht, J.: *The Origins of Muhammadan Jurisprudence,* Oxford 1950

Serjeant, R.B. *Customary and Shari'ah Law in Arabian Society.* Aldershot: Ashgate/Variorum, 1991.

Sonbol, Amira El Azhary: *Women, The Family, and Divorce Laws in Islamic History.* Syracuse, NY: Syracuse University Press, 1996.

Starr, June. *Law as Metaphor: From Islamic Courts to the Palace of Justice.* Albany, NY: State University of New York Press, 1992.

Stewart, Devon J. *Islamic Legal Orthodoxy: Twelver Shiite Responses to the Sunni Legal System.* Provo, UT: University of Utah Press, 1998.

Vogel, Frank E. *Islamic Law and Legal Systems: Studies of Saudi Arabia.* Leiden: E.J. Brill, 2000.

Weiss, Bernard G. *The Spirit of Islamic Law.* Athens, GA: University of Georgia Press, 1998.

Welchman, Lynn. *Beyond the Code: Muslim Family Law and the Shari'a Judiciary in the Palestinian West Bank.* The Hague: Kluwer Law Int'l., 2000.

Index

❑❑❑